THE NORTH KOREAN ECONOMY

Hoover Institution Publications 132

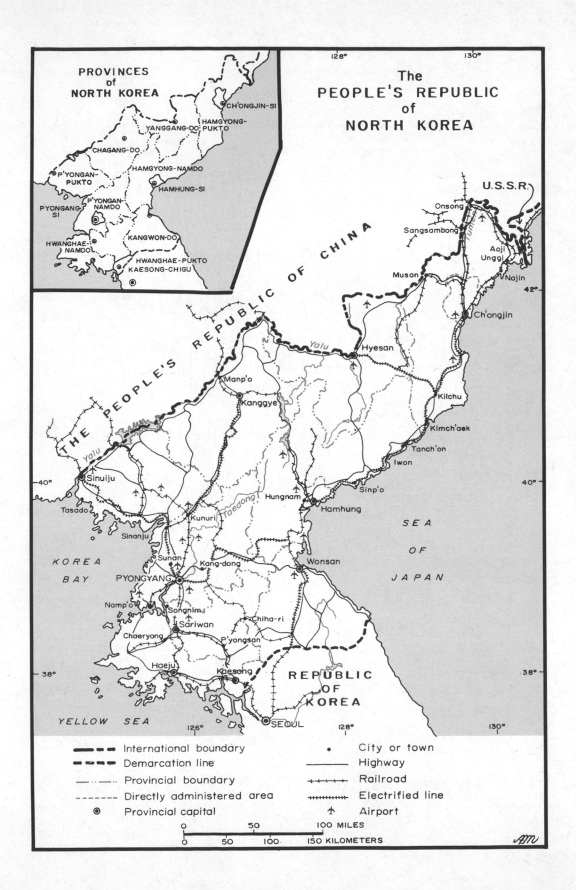

PROVINCES
of
NORTH KOREA

CH'ONGJIN-SI

HAMGYONG-
PUKTO

YANGGANG-DO

CHAGANG-DO

HAMGYONG-NAMDO

P'YONGAN-
PUKTO

P'YONGAN-
NAMDO

HAMHUNG-SI

PYONGANG-
SI

HWANGHAE-
NAMDO

KANGWON-DO

HWANGHAE-PUKTO
KAESONG-CHIGU

The
PEOPLE'S REPUBLIC
of
NORTH KOREA

U.S.S.R.

Onsong

Sangsambong

Aoji
Unggi

Musan

Najin

Ch'ongjin

Hyesan

Manp'o

Kanggye

Kilchu

Kimch'aek

Tanch'on

Iwon

Sinuiju

Sinp'o

Tasado

Hungnam

Kunuri

Hamhung

Sinanju

Sunan

Kang-dong

Wonsan

PYONGYANG

Namp'o

Songnim

Chiha-ri

Sariwan

Chaeryong

P'yongsan

Haeju

Kaesong

SEOUL

REPUBLIC
OF
KOREA

THE PEOPLE'S REPUBLIC OF CHINA

Yalu

Taedong

KOREA
BAY

SEA
OF
JAPAN

YELLOW SEA

- - - International boundary
- - - Demarcation line
—·—·— Provincial boundary
- - - - Directly administered area
⊚ Provincial capital

• City or town
——— Highway
+++++ Railroad
++++++ Electrified line
✈ Airport

0   50   100 MILES
0   50   100   150 KILOMETERS

THE NORTH KOREAN ECONOMY

STRUCTURE AND DEVELOPMENT

Joseph Sang-hoon Chung

**Hoover Institution Press
Stanford University
Stanford, California**

Hoover Institution Publications 132
International Standard Book Number 0-8179-1321-1
Library of Congress Card Number 75-187263
© 1974 by the Board of Trustees of the
    Leland Stanford Junior University
Printed in the United States of America

Contents

About this Book

This book, the only comprehensive study of the North Korean economy ever published in English, describes the transformation of the economy since 1945 and assesses the role of collectivism and central command in effecting this transformation.

With extensive documentation, including numerous charts, the author shows that the economy has grown 12.7 percent per year; achieved a significant degree of industrialization, particularly in heavy industry; undergone a fundamental change in its structure; and shifted from exporting almost solely raw materials to exporting largely semi-finished goods. Throughout the transformation, the author shows, North Korea has remained one of the world's most highly centralized and rigidly controlled economies.

While collectivism undoubtedly helped this transformation--through taxing peasants, rationing and mobilizing manpower, and shifting capital to the industrial sector--it was not the only cause of rapid economic growth. The Japanese left a substantial capital residue, and extensive economic aid and technical assistance from the communist countries, particularly the Soviet Union, contributed toward impressive post-Korean War growth.

In fact, collectivism seems to have detracted from growth in the agricultural sector, where the increase in output did not match the increase of such input factors as mechanization, fertilizers, irrigation, land utilization and farm labor. The author attributes this failure to collectivism's inability to provide material incentives.

Furthermore, the disadvantages of central command seemed to increase as the North Korean economy grew larger and more complex. The inherent inefficiencies of central planning--inflexible bureaucrats, excessive political input into economic decisions, insensitivity to local conditions-- became increasingly detrimental to economic efficiency, and for this reason, the growth rate of the North Korean economy slowed considerably during the 1960's.

As a specific study of the North Korean economy and as a contribution to the fields of economic development and comparative economic systems, this book is highly valuable.

Joseph Sang-hoon Chung is Professor of Economics and the Head of the Economics Faulty at Illinois Institute of Technology. He has edited Patterns of Economic Development: Korea and has contributed to numerous scholarly journals and monographs. Among other honors, he received a Fulbright Lectureship at Seoul National University for 1966-68 and a Social Science Research Council Fellowship in 1962. He has a Ph.D. in Economics from Wayne State University. Dr. Chung is a native of South Korea and has been a naturalized citizen of the United States since 1961.

Tables

Charts

Preface

In August 1945, following the conclusion of World War II, Soviet and U.S. troops entered and occupied the northern and southern parts of Korea, respectively, pursuant to Allied wartime agreements. The Allied occupation, while it liberated Korea from nearly four decades (1910-45) of Japanese colonial rule, marked the beginning of the partition of Korea and the birth of a communist regime in the North. The Korean War (1950-53) that followed was the tragic consequence of that division.

Severed from Japan and South Korea, North Korea was faced with the task of developing a viable economy, reoriented toward the communist bloc countries, having adopted a planned economic system. Her problems were heightened by the destruction of some of its productive facilities by the outgoing Japanese and debilitation by the Korean War. Various economic plans and massive programs of industrialization were introduced for rehabilitation and development.

Thus the North Korean model of economic development offers a unique case study of a divided and war-torn country attempting to rehabilitate, restructure, and develop its economy after having severed its contacts with the other half of the country which complemented its economy. It also provides a study of a Soviet-type of economy in action in the Asian context. Since both North and South Korea have been window-dressed as showpieces for the communist system and the free world, respectively, the success (or failure) of the North Korean economy will have obvious ideological implications. Moreover, a careful analysis of the type of economic system into which North Korea has been transformed and the pattern of economic development the country has undergone must serve as a basis of any plan or measure designed toward integrating the two polarized economies in the event of Korean reunification in the future.

Very few studies on the subject exist, except for a few journalistic accounts. This lack of material is owing to two factors. The first deals with the nature of the communist regime: North Korea must surely rank as one of the most secretive countries in the world, even by communist standards. Economic statistics, particularly when the economy does not fair well, are prime objects of the secret stamp. Further, even those few statistics that are available are fragmentary, often misleading and discontinuous. The second factor is related to the languages in which data are made available. Most first-hand materials appear in Korean and Japanese and, to a lesser extent, in Russian; rarely do they appear in English. The present study is an attempt to fill the gap in this vital, yet little explored, field of economics, using Korean and Japanese sources as well as the available English materials. As far as can be determined, this is the first comprehensive study of the North Korean economy ever made in the West and will be of interest to students of comparative economic systems, comparative governments, economic development, and Asian and Korean studies.

Translation of direct quotations from Korean and Japanese sources, unless otherwise indicated, are the author's. The principle of surnames first is used in citing Oriental names (such as Kim Il-song) unless they are Anglicized (such as Walter W. Wang and the like). For transliteration (Romanization), the Hepburn and the McCune-Reichauer system have been generally followed, respectively, for Japanese and Korean words.

I have received general assistance from many individuals and institutions in writing this book. My book owes primary thanks to Professor Yuan-li Wu for the initial suggestion and encouragement that led to the selection of this vital topic, for his constant moral support, and for reading the earlier manuscript and offering invaluable critical comments. I am also grateful to Professors David Felix and Shanti Tangri for spending endless hours editing and offering invaluable comments regarding content and style, which greatly improved the earlier draft.

I am grateful to The Hoover Institution at Stanford University for its timely research and publications grant and for its logistical support, which enabled me to devote two summers of concentrated research on this project. I owe a special debt to Dr. W. Glenn Campbell, Director of the Institution, and to the librarians at the Hoover East Asian Collection. Acknowledgment is also due to Mr. Key P. Yang of the Library of Congress whose assistance in making many of the documentary sources accessible to me greatly facilitated the data collection. I especially valued those informal chats I had with him during my many visits to the Library, benefiting immeasurably from his comprehensive and up-to-date knowledge on North Korean affairs. My thanks also go to Dr. Thomas H. Kang, also of the Library of Congress, whose ready assistance made the chore of data collecting a pleasant experience. I am also grateful to Dr. Jun-yop Kim, Director of the Asiatic Research Center, Korea University, Seoul, Korea, and to his staff for their cooperation in making research materials available to me during my stay in Korea. To the Stuart School of Management and Finance of the Illinois Institute of Technology goes my vote of thanks for its support in typing the manuscript. I owe a debt of thanks to Kay Kane and Karen Smolak, both secretaries at Stuart School, for their cooperation and excellent work in typing some of my manuscript. I am indebted to Christine E. Tapley, my editor, whose painstaking work made this book more readable and presentable. I also offer my gratitude to the unknown readers whose criticism provided fresh viewpoints and guidelines, so important for subsequent revision. Of course, I alone am responsible for the content.

Last, but not least, my gratitude goes to Louise Carol Guenther, my wife, for her editorial advice and for her moral support and devotion.

May 1973   Joseph Chung
Chicago

List of Abbreviations
and Korean Terms

Abbreviations

CCY	Chosŏn chungang yŏngam (Korean Central Yearbook)
CSB	Central Statistical Bureau (of State Planning Commission)
DPRK	Democratic People's Republic of Korea
ERNK	Economic Report on North Korea (JPRS)
FEER	Far Eastern Economic Review
GAP	Gross agricultural product
GIP	Gross industrial product
JPRS	Joint Publications Research Service
MTS	Machine-tractor stations
UNCURK	United Nations Commission for the Unification and Rehabilitation of Korea

Korean Terms

Bunjo	Sub-workteam
Chaejŏng	Finance; public finance
Chagŏpban	Workteam
Chisik	Knowledge
Chŏngbo	One chŏngbo equals 2.45072 acres or nearly 1 hectare (0.992)
Chosŏn	Korea
Hyŏpdong chohap	Cooperatives
Kongŏp	Industry
Kŏnsŏl	Construction
Kŭlloja	Workers
Kŭmyung	Money; monetary affairs; finance
Kun	County (administrative unit)
Kyŏngje	Economy
Kyŏngjehak	Economics
Nodong	Work; labor

Nodongja	Workers
Nongmin	Farmers; peasants
Nongŏp	Agriculture; farming
Ri	Village (lowest administrative unit)
Sangŏp	Commerce
Sinmun	Newspaper; daily
Wŏn	Unit of North Korean currency
Yŏnbo	Yearbook; annual report
Yŏngam	Annual survey; yearbook
Yŏnku	Study; research

CHAPTER
1
Introduction

North Korea ranks as one of the world's most highly centralized, socialized, and planned economies, even by communist standards. Like other Soviet-
type or "command" economies, North Korea's economy is run by means of commands
from a central planning group. All economic decisions concerning the selection
of output, output targets, allocation of inputs, prices, distribution of
national income, and growth are carried out by the long-range and short-run
economic plans from the center, "blueprinted" by the State Planning Commission
(SPC).

North Korea has so far instituted the following distinct economic plans
starting with the One Year Plan of 1947, each of which expresses the broad and
specific economic objectives to be achieved during the period covered by the
plan. (Plans in detail are given in Appendix A.)

      <u>One</u> <u>Year</u> <u>Plan</u>, <u>1947</u> ("Peaceful Construction Period")
      <u>One</u> <u>Year</u> <u>Plan</u>, <u>1948</u>   "   "   "
      <u>Two</u> <u>Year</u> <u>Plan</u>, <u>1949-50</u>   "   "   "
      <u>Three</u> <u>Year</u> <u>Plan</u>, <u>1954-56</u> ("Post-War Reconstruction Period")
      <u>Five</u> <u>Year</u> <u>Plan</u>, <u>1957-61 (60)</u> A <u>de</u> <u>facto</u> Four Year Plan
      <u>Seven</u> <u>Year</u> <u>Plan</u>, <u>1961-67 (70)</u> A <u>de</u> <u>facto</u> Ten Year Plan
      <u>Six</u> <u>Year</u> <u>Plan</u>, <u>1971-76</u>

During the so-called "peaceful construction" period preceding the Korean
War, the basic goal of the North Korean economy as embodied in the two successive One Year Plans of 1947 and 1948 and the Two Year Plan of 1949-50 was to
overtake the peak output level and efficiency attained during the Japanese
colonial period. This was necessitated by the deterioration of productive
facilities toward the end of World War II, some willful destruction by the
outgoing Japanese, and the chaos created by the withdrawal <u>en</u> <u>masse</u> of trained
Japanese personnel at all levels of productive activity. Subsequently, however, the North Korean economy had to repeat the task of rehabilitation all

over, this time reconstructing an economy ravaged by the Korean War. This was
the main task of the Three Year "Reconstruction" Plan of 1954-56.

The basic task of the Five Year Plan was to establish a firm foundation
for industrialization with continued emphasis on heavy industry as well as to
"solve problems of food, shelter and clothing." The North Korean planners en-
visioned a real departure toward industrialization once reconstruction was
completed. However, as it turned out, despite the official designation of the
Three Year Plan as a reconstruction plan, the actual overtaking of the pre-
Korean War output level for the majority of industrial products was not attained until the Five Year Plan.

With the successful fulfillment of the Seven Year Plan, the planners predicted a "decisive strengthening of the material and technical basis for
socialism," through continued development of heavy industry, particularly the
machine-building industry. In fact, however, the Seven Year Plan was from inception beset by slowdowns and setbacks which compelled the extension of the
Plan for three additional years to 1970, making it a de facto Ten Year Plan.
This was in sharp contrast to the unparalleled and continuous high growth during the Three and Five Year Plans. Understandably, the current Six Year Plan,
save for a few specifics, fails to disclose any deviation from the basic tenets
of the Seven Year Plan.

Through these plans North Korea has made impressive progress in her striv-
ing toward industrialization and economic viability, albeit setbacks, instabil-
ity, and uneven growth. Concomitantly, the structure and institutions of its
economy have undergone drastic changes. Important among these changes are:
patterns in ownership and control of productive enterprises (nationalization
of industry, collectivization of agriculture), a shift in the composition of
national output, labor force, and international trade.

This study has undertaken an analysis of these changes and other facets
of the North Korean economy, and in so doing has made to the field several
unique contributions. Specifically, it offers:

1. A description and analysis of the principle of the operation of the
    North Korean economic system. Patterns in the institutional arrange-
    ments, organizational structure, plant sizes, decision-making mechan-
    ism, incentive systems, and the like of industry and agriculture.

2. Reconstruction of a comprehensive series of statistical data for major
    economic indicators.

3. Analysis of the nature, extent, and causal relationships of economic development and the accompanying transformation in the structure of the economy.

4. Construction of the North Korean model of economic development for possible lessons for development.

Although a formal economic analysis has been emphasized in the study, historical, institutional, and descriptive approaches have also been employed. The state of research on the North Korean economy being what it is, any venture at filling the gap at this stage must entail a judicious combination of all these methods. The paucity of quantitative data and the lack of accumulated knowledge on the subject prevent application of a more sophisticated technique of economic analysis.

The organization of the book is topical rather than historical, as the main thrust of the study is development in the various sectors—agriculture, industry, and foreign trade, each of which is treated as a separate entity. Since agriculture has been and still remains the most important sector in terms of the share of the labor force and as a way of life, the chapter on agricultural development precedes chapters on industrial development and external trade. The book concludes with a chapter on the overall economic performance and change, and a summary. It is admitted that many other important topics beg for inclusion, but these must be left for future exploration. A beginning must be made somewhere.

Although all available sources covering up to the end of 1970 have been used, the discrepancies in cut-off dates between certain series will be obvious throughout the study. The reader should be assured that in each the latest available data have been used, and statistical biases of many origins such as misleading definitions, deliberate inflation, doublecounting, and the like have been noted wherever applicable. Also, attempts have been made to correlate the various related series for consistency. Beyond the published compendia of statistics, the author has resorted to searching for statistics and "reading between the lines" in leaders' speeches, an unavoidable but all-important source of data at this infant stage of North Korean study. (For a detailed description of the availability and reliability of North Korean statistics, see Appendix B.)

CHAPTER 2

The Agricultural Sector

Introduction

When the communists took over in 1945, the North Korean economy was primarily agricultural. Nearly two-thirds of its total national output originated in agriculture, and a much larger proportion of the total population derived livelihood from this sector, engaged predominantly in the production of grains. Trailing behind the South in rice and barley and in total agricultural output, the North was the leading producer of wheat, corn, and soy beans and chief supplier of chemical fertilizers in Korea.[1]

The Japanese left behind an agrarian structure—land tenure system, size of landholdings and farm operation, pattern of land utilization, and farm income—in need of reform due to unfavorable developments during their colonial rule. During the Japanese period there had been a gradual and persistent shift in the nature of land ownership and farm management which turned owner-farmers at the beginning into tenants and farm laborers. This trend continued until the end of the Japanese occupation, so that in 1943 nearly 44 percent of the total farm households in North Korea were actual tenants, somewhat less than the ratio in South Korea (table 1). Actual tenants differ from owner-tenants in that the latter are part—owners and part—tenants of the land they cultivate. When these (owner-tenants) are included, the tenancy ratio is even higher, that is, three out of every four farm households were either without land or at least rented part of it. Fragmentation (division of land into small plots) in the use of land and extreme inequality in land ownership were characteristics of both North and South Korea. The small scale of farm production is evident in the data for 1940 for the whole of Korea. In that year 72 percent of all the farms were operating at a size less than 1 chŏngbo* while only 4 percent of

_____

*One chŏngbo equals 2.45072 acres or approximately 1 hectare (0.992).

the farms were larger than 5 chŏngbo.[2] In 1943, a small group of landlords who made up only 4 percent of the total farm households owned 58 percent of the total arable land in North Korea.[3]

TABLE 1

FARM OWNERSHIP PATTERN, 1911 AND 1943

| | North Korea, 1943 | | (Household Units) All Korea | | |
			1919*	1943	
Owner-farmers	251,261	(25.0%)	(22.0%)	536,098	(17.6%)
Owner-tenants	309,143	(30.8%)	(35.2%)	984,415	(32.4%)
Tenants	435,789	(43.4%)	(41.0%)	1,481,357	(48.6%)
Farm laborers	8,316	(0.8%)	*	44,231	(1.5%)
Total	1,004,509			3,046,101	

*Figures for 1919 are based on the total of farm households, which excludes farm laborers but includes landlords, who constitute 1.8%.

Sources: For 1943, Chosŏn kyŏngje yŏnpo, 1948, pp. 1-375.

For 1919, Bank of Korea, Kyŏngje yŏngam, 1949 (Economic Yearbook, 1949), Seoul: Bank of Korea, 1949, pp. 1-3.

Scarcity of available land for cultivation, expanding population, land fragmentation, small scale of farm operation, an extreme concentration of land-holdings in a few hands, and the mass transformation of peasants into tenant farmers are all factors that eventually led to low productivity and high rents, consequently depressing the economic position of the peasants toward the end of Japanese rule. It is against this background the communists began to introduce several reforms in agriculture.

Land Reform

Following a typical communist pattern, North Korea went through two cycles of change in agriculture—land reform (1946) and collectivization (1954-58)—affecting the organization and management of agricultural production and the structure of land ownership and utilization.

The law[4] on land reform was proclaimed on March 5, 1946, by the Provisional People's Committee, and the reform was completed in less than one month. The extent of economic and social disruptions and dislocation of the peasants in a reform carried out in such a short time, affecting 54 percent of the total cultivated land, must have been stupendous.

Outright confiscation and free distribution of land were the general rule in redistribution. Article 5 of the law stipulated that the land was to be transferred free of charge to peasants in permanent ownership. This provision for the right of ownership, however, was limited by Article 10 of the same law, which prohibited peasants from selling, buying, renting, or mortgaging the redistributed land. Land belonging to certain preferred groups (e.g., anti-Japanese revolutionaries, schools, hospitals) was compensated.[5] Thus, the reform abolished landlords as a class, eliminating them as an effective economic and political force in the villages.

Actual distribution of land was based on a system of assigning points to each member of the farm family according to sex and age, as shown below. Productivity rather than need seemed to have been the yardstick in assigning points, the highest points being given to males and females of working ages. The maximum limit of ownership was set at 5 chŏngbo and the quality of land was also a factor in determining the size of the land redistributed.

	Age	Points
Male	18-60	1
Female	18-50	1
Youth	15-17	0.7
Child	10-14	0.4
Child	9 or under	0.1
Male	61 or above	0.3
Female	51 or above	0.3

Source: Chosŏn kyŏngje yongo, 1948, p. 1-376.

According to the accounts of refugees from North Korea, however, there was considerable room for arbitrary action by the people's committee in favor of the members of the communist party and its sympathizers in determining the size of land confiscated and redistributed. When certificates of ownership were actually rescinded and reissued in 1948, those who did not collaborate with the party were deprived of their land on the ground that they were "traitors." And in practice, no appeal was possible against any decisions made by the people's committee.[6]

The reform also exempted peasants from all debts and mortgages on the land they were given and freed them from all previous obligations to the landlords whose land they were granted. The law also made provisions for the appropriation of livestock, agricultural implements, buildings, irrigation facilities, and all forest lands except the small holdings of peasants.

In addition to the arable land redistributed (as shown in table 2, which summarizes the results of the reform as well as the objects of confiscation and redistribution), a total of 3,432,936 chŏngbo of forest land; 1,165 irrigation units with facilities to water 50,502 chŏngbo; 14,477 buildings; 4,650 and 116 head of cattle and horses, respectively, were all turned over to the "disposition" of the people's committees.[7] The number of cattle and horses appropriated was almost insignificant compared to the total population: at the end of 1946 there were 1,238,000 cattle and 10,000 horses (table 15).

Immediate economic effects of the reform were that the average (mean) size of a farm decreased beyond its already small size, and the inequality in landholdings declined. About one million chŏngbo of land (amounting to 53.8 percent of the total arable land) owned by about 423,000 farm units were redistributed among 724,000 farm households. This means that the average size of the confiscated farms was 2.4 chŏngbo whereas 98 percent of the confiscated land was redistributed at the average rate of 1.4 chŏngbo per farm household. Also, since land was confiscated from large holdings held by a smaller number of landlords and redistributed more or less equally to a larger number of tenant farm households, concentration of landholdings obviously declined substantially. Fragmentary evidence, in the form of an official claim, points to the fact that the average (mean) land holdings of "poor" (undefined) peasant households were raised from 0.2 chŏngbo to 2.1, and those of the landlords were reduced from 14.5 to 2.1 chŏngbo due to the reform.[8]

Smaller scale of operation, other things being equal, would tend to lower farm productivity through declining farm investment: smaller size implies lower income on the part of the peasants and, in turn, leads to lower savings and lower farm improvements. Since fragmentation of land goes hand-in-hand with small holdings, land reform must obviously have caused its increase. Increased fragmentation, in turn, must have further lowered the productivity. Clearly, further division of already small scattered patches of land producing, more often than not, different crops on each tract lowers efficiency. Among other things, it diminishes opportunities for increased productivity through mechanization and more specialization, since these require larger plots with single crops.

On the other hand, land reform undoubtedly had a favorable effect on peasants' incentives and farm improvements, since they were freed from obligations

7

TABLE 2

SUMMARY* OF THE RESULTS OF LAND REFORM IN NORTH KOREA, 1946

| | Area | | Households | | Area Per Household |
	Chŏngbo	Percent	Number	Percent	
A. Agricultural land confiscated, total	1,000,325	100.0	482,646	100.0	2.4
Land owned by Japanese	112,623	11.3	12,919	3.1	8.7
Land owned by "traitors"**	13,272	1.3	1,366	0.8	9.7
Land owned by landlords in excess of 5 chŏngbo	237,746	23.8	29,683	7.0	8.0
Land owned by owners who rent all of their holdings	263,436	26.3	145,688	34.5	1.8
Land owned by those who continuously rent the land	358,053	35.8	288,866	54.1	1.6
Land owned by churches & temples	15,195	1.5	4,124	1.0	3.7
B. Agricultural land redistributed, total	981,390	100.0	744,527	100.0	1.4
To farm laborers	22,387	2.3	17,137	2.4	1.3
To landless peasants	603,407	61.5	442,978	61.1	1.4
To peasants with too little land	345,974	35.3	280,501	38.0	1.3
To relocated landlords	9,622	1.0	3,911	0.5	2.5
C. Agricultural land held by people's committees	18,935	1.9***			
D. Total forest land confiscated	3,432,936				

*There are some discrepancies in the official statistics on the reform because of later revision. Revision was necessitated by the confusion created by the lack of accurate records of landholdings at the time reform was instituted as well as controversies after the reform as to the exact borderlines among the newly redistributed holdings. A complete survey of all landholdings was carried out during 1947. Revised figures are used here. See, in this connection, Kita chosenni okeru tochi kaikaku (Land Reform in North Korea), Tokyo: Chosen Keizai Kenkyusho, 1948, p. 52.

**No explanation of the term is given but is presumed to refer to those who collaborated with the Japanese.

***Represents proportion to the total confiscated.

Sources: A, B, C, Joint Publications Research Service (JPRS), Economic Report on North Korea, No. 79 (Washington, D.C.: JPRS, 1963), pp. 30-31; D, CCY, 1949, p. 71.

to former landlords and came to own the land they cultivated, although some of these favorable effects were neutralized by the agricultural tax-in-kind introduced later. Also, since sale or purchase of farm properties was forbidden by law, land ceased to be the object of speculative investment, thus making funds available for productive investment projects (farm improvements, mechanization, and irrigation). In spite of the law, however, before the Korean War there were, reportedly, some scattered cases of peasants who speculated in urban areas with funds obtained from the sale or renting of land.[9] In addition, land reform paid off politically for the regime insofar as it did earn some good will and popular support by satisfying the peasants' centuries-old hunger for land. A limited number of North Korean peasants interviewed during the Korean War indicated that they preferred ownership status to that before the reform.[10]

These factors suggest that land reform in North Korea created some favorable conditions for increased productivity, but there were negative effects to offset them. The net result is that the reform simply changed ownership of land without any significant reorganization in the agrarian structure conducive to raising the farm productivity and income. A firm evaluation of the success (or failure) of the reform must come from a quantitative study of agricultural production before and after the reform. Such a study is not possible because no comparable prereform data are available. In addition, drastic changes occurred in so many other factors around the time of the reform (withdrawal of the Japanese, communist takeover, division of the country) that it is impossible to isolate the effect of changes due to land reform alone.

Several motives may be advanced as to why North Korea went through the motion of land reform in 1946 only to undo the whole transfer of ownership and collectivize later (by 1958), especially when land reform could not be counted upon to remove the economic disadvantages of small-scale operation with parceling of land and other undesirable arrangements in the existing agrarian structure. First of all, the communists are ideologically committed to the elimination of landlords as a class that exploits the poor tenant farmers. Politically, this has the effect of removing the last remnants of opposition from the traditional power elite in the villages. Second, popular support of the peasants is needed as the communists embark on their new program. New owner-peasants can be used as instruments for producing the agricultural surplus necessary to finance and support industrialization: what the peasants used to pay their landlords in terms of rents is now transferred to the government through agricultural

9

tax-in-kind introduced immediately after the reform. This seems to be a politically wise policy of the communist regime, since taxing the landlords on their
rental incomes without the land reform that eliminated the class would meet
with strong opposition from them. Third, the communists considered the introduction of collectivization in the early stages as unfeasible on both political
and economic grounds. Politically, the regime needed further consolidation of
its power before such drastic change was attempted. Ironically, it needed the
political support of the very peasants it planned to collectivize. Apart from
political considerations, economic reasons such as lack of entrepreneurship and
experience in the mechanics of managing larger farm units, trained bureaucrats,
and farm machinery and equipment might have caused the regime to delay collectivization. The first agrarian reform, however, was only the initial stage in
transforming individual farm units subsequently into larger collectivized
units. The operational requirements of central planning demanded more strin-
gent and direct control of agricultural production, consumption, and farm labor
than was required under private farming; there were serious economic disadvantages in having small, fragmented operations; and ideologically the communist
regime was committed to complete "socialization" of agricultural management and
production.

The Collective Farms[11]

Organizational Evolution

     Private farming which, ironically, was given a boost by the regime's land
reform in 1946 declined rapidly after the Korean War. In 1953, the year of the
armistice, private farming was still predominant, contributing 92 percent of
the total agricultural output and 95 percent of the cultivated land (table 3).
Starting in 1954 the drive for collectivization intensified, and individual
farmers began to be rapidly absorbed by the collectives. By August 1958, private farming as a type of agricultural organization and as a way of life had
totally disappeared from North Korea. Since then, agricultural production has
been carried on by two types of farms—collective and state.
     Although the first formal announcement of the policy concerning agricultural

TABLE 3

CHANGE IN THE RELATIVE IMPORTANCE
OF COLLECTIVE, STATE, AND PRIVATE FARMS,
1946-1953

	1946	1949	1953	1954	1955	1956	1957	1959	1960	1963
A. Composition of gross agricultural products (%)										
Collectives	-	-	0.5	3.3	43.2	65.4	77.9	n.a.	83.9	84.0
State farms	-	3.2	8.0	8.2	12.2	9.6	10.3	n.a.	16.1	16.0
Private farms	100.0	96.8	91.5	88.6	44.6	25.0	11.8	-	-	-
B. Breakdown of cultivated area (%)										
Collectives*	-	-	0.6	n.a.	n.a.	63.5	80.6	92.0	94.0	92.0
State farms	-	1.9	4.6	n.a.	n.a.	5.3	5.1	8.0	6.0	8.0
Private farms	100.0	98.1	94.8	n.a.	n.a.	31.2	14.3	-	-	-

*Includes private plots of the members.

Sources: For 1946, 1949, 1953, 1956, and 1957, CCY, 1958, pp. 189, 192.

For 1954 and 1955, Democratic Peoples' Republic of Korea (DPRK) (Pyŏngyang: Foreign Language Publishing House, 1958), p. 216.

For 1959-60, CCY, 1961, pp. 180, 328-330.

For 1963, Chosen minshushugi jinmin kyowakoku kokumin keizai hatten tokeishu, 1946-1963 (Statistical Summary of the Development of the Peoples' Economy in the Democratic Peoples' Republic of Korea, 1946-63) (Tokyo: Chosen kenkyusho, 1965), pp. 19-20. To be now called Statistical Summary of DPRK, 1946-63.

cooperatives* was not made until August 1953, in Premier Kim Il-song's speech at the Sixth Plenum of the Central Committee of the Party, there already existed various work teams and brigades which were agricultural cooperatives in a germinal form. These were "labor-exchange teams," "share-ox teams," "front-line mutual work brigades," and the like organized to pool the scarce resources under the conditions of the Korean War. As of July 1953, at the conclusion of the war there were 174 such cooperatives.[12]

---

*Although, strictly, only certain forms of cooperatives should be considered collectives, these two terms are used interchangeably in this study. The official North Korean term is cooperatives, but in their present form (Type III) they should be designated as collectives.

Since Kim Il-song's announcement, collectivization was carried out via three stages according to the stated policy of the government: experimental stage (August 1953-November 1954); mass movement stage (November 1954-December 1956); and completion stage (January 1957-August 1958). During the experimental stage the regime established a number of cooperatives in each county ostensibly for the purpose of "demonstrating the superiority of the new system and its economic advantages." It has been claimed by the regime that membership was strictly based on the principle of "voluntary application." However, it has been openly admitted that in the early stage of collectivization some of the peasants with medium-sized holdings were led into the collectives "through persistent indoctrination and persuasion"; a segment of rich farmers who opposed collectivization were "silenced"; and those who argued that collectivization was premature were "dealt a blow at appropriate occasions."[13] On the other hand, there is no evidence of the kind of bloodshed that swept the U.S.S.R. at the time of its collectivization. This may have been chiefly because of the weakened influence of rich farmers and landlords as a consequence of land reform, prohibition of the resale of land, and the "intensive class struggle" during the Korean War. It was reported that immediately after the armistice the number of "rich farmers" made up only 0.6 percent of the total farm households.[14] In addition, a majority of the peasants had come out of the war impoverished by heavy property losses and damage to their already small farms. Yet, as late as the end of December 1957 there were "relatively well-to-do" farmers who were "not inclined" to join the collectives. Together with those who lived in scattered remote areas they constituted the last remnant of private farming, amounting to 4.4 percent of the total peasant households.[15] In North Korea, as in other communist economies, various organizational forms of collectives have been devised, distinguished by varying degrees of private ownership and distribution of output. Until 1958, three types of cooperatives had existed, at which time Type I and Type II were completely transformed into Type III. Following is a summary of the characteristics of each organizational form.[16]

Type I: Private ownership of land, draft animals, and agricultural implements; individual tillage and reaping of private plots; collective use of draft animals and implements for performing basic tasks; pooling of labor; use of draft animals and implements compensated to the owner in the form of produce and/or labor.

Type II: Private ownership of land; draft animals and agricultural implements may be owned privately or purchased by the cooperative; collective use of land; collective sowing, plowing, and harvesting; 20 percent of the crop distributed according to the land contributed and 80 percent according to labor contribution.

Type III: De jure private ownership of land but de facto collective ownership as the distribution of output is based solely on labor
contribution; collective use of land, draft animals, and implements; purchase of draft animals and implements by the cooperative; collective sowing, plowing, and harvesting.

Type I was a kind of mutual-aid arrangement based on pooling of labor,
draft animals, and agricultural implements while retaining basically the individual management of private plots of land and the control of harvests. This
form is considered to be "primitive" and "inferior." In Type II, land is collectively used, but distribution of output is based on the amount of labor and
land contributed. In computing the share of land, both quantity and quality of
land were taken into consideration. In order to be entitled to receive divi-
dends on the share of the land, the technical owner had to put in more than 120
workdays a year.[17] Before the harvest was distributed, all production costs
and tax-in-kind were put aside along with common reserve and social-cultural
funds, which amounted to 5 to 10 percent and 2 to 3 percent, respectively, of
the total harvest. This form is considered "intermediate" and "transitional"
to the extent that rent from land and private ownership of the property was
still allowed. The third form is considered "superior" and most "advanced,"
since it is completely "socialistic." Ownership of land was initially allowed,
but in actuality it had no bearing on the distribution of output since the latter was based solely on labor contribution. New rules, adopted in January
1959,[18] concerning the operation of the cooperatives dispelled even the pre-
tense of private ownership of land by proclaiming its complete abolition.
Since then all means of production, including draft animals and agricultural
implements, came to be owned jointly by the cooperative farm, making Type III a
collective farm in all respects. Ownership of small "garden plots" and fruit
trees as well as the raising of poultry, pigs, rabbits, and bees has been permitted both for consumption at home and sale at the peasant market.[19] The rule
sets the maximum for the private plot at 50 pyŏng (0.04 acres).

Agricultural cooperatives of the Type I form, which was the only kind existing up to 1953, completely disappeared in 1954 when Type II and Type III began to appear in large numbers (2,176 and 7,922, respectively). Since then
Type II, which had been steadily on the decline, was altogether absorbed into
Type III by August 1958, the only form currently in existence.[20] Thus, the
drive toward complete collectivization of all private farms (other than those
absorbed into state-operated farms) went through various intermediate stages.

Such a progression must have made the peasants' transition easier and minimized any possible violent opposition on their part.

Scale of Operation

During the period of collectivization (1954-58) the average size of cooperative farms, while steadily rising, was kept relatively small in terms of both number of farm households and the acreage under cultivation. In October 1958, immediately following the completion of collectivization, the regime shifted its policy on the size of collective farms by deciding to merge them into larger units.[21] According to that decision, all collective farms in each Ri (village—the lowest administrative unit) were amalgamated into a single collective. The merging is said to have been completed in two months.[22] Consequently, the number of collectives declined drastically but the average size was more than quadrupled (table 4). The sudden leap in the size of a typical (average) farm from 1957 to 1958 was also accompanied by the emergence of relatively giant-sized collectives. For example, in 1957 there were no collectives larger than 400 households; in 1958 there were 753 collectives with more than 400 households, constituting nearly 20 percent of all collectives. Also, since 1958 there appeared some collectives (8 and 11, respectively, for 1958 and 1960) whose size exceeded 1,000 households.[23] Geographically, of the 11 collectives having more than 1,000 households in 1960, 9 were concentrated in the province of South Hwanghae, one of the provinces that border South Korea; the provinces of South Pyŏngan and South Hamgyŏng each claimed one.[24] Analysis of the size distribution of collectives in terms of the number of households for 1960 shows no appreciable change over 1958.[25]

After a further decline in 1959, the number of collectives has remained relatively stable with increasing tendencies for the average size of the collective farms in terms of both the number of households and area under cultivation (around 300 households and 500 chŏngbo). In 1963, an average collective farm contained a farm population of about 1,300.

Administration of the newly amalgamated collectives in 1958 was under the control of the chairman of the village (Ri) people's committee. The new collectives also consolidated the work of such hitherto independent organizations as the stores operated by rural consumers' cooperatives and the agricultural credit cooperatives in each Ri under the control of the chairman of the Ri people's committee.

TABLE 4

SOME INDICATORS OF COLLECTIVIZATION IN NORTH KOREA, 1953-1964 (End of Year)

	July 1953	1953	1954	1955	1956	1957	1958	1959	1960	1963	1964
1. Agricultural collectives, total number	174	806	10,098	12,132	15,825	16,032	3,843	3,739	3,736	3,732	3,778
2. No. of agricultural collectives as % of 1953		100.0%	1,252.9%	1,505.2	1,963.4	1,989.1	476.7	463.8	463.5	464.8	468.7
3. No. of farm households in collectives (1,000)		12	333	511	865	1,025	1,055	n.a.	n.a.	1,067	n.a.
4. (3) as % of total farm households in North Korea		1.2%	31.8%	49.0%	80.9	95.6	100.0	100.0	100.0	100.0	100.0
5. Area under cultivation by collectives (1,000 chŏngbo)		11	576	885	1,397	1,684	1,791	n.a.	1,789	1,837	n.a.
6. (5) as % of total farm area (excluding state farms)		0.6%	30.9%	48.6%	77.9	93.7	100.0	100.0	100.0	100.0	100.0
7. Farm households per collective		14.7	32.9	42.1	54.7	63.9	274.5	n.a.	n.a.	286.0	n.a.
8. Cultivated area per collective (chŏngbo)		13.6	57.0	72.9	88.3	105.0	466.0	n.a.	466.4	492.2	n.a.
9. Percent of total population in collectives		n.a.	17.1[a]	17.1[a]	26.1	40.0[b]	n.a.	45.7[a]	44.4	42.8[c]	n.a.

[a]Population as of December 1; [b]population as of September 1; [c]population as of October 1.

Sources: For 1953-58, CCY, 1958, p. 190.

For 1959-60, CCY, 1961, pp. 328-329.

For percent of total population in collectives: 1959-60, ibid., p. 470; 1958, ibid., p. 322; 1955, Cho chae-son, Kwadogie issŏsŏ e chosŏn nodongdang ŭi kyŏngje chŏngch'aek (Economic Policy of the Korean Labor Party During the Period of Transition) (Pyongyang: Korean Labor Party Publishing House, 1958), p. 120.

For 1963, Statistical Summary of DPRK, 1946-63, p. 18.

For 1964, CCY, 1965, p. 479.

No doubt the decision to increase the size of the collectives was a consequence of the inefficiency arising from the small scale of farm operations.
Moreover, some mechanization had been achieved and the administrative experience
and technical competence of the members had increased so as to make larger units
feasible. Yet the policy change had been sudden: as late as a year before
(January, 1957) the 1958 consolidation, Kim Il-song, at the South Pyŏngyang
Agricultural Cooperative Managerial Personnel's Conference, suggested 40 to 100
households as the "reasonable" size of the collective farm.[26] Significantly,
the decision came in the wake of the implementation of communes in China. New
rules, like those in the communes, called for the establishment and operation by
the collectives of such nonagricultural institutions as clinics, rest homes, day
nurseries, schools, and community dining halls.

Organization of Farm Labor

Peasant workers are grouped into work teams (brigades) on the basis of
their geographical proximity, specific abilities, and qualifications as well as
the requirements of the type of work, so that productive efficiency will be max-
imized. These brigades are identified according to the nature of the work involved such as agricultural, livestock, farm machinery repair, and farm machinery
operation. They are of three types: specialized, mixed, and all-purpose teams.
A specialized work team concentrates on one crop or one species of livestock; a
mixed team works on more than one specialized product; and an all-purpose work
team engages in more than one sector of agriculture, such as raising both crops
and livestock.

Work brigades have been established on a permanent basis, known as the
"fixed" work brigade system, advantages of which are as follows.[27] First of
all, since the members belong permanently to a particular brigade engaged in a
well-defined task, precise clarification of responsibilities concerning work and
maintenance of land, equipment, and facilities is possible. Second, the brigade
system raises the efficiency of labor through specialization of a brigade on a
certain task. Third, the fixed system through accurate definition of work standards simplifies the evaluation of actual work performed, thus making easier the
application of compensation based on a piece-work system.

Average size of the brigades as well as the amount of acreage assigned per
brigade has been increasing (between 1957 and 1961, table 5). All this, of

course, is consistent with the trend toward a larger scale of operation since
the consolidation of 1958.

TABLE 5

NUMBER AND SIZE DISTRIBUTION OF WORK BRIGADES,
1957 AND 1961

	1957	1961
Total number of brigades.........................	58,550	30,365
Number of workers per brigade...................	27	65
Number of brigades per collective farm..........	4	8
Chŏngbo of arable land per brigade..............	29	61
Size distribution (percent): 20 or less workers		20.4%
21 - 35 "		62.5
36 - 50 "		15.1
51 - 70 "		1.7
71 or more "		0.3

Sources: For 1957, Ro Hang-mok, op. cit., p. 23.
          For 1961, Hong Tal-son, op. cit., p. 101.

A subteam group contract system was introduced in 1965 (see p. 27 under
Farm Income), and these subteams, within the work brigade, have increasingly become the basic units of farm labor organization both for production and income
distribution. It was reported (presumably in 1966) that an average subteam is
made up of 4 to 5 neighboring farm households with 15 to 25 workers and has
under its cultivation 20 to 30 chŏngbo of land.[28]

Agricultural Taxes

In June 1946, three months after land reform was proclaimed, a law[29] de-
creed the adoption of an agricultural tax-in-kind in an attempt to reform the
existing tax structure. This tax was to "free peasants forever" from the "pred-
atory" tax system which existed during the days of the Japanese colonial rule,
when between 30 to 70 percent of the peasants' harvest had been taken away,
partly by the government and partly by the landlords. Article 1 of the law established tax-in-kind as the only form of agricultural taxation, thereby abolishing all other taxes, such as land tax and income tax, in the agricultural
sector.

17

The tax was set at 25 percent of the harvest, including such crops as rice, barley, wheat, potatoes, and beans of each farm household, and the remainder was to be placed at the free disposition of the peasants. There were no provisions for differentiating between dry fields and irrigated fields and between various grades within the same category of land. In May 1947, the law was changed[30] to impose differential rates on different kinds of fields: 27 percent for irrigated fields; 23 percent for dry fields; and 10 percent for firefields.[31]

These tax rates seem fair. However, the rates should not be used as such to evaluate the real burden of the tax on the peasants for the following reasons. First, the manner in which the tax was assessed made the effective rates of tax much higher than the proclaimed official rates. For example, the assessment of tax was not based on the actual harvest but on the planned harvest prepared by the bureaucrats who tended to inflate their planned output. According to one estimate,[32] such practices raised effective rates almost 50 percent and in some cases as high as 70 percent of the actual harvest. Also, the government insisted that only the best quality grain could be used as tax payment.[33] Some less frequent but bizarre practices were attributed to overzealous local officials who collected grains even before they were ripe so as to accelerate the rate of tax collection. Also, a case was reported of a flood-ruined area where peasants were actually forced to purchase the amount of grains necessary for the tax-in-kind.[34] These practices raised the effective rates of tax in terms of value of the actual harvested grains. Also, from 1949-50 the government began increasing pressure on the peasants to sell the after-tax surplus farm products directly to the government rather than dispose of them in the free market. The government-set prices were lower than those in the free market, thus reducing the peasants' real income.[35] To make matters worse, there were a number of special taxes disguised under such names as social organization dues, patriotic contributions, shares of irrigation, local autonomy, schools, army, and so on. Also, peasants had to contribute one or two months of uncompensated labor for local construction projects such as roads, bridges, and schools. In addition, the entire farm population between the ages of 18 and 55 was subject to 20 days annually of compulsory labor in such national projects as factories and mines.[36]

Succumbing to pressure and dissatisfaction with the indiscriminate nature of the existing tax rates, which did not take productivity differences into consideration, the regime introduced a reform in the tax law in January 1956. The reform assigned four distinct rates: 27, 25, 23, and 20 percent, respectively, to

18

four grades of irrigated fields; 23, 20, 17, 15, 12, and 10 percent, respectively, to six grades of dry fields; and 25 and 23 percent to orchards.[37] Assessment of the tax was to be based on an average actual harvest, which amount was to remain fixed for a given period of time. Also, provisions were made to either exempt or reduce the tax on newly reclaimed, improved, or rehabilitated land for a set period of time. This was a policy expression of government attempts to encourage land reclamation and cultivation of virgin or less fertile land. The government also tried, through the tax reform, to encourage formation of agricultural cooperatives by giving a 5 percent reduction in taxes to members of cooperative farms.[38] The reformed tax law made illegal free disposition of harvest left after tax and household consumption, by making it compulsory for peasants to sell the surplus to the government; thus government organizations became the sole dealers of agricultural products.[39] The only exception was such nongrain surplus products as eggs, milk, vegetables, fish, poultry, rabbit, seasonings, and the like which the peasants could sell at the peasant markets at free market prices (see chapter 5).

In 1959, one year after collectivization was completed, agricultural tax-in-kind was lowered to an average rate of 8.4 percent for all crops harvested (13.7 percent for rice and 10 percent for other grains) while tax on such industrial crops as cotton, flax, and tobacco was abolished at the same time. The most significant policy statement on recent agricultural development in North Korea is embodied in Kim Il-song's "Thesis on the Socialist Agrarian Question in Our Country"[40] adopted formally at the Eighth Plenary Meeting of the Fourth Central Committee of the Workers' Party on February 25, 1964. In the document, Kim proposed to abolish the agricultural tax-in-kind over the three years between 1964-66. Exemption was to start with "weak" farms in the first year, "medium"-level farms in the second, and "comparatively well-to-do" farms in the last year. Accordingly, all the collective farms in the districts tabulated below were totally exempt from the tax starting with the late harvest of 1964.[41] The list gives a

Provinces	Areas exempted
Chagang	All cities and counties
Yanggang	All cities and counties
South Pyŏngan	The Sŏngyo district of Pyŏngyang; Hoech'ang & Sinyang counties
North Pyŏngan	The Sakchu, Tongchang, and Pyŏktong counties
South Hwanghae	Sinwŏn county
North Hwanghae	Insan and Yŏnsan counties
Kangwŏn	Pŏptong, Sepo, and Pyŏngyang counties
South Hamgyŏng	Changjin, Taeheung, Sutong, and Hŏch'ŏn counties
North Hamgyŏng	Yŏnsa, Musan, and Najin counties

general picture of localities where productivity and income levels of farms are relatively the lowest. In addition, 643 farms in other scattered cities and counties received complete tax relief.

Even before systematic steps were taken to abolish the tax, partial exemption was initiated. Thus it was reported that in 1962 the government canceled the taxes for 469 collectives in mountain areas.[42] By the end of 1963 a total of 1,331 collective farms had been freed from the tax burden. By the end of 1964, the year Kim's thesis was announced, about half the farms were exempt.[43] The tax-in-kind, the only agricultural tax in existence, from which nearly all the farms were exempt by 1965, was formally abolished by a decree in April 1966.[44]

Agricultural tax had been a major source for financing the Korean War and industrialization programs. This was openly admitted by Kim Il-song when he boasted that "we fought the war as well as developed industry through the tax-in-kind we received from the farmers."[45] Several motives can be advanced for the regime's drastic measure of abolishing this important source for forced savings on the part of the peasants. First of all, a foundation had been built for industry and with it industry's internal capacity to generate capital had been strengthened. In the words of Kim Il-song,

> Now that the might of our industry has grown and the foundation of an independent economy of the country has been laid more firmly, we can take a series of important measures for alleviating the burdens of the co-operative farms and the peasants and rendering them greater state benefits. Such measures are: first, complete abolition of the agricultural tax-in-kind;...[46]

Second, this was another manifestation of the North Korean effort to rectify the industry-agriculture discrepancy and ensure a more balanced growth in the economy. Third, the government through tax relief was attempting to eliminate partially the gap in the living standards and incomes of industrial workers and peasants. Fourth, and perhaps the most important motive, was to furnish the peasants with added material incentives for stimulating output. Abolition of the agricultural tax was accompanied by the government's undertaking of rural capital and housing construction projects which had hitherto been the main responsibility of the collective farms themselves.[47] Finally, the government could devise ways, if it so desired, to regain grains freed by the tax relief. For instance, since 1964 some of the facilities owned by the collectives—namely, milling houses, small and medium power plants, irrigation facilities, stores—have been transferred to state ownership. This has increased state access to grains through the fees-in-kind it charges for the use of these facilities. Also, by January 1966 state-owned retail stores began to be newly established or expanded at every village in order to intensify the government's grain purchase activities.[48]

The Kun (County) Agricultural Management Committees

The trend toward a larger scale of agricultural operation in North Korea received a new boost in 1961. The regime, not stopping at the consolidation of collectives at the Ri level decided, in December 1961, to organize Agricultural Cooperative Management Committees on the Kun (county) level. The primary purpose behind the decision unquestionably was to coordinate and integrate all the resources within the county so as to carry out agricultural production on an even larger scale than that based on the Ri and with more direct state control and guidance. Under the new scheme, the Kun farm management committee is charged with the responsibility of supervising and controlling all organizations and enterprises providing goods and services to agriculture such as the machine-tractor stations, the irrigation administration offices, and farm implement shops. The committee has also become the agency for guiding as well as channeling state directives and assistance to the collective farms within the county. Specific functions of the new committee include assisting the collectives in planning their production and supervising such farming operations as seed selection, soil improvement, fertilization, farm implement maintenance, labor administration, bookkeeping, collective construction work, and so on.[49]

Until the management committee was formed, the Kun people's committee supervised the collective farms within the county merely through formal administrative directives in the form of memoranda and notes; it did not have the capacity and authority to provide technical guidance simply because farm machinery and implements, repair shops, purchasing centers for construction materials, and so on were under the control of different agencies.

Considering the number of counties in North Korea, the average Kun, in 1963-64, had approximately 22 collective farms comprising 6,300 households and 10,800 chŏngbo of cultivated land. Around 1965, 78 percent of all the counties were those having between 5,000 and 15,000 chŏngbo of land. Of these, most counties with a larger area of cultivated land (those belonging to the class of 10,000 chŏngbo or more) are situated in the plains, whereas those with a smaller area (below 10,000 chŏngbo) tend to be located in the mountains.[50] Since the population density is higher in the plains, discrepancy in the acreage per capita in each Kun would not be as high as indicated by the size of cultivated land.

Significantly, the new arrangement brought local agricultural activities under closer and tighter control of the central government under the guise of the so-called enterprise method. The enterprise method essentially entails bringing the method of management and operation of agricultural production as close as possible to that of industrial enterprises. The superiority of the Kun-level collective farm management committee was said to lie in "state guidance of the agricultural economy with the enterprise method." Kim Il-song's own defini-tion of the enterprise method of guidance points eloquently to the nature of the new approach in agricultural organization and production:

> What is the enterprise method? Starting with the formation of the plan, it means direct control and organization of all activities of the enterprise such as the organization of production, technical development, the guarantee of materials, the allocation and organization of labor force, and the finan-cial activities of enterprise for concrete guidance.[51]

Thus the new committee became a unified Kun-wide agency carrying out and controlling central government directives as well as providing technical guidance for all aspects of agricultural production for the collective mobilization of all available resources throughout the county.[52] A concrete example of how the en-terprise method is translated into action is the monthly work-directing system initiated in some counties. Under this system the Kun management committee issues the monthly work directives indicating, for each collective farm, major work indices, work volumes, time of work, and workday points to be invested in the various projects. In turn, the chairman of the collective farm gives a 10-day work plan to each work team to implement the Kun-planned monthly quotas. At least in the case of one county (Sŏkch'ŏn County), the Kun management com-mittee, through the monthly work-directing system, controls over 80 percent of the total labor force of the collective farms while the remaining 15 percent and 5 percent are allowed to be controlled by each collective farm and work team, respectively.[53]

The management committee is composed of "leading workers," agricultural ex-perts, technicians, the directors of the Kun-level agricultural organizations, the chairman of the collective farms, and others.[54] This committee, for example, has been credited with raising the managerial and technical standards of the farm workers in 1964 by assisting the collective farms in such managerial activ-ities as production schedules, soil utilization, irrigation systems, material storage, allocation and organization of technicians and other workers, distribution of products, farm tools, and financial management.[55]

In spite of its accomplishments in certain respects, many defects have been found in the actual operation of the management committee. These, admittedly, have arisen from the organizational structure of the committee: responsibilities, functions, and work of all units under the committee's auspices have been ill-defined and lacked elaboration; lines of communication and coordination between the committee and its field units, and between individual committee workers, have been unsatisfactory; and, in the selection of the leading committee members, standards for their technical and administrative training and experience have been low.[56]

The regime's attempt toward more centralization in the farm decision-making and the role of the Kun as the lowest administrative control unit in the execution of this policy is evident in the following excerpts from an article in Nodong sinmun (March 13, 1964) which paraphrases and analyzes Kim Il-song's pronouncements:

> One of the difficulties of managing farms is the high degree of decentralization of farms. Therefore, it is necessary to establish control districts. The Kun has all the attributes to become a unit of control. As the socialistic transformation goes on, each Kun is expected to play an increasingly important role in supervising farms.
>
> Thus, today the Kun has become an important mediating point between the rural and urban areas; it has become a focal point of organizing light industry and agriculture in the local areas;....In other words, the Kun is the lowest administrative body providing leadership, a mainstay of cultural and economic development in rural areas, and the basic point of uniting urban and rural areas.

Enhancing the role of the Kun continues to be emphasized as a prime strategy for solving farm problems, as demonstrated in Kim Il-song's report to the Fifth Congress of the Workers' Party held November 1970.[57]

Farm Income

Principles of Distribution

The net income (cash and noncash) available for distribution among the members of the collective farm is derived by subtracting from the total output the following stipulated deductions for various purposes indicated.[58] Until it was

abolished in 1966 the agricultural tax-in-kind constituted the major component
of the state obligations.

  I. State obligations:

    1. Machine and tractor fees—2 percent (with better quality grains)

    2. Irrigation fees—an average of 4 percent

      a. Paddy fields—5 percent of tax base if water is directly supplied
        by the state irrigation authorities; 2 percent if water is under
        the control of the collectives

      b. Dry fields—20 won per chŏngbo

  II. Productive fund:

    1. Seeds—stipulated according to kind (2 to 3 percent)

    2. Feed grains (0.7 to 1 percent)

    3. Fertilizer fund—amount based on the state allocation of fertilizer
      for the coming Plan year (2 to 4 percent)

    4. Other productive funds—fund for repairing and purchasing implements
      as well as purchasing seeds (10 percent)

  III. Common accumulation fund:

Basic source for purchasing agricultural machinery and constructing productive and cultural facilities; made up of 15 to 30 percent of output
left over after all the deductions under I and II above are made.

  IV. Social and cultural fund:

Maintenance of nurseries, kindergartens, libraries, and other cultural,
social, and welfare activities; between 3 to 7 percent of output after all
deductions under I and II are made.

  V. Assistance fund:

Living and educational expenses of needy families of deceased patriots and
of soldiers as well as the old and disabled (1.5 percent)

  VI. Distribution fund: (about 37.1 to 51.4 percent)

Net income available for distribution among the members after all the
above deductions (48.6 to 62.9 percent) are made. (Before the abolition
of tax-in-kind, deductions amounted to 48.6 to 70.9 percent.)

Distribution of the net income among the members is made according to a
somewhat complicated work-point system. Specifically, work is rewarded on the
basis of the number of workday (nodong il) points accumulated by each member.
The number of workday points, in turn, is determined by the type of job performed, actual amount of work performed, the standard amount of work specified
for the job, and the quality of work.[59]

All farm jobs, depending on "whether they require heavy or light labor,
technical or common labor, complicated or simple labor, important or subsidiary
labor,"[60] are assigned workday rates (amount of workday points earned for one

calendar day's work), following the Soviet model. Table 6 shows the allocation of workday rates (coefficients) for managerial workers of collective farms. The same principle applies to the field workers of the collectives. In order to earn the stipulated workday points, the chairman must actively participate in the field at least 50 workdays. The minimum for the rest of his staff is 70 workdays. Stipulations have also been provided to fine those who do not fulfill the fieldwork requirements.

TABLE 6

COEFFICIENTS OF WORKDAY RATES
FOR MANAGERIAL WORKERS AND FOREMEN OF WORK BRIGADES

A. Managerial workers:

Size of Collectives (Households)	Chairman	Vice-chairman, chief clerk, agr. engineer	Chief accountant, agricultural technician	Statistician, bookkeeper
200 or less	1.10	1.00	0.95	0.80-0.85
201 - 400	1.13	1.03	1.00	0.85-0.90
401 - 600	1.17	1.07	1.05	0.90-0.95
601 & above	1.22	1.12	1.10	0.95-1.10

B. Foremen of work brigades:

Size of work brigades (workers)	Workday rates
60 or less	0.65-0.70
61 - 80	0.70-0.75
81 & above	0.75-0.80

Source: Kyŏngje sangsik:kongŏp, nongŏp, sangŏp (Commonsense of Economics: Industry, Agriculture and Commerce) (Korean Labor Party Publishing House, 1960), pp. 161-162.

An example of the standard quantity of work specified for a particular job per day as applied to livestock workers[61] is given in table 7. In the event

TABLE 7

STANDARD WORK PER DAY PER LIVESTOCK WORKER

	Standard no. of animals to be tended per day
Honey bees........................	30- 40 (hives)
Dairy cows........................	4- 6
Calves............................	20- 30
Hogs for breeding.................	13- 15
Hogs for fattening................	30- 40
Sheep.............................	80-100
Chickens and ducks................	300-400
Rabbits...........................	80-100

Source: Saikinno chosenno kyodonojo, p. 119.

25

that the quality of the work does not meet standard requirements, work points are discounted accordingly.[62]

According to this piece-rate reward system* once a particular job is assigned, the number of workday points earned is proportional to the quantity and quality of actual work performed in relation to the work standard. Thus the system has some built-in incentives.

The final income share of a member at the end of the year is, in turn, determined by the share of his cumulative total workday points earned relative to the grand total work points of all members of the collective for the year.**

It is clear that under this system a collective farmer cannot precisely anticipate the real value of his current work and hence his income, since they are undeterminable until after harvest and even then his share of it depends on the number of workday points he has accumulated as well as that credited to other members. As a result, there may be marked differences in the actual value of a workday point between any two collectives, and it may vary from one year to another.

In the beginning of collectivization, when establishing the work standard was in the hands of each collective farm, the authorities made frequent complaints that the standards set were very low.[63]

---

*For each day worked, work points earned are calculated as

$$W = R\left(\frac{A}{S}\right)Q, \quad 0 \leq Q \leq 1$$

where W stands for the number of workday points earned per working day; R, rate (coefficient) of workday points per job, per day; A, actual amount of work performed per day; S, standard amount of work specified per day, per job; and Q, quality coefficient.

**Thus the actual amount of income received by a member at the end of the year is calculated as:

$$F_i = H \; \frac{\sum_j W_{ij}}{\sum_i \sum_j W_{ij}}$$

where F_i represents the final output received by the $\underline{i}$th member; H, the residual income available for distribution; W_{ij}, the number of workday units accumulated by $\underline{i}$th member on $\underline{j}$th working day; and $\sum_i \sum_j W_{ij}$, the total number of workday units earned by all the members of the collective farm during the entire year. $\sum_j W_{ij} / \sum_i \sum_j W_{ij}$, the relative share of the income to the $\underline{i}$th member, depends not only on the number of workday points he earns but also on the number of workday points others earn.

Since the gestation period of crops is quite long, the method of handling payments before harvest would pose a serious problem and have a far-reaching effect on the incentive and consumption patterns of the collectives' workers. Advance payments are made either in cash or in kind and in the case of some collectives early crops are distributed as advance payments until major crops are harvested.[64] Advance payment in cash was not known until 1959 when some collectives initiated monthly cash payments in advance on an experimental basis.[65]

Since 1960 a work-team bonus system (Chagŏpban udaeje) has been used in which the actual output in excess of 90 percent of the government quota is awarded to every member of the work brigade involved.[66] At the same time, if any work brigade falls short of the assigned standard of work, it must contribute 5 to 15 percent of the deficiency to make up the difference.[67] Certain incentives are also provided for the chairman of the local party committee and management committee in seeing that output targets of the collectives under their supervision are fulfilled. If, for instance, 70 percent of the work brigades or 360 out of 500 members of the collectives are awarded a premium, the chairman will receive a premium equal to 70 percent of the average premium distributed to the members of the collectives, while other members of the management committee will be awarded the bonus "in proportion to the rate based on the amount of premium awarded to the chairman." Each management worker must have worked more than 230 days of that year for a particular collective farm to be eligible for the reward.[68]

In addition to the team bonus system, there is also the subteam group contract system (punjo togŏpje). This began on an experimental basis in May 1965 and, strongly encouraged by the government, became fully operative in 1966.[69] Under this system a subteam comprising 10 to 20 members is allocated a specific number of workday points for performing a planned task on an assigned area of land. Depending upon whether it over- or underfulfills the planned task (quota) the planned workday points are adjusted upward or downward. Once the workday points earned by the subteam as a group are determined, they are in turn divided among the individual members according to the share of the work performed.

There is no essential difference between the subteam group contract system and the individual piece-rate system* except that the former is expressed in

---

*The subteam group contract system can be expressed as:

$$W_a = Lw_p + L(Y_a - Y_p)\left(\frac{Lw_p}{LY_p}\right)$$

27

terms of the total number of workday points for the year and for the subteam (as a group) rather than for each individual peasant worker. There is, however, one important difference: the former emphasizes subteams as the basic work units of production as well as income distribution. Each member of the team is made more directly responsible for his part in fulfilling the government assigned quota. There are more built-in incentives in the subgroup system because the actual workday points earned by the peasants are directly and immediately the consequence of the performance of the very small group of which he is a member. Also, reevaluating the workday points earned for the entire year on the basis of the actual output at the end of the year makes the peasants concentrate their efforts on, and be more aware of, the quantity and quality of the final products at the time of the harvest, rather than attempt to earn as many workday points as possible on the day-to-day basis. Fixed assignment of all the means of production including land, farm implements, and draft animals to a small group like the subteam for its exclusive use and maintenance also makes the team members more responsible for them. Previously their use was widely diffused among larger groups without clear definition of responsibility. The new system is another means by which the government can raise the effective rate of utilization of available land and farm capital.[70] In addition, the new system may be regarded as a further application of the industrial enterprise system to agriculture: just as one or two operators are permanently assigned to a lathe, so is a subteam

---

which can be alternatively written as:

$$W_a = L \left[w_p + (Y_a - Y_p) \left(\frac{w_p}{Y_p} \right) \right]$$

where W_a = actual or reevaluated total workday points earned for the subteam for the year; L = assigned <u>chŏngbo</u> of land for the year; w_p = number of workday points allocated (planned) per <u>chŏngbo</u> per year; Y_a = actual yield per <u>chŏngbo</u> per year; Y_p = planned yield per <u>chŏngbo</u> per year. To be sure, Lw_p is the total allocated workday points for the group, which it will receive if it exactly fulfills the quota. $L(Y_a - Y_p)$ represents the amount of output in excess or below the quota while w_p/Y_p stands for (planned) number of workday points per unit of (planned) output. Since the formula can be reduced simply to the expression

$$W_a = Lw_p \left(\frac{Y_a}{Y_p} \right)$$

it is clear that there is a substantial similarity between the two systems.

made responsible for a fixed tract of land and given farm capital for doing assigned work.

There are also interesting features regarding the mechanics of distribution. If fruits, vegetables, and industrial products which account for a sizable portion of cash incomes cannot be sold in a particular year, income derived from them is carried over to the following year rather than included in the initial year's income. Grains must, of course, be sold to the government as required by law. Another feature is that the children of "patriotic" families—families of the war dead, and soldiers' families in need—can obtain financial assistance from the common funds of the collective farm. Lastly, labor supplied by the school boys and girls who work on holidays or after school is credited to their parents' workdays.[71]

Composition and Growth

Official data on the cash and noncash income per family of the collectives show a marked improvement in the standard of living of the peasant families since 1954 (table 8). However, even by 1968 the Seven Year Plan target of 1,000 won of cash income per peasant family was not achieved as planned.

Growth in the purchasing power of cash income was even greater, owing to the steadily declining general price level throughout the period. Since the average size of farm households was 4.64 persons in 1963, the last year for which such information can be estimated, cash income of 480 won per farm family in 1963 amounts to about 103 won per capita for the entire collective farm households. In the same year the official per capita income for the whole of North Korea (see chapter 5) was at most 445 won. If farm income were entirely made up of cash and if peasants received the national average income, each farm household should have received 2,065 won on the average in 1963 as compared to the actual cash income of 480. The discrepancy, of course, is explained by income-in-kind and lower-than-average farm income. Cash values of grains and tubers distributed to the peasants in 1963 should not exceed the maximum of 1,585 won per family. To put it another way, cash income must have constituted at least one-fourth of the total farm income.

Noncash income consists of grains and tubers. The share of grains distributed per member family has also been growing steadily since 1954 for all the years covered except 1964 when there was a decline of 321 kilograms over the

29

TABLE 8

GROWTH IN THE CASH AND NONCASH INCOME
PER PEASANT FAMILY, 1954-1968

Year	Grains		Tubers		Cash	
	Kg.	% of 1960	Kg.	% of 1960	Won	% of 1960
1954	764	36.4	n.a.	-	40	13.3
1955	1250	59.5	193	35.7	56	18.7
1956	1616	77.0	357	66.1	95	31.7
1957	1742	83.0	434	80.4	137	45.7
1958	1826	87.0	501	92.8	203	67.7
1960	2100	100.0	540	100.0	300	100.0
1961	2700	128.6	n.a.	-	400	133.3
1963	2842	135.3	n.a.	-	480	160.0
1964	2521	120.0	n.a.	-	600	200.0
1967	3316	157.9	n.a.	-	531	177.0
1968	3780	180.0	n.a.	-	600	200.0
1970*	(3000)	(142.6)			(1000)	(333.3)
1976**					(1800)	

*The Seven Year Plan target (originally for 1967).

**The Six Year Plan target.

Sources: For 1955, Kyŏngje kŏnsŏl, June 1958, p. 36.

For 1956-57-58, Yi Myong-so, Chi Un-sŏp and Kim Hyŏk-chin, Uri nara esŏŭi sahoejuŭi kŏnsŏlŭi taekojo (Greater Progress in the Socialist Construction of Our Country) (Pyŏngyang: Academy of Science Publishing House, 1959), p. 65.

For 1960, Kyŏngje chisik, February 1962, p. 43.

For 1961, Facts About Korea (Pyŏngyang: Foreign Language Publishing House, 1961), p. 153.

For 1954, 1963-64, and 1970 (Plan target), Saikinno chosenno kyodonojo, p. 10.

For 1967, The People's Korea, February 12, 1957.

For 1968 and 1976 (Plan target), Nodong sinmun, November 10, 1970.

previous year. The fact that total output of grains in 1964 remained at the same level as in 1963 in the face of increasing population must explain the decline. Substantial increase in the share of grains starting from 1967 must be at least partially explained by the abolition of tax-in-kind in 1966. Increased income from grains in 1967, however, was partly offset by a decline in cash income in that year. Since grains are expressed in terms of aggregated weight of composite items, it is more than plausible to conclude that the grains distributed to the peasants contained an increasing proportion of corn relative to rice since the postwar growth rate of corn production has been overwhelmingly higher than that of rice. Thus the monetary value of farm income originating from grains has not improved in the degree indicated by growth in the weight of grains.

North Korea's withholding of statistics on the amount of tubers distributed since 1960 leads one to suspect slow growth or decline in this category. Omission of production data on potatoes and the like since about the same time in official statistics seems to confirm the suspicion.

Geographical Distribution

As an indication of the geographical dispersion of farm income among different regions it was reported, for instance, that in 1961 Pŏptong County, Kangwŏn Province, enjoyed the nation's highest in cash and grain payments per farm family. A cash payment of 500 won and grain distribution of 3,560 kilograms were reported as compared to the national average of 400 won and 2,700 kilograms, respectively, for that year. In terms of individual collective farms, Chŏngjin Collective Farm in Ryongchon County, North Pyŏngan Province, reportedly paid the highest income per family in 1961 with 617 won of cash and 5,000 kilograms of grains.[72]

Mountain areas, because of their less fertile land, have been lagging behind in productivity and income. These and adjacent areas have been considered depressed areas even by official accounts. The regime has been campaigning to equalize farm income among the three major groups—plains, intermediary areas, and mountain areas. This was the reason why the agricultural tax was canceled by the government for 469 collectives in mountain areas in 1962, four years before the tax was completely abolished.

The mean family income among the three major regions for 1962 (table 9) shows the result of the campaign. Mountain areas far exceed the national average

31

in their share of potatoes but are still behind that of grains. Mountain areas still fall below the national average in the all-important category of grains, which includes rice and other cereals. However, this is offset by the above average cash income. The relative position of mountain areas before the tax exemption must have been worse than is shown in the table. Abolition by 1966 of the agricultural tax for the collectives in all areas, including those in the plains and intermediate areas, must in all probability have increased the geographical difference since then. The table also suggests a diet among the peasants of the mountainous areas heavily weighted toward potatoes and the like.

TABLE 9

MEAN CASH AND NONCASH INCOME PER COLLECTIVE FAMILY, 1962:
A GEOGRAPHICAL COMPARISON (PERCENT)

	National Average	Plains Areas	Inter-mediary Areas	Moun-tain Areas
Grains	100%	105%	99%	92%
Tubers	100	45	89	193
Cash	100	68	91	116

Source: Kim Song-jin, op. cit., p. 391.

State Farms

Since private farming disappeared in 1958 with the completion of "socialization" in agriculture, there remain only two forms of agricultural production—the collective farm and the state farm. Notwithstanding the official communist attitude that the latter is the superior form of ownership, the former predominates in North Korea (table 4) as in the U.S.S.R. and other communist economies.

The state farm is a sort of state-operated factory that produces such items as grains, milk, meat, and wool. Like the managers in industrial enterprises, those of state farms are appointed by the state, which owns the land, the machinery, and all other means of production. The system of independent economic accounting used by industrial enterprises has also been adopted by the state farms.

The number of state farms has increased considerably since 1949 (table 10). This growth is mainly owing to the increase in the number of province-managed state farms which came to comprise 94 percent of the total state farms (in 1965).

Centrally managed state farms are larger in scale than those managed by provinces. The average size of a state farm in terms of acreage under cultivation more than quadrupled between 1957 and 1960, following the regime's new policy of consolidating small-scale state farms into larger ones.[73] This is in line with similar consolidation in collective farms starting from 1958.

TABLE 10

TRENDS IN STATE FARMS, 1949-1965

Year	Number of state farms			Cultivated area under state farms (1,000 chŏngbo)	Chŏngbo per state farm	Chŏngbo per collective farm
	Total	Central	Pro-vincial			
1949	37	37	–	39	1,044	n.a.
1953	213	37	176	n.a.	–	14
1956	188	49	139	101	536	88
1957	165	53	112	n.a.	–	105
1960	169	39	130	124	734	466
1961	172	41	131	n.a.	–	n.a.
1962	182	31	151	n.a.	–	n.a.
1963	190	n.a.	n.a.	159	832	492
1964	191	n.a.	n.a.	n.a.	n.a.	n.a.
1965	180	11	169	n.a.	n.a.	n.a.

Sources: Number of state farms: 1949-57, CCY, 1958, p. 120; 1960, ERNK, No. 79, p. 35; 1961-62, JPRS, 1963 North Korean Central Yearbook, p. 164; 1963, Statistical Summary of DPRK, 1946-63, pp. 18-20; 1964, One Korea Yearbook, 1967-68, p. 838; 1965, Pukhan yoram, 1968, pp. 119-120. Cultivated land: ERNK, No. 79, p. 33; Statistical Summary of DPRK 1946-63, pp. 18-20.

The acreage of the average state farm is considerably larger than that of the average collective farm. On the other hand, state farms as a whole had under their control a relatively small percentage of the total cultivated land (only 8 percent in 1963) but contributed more than a proportionate share (16 percent in 1963) of the total agricultural output. The relatively higher level of mechanization and efficiency because of a larger scale of operation in the state farms undoubtedly contributed toward the state-collective farm productivity gap.

It is not known why there had been a reduction of 11 state farms between 1964 and 1965. These farms must have been either absorbed by other state farms or converted or absorbed into the collective farms. This was the first time since 1957 that the number of state farms showed a decline. For one thing, it was reported that as of the end of 1965 all centrally managed state farms specializing in rice crops were abolished to be converted into collective farms starting from 1966.[74] Low productivity and inefficient management were blamed. It is possible that even before the formal decision was made some of these farms were converted into collectives, which may explain the reduction in the number of state farms between 1964-65.

The trend toward a larger scale in agriculture has taken a new turn since 1959, when two new state farms were created in Unggi County, North Hamgyŏng Province, and Ryongyun County, South Hwanghae Province. Each of these farms was created by consolidating all the state and collective farms within the county into a single unit.[75] These large-scale farms have been officially designated as state general farms (Chonghap nongjang); they are formed by consolidating not only farms but also marine and industrial enterprises, be they state or cooperative. In addition, the general farm coordinates all education, cultural, health, and welfare activities in the county. The formation of these countywide monolithic state agro-industry complexes reflects North Korea's efforts to utilize effectively local resources for a unified, comprehensive, and all-round economic development and "technical revolution" in the countryside.[76] In assessing the significance of this new development, the following two related but distinct factors are relevant. First, what happened was clearly a movement toward transforming collective farms into state farms. Second, the new development introduced a larger scale of operation into agriculture. This was a further step from the consolidation and merger of collectives carried out toward the end of 1958 and the confirmation of basic policy lines. The large size of these newly created state farms can be seen by the fact that there are about 23 villages per county on the average in North Korea.[77]

That the transformation of collective farms to state farms, which are considered ideologically superior to the former, will become an integral part of the North Korean agricultural policy seems unlikely, at least in the immediate future. For one thing, contrary to the national trend, state farms in the two counties had occupied a predominant position even before the consolidation. For instance, in March 1959 on the eve of the transformation, only 14 percent of the cultivated land in Ryongyun County was in the hands of collectives while 86 percent belonged to state farms. Significantly, in the same county the proportion of agricultural population was only 30 percent, a very small proportion relative to other areas.[78]

Conversion of some state farms into collectives around 1966 is another sign. Additional evidence supporting the negative answer comes from the formation of the Kun management committee, in that another point of superiority of the Kun collective farm management committee is said to lie in the fact that "it establishes a relationship between the people and cooperative ownership and that it strengthens state assistance to the agricultural economy....The essential characteristic of this measure is to maintain the combination of state and cooperative ownership through enterprise guidance and to rapidly raise the level of cooperative ownership by further strengthening the guiding function of state ownership."[79] Kim Il-song was quoted as stating that the "development of an organic relationship between state and cooperative ownership does not mean the weakening or eliminating of the cooperative ownership. It rather strengthens the cooperative form of ownership."[80] The new system of guidance is seen to narrow the difference between cooperative and state ownership.[81] From all indications it appears that the regime does not plan to transform the collectives into state farms for some time to come.

State farms assume the function of agricultural experimental stations for themselves and especially for the surrounding collective farms. New methods of seeding and crossbreeding and advanced techniques of crop and livestock raising are first tested and experimented by the state farms, later to be disseminated gradually among the neighboring collectives. Equipped with tractors, harvesters, trucks, and other relatively advanced agricultural machinery, state farms serve to demonstrate the economic advantages of large-scale, highly mechanized agricultural operations.[82] For instance, it was reported that in 1960 state farms supplied more than 50,000 pigs, 105,000 rabbits, and more than 501,000 chickens to the collective farms. These, produced by state farms, were said to be of a superior quality and were used to improve the breeding livestock of the collectives.[83]

Before 1960 the incomes of workers at state farms were not tied to the amount of output they produced: the entire output (net of the reserve for seeding and livestock feeding for the following year) was turned over to the state, and workers were paid according to the nationally set wage standard in the manner of industrial workers. Since 1960 state farms have been allowed to keep produce in excess of the state delivery quota.[84] The surplus which was placed

at the disposal of state farms is largely distributed as bonus among the workers
in addition to their regular wages. The major purpose behind the change is to
infuse more material incentives by relating a portion of a worker's income to
his productivity. However, it also makes the incomes of workers less stable
than before since a part of their income now fluctuates with the harvest. Accompanying this innovation was an emphasis on combining livestock breeding and
crop raising activities and the reorganization in the work brigades so as to
"eliminate the nonproductive work force." This was accomplished by sending out
"a great many technicians who had been concentrated in management offices...to
work teams."[85]

The Machine-Tractor Stations and Farm Mechanization

Following the example set by the Soviet Union, North Korea introduced
machine and tractor stations (MTS) in 1950 when three stations were set up on an
experimental basis. Most agricultural machinery in North Korea has been concentrated in the hands of MTS (table 11), which is an independent state enterprise
controlled by the Kun Farm Management Committee.[86] The reason for establishing
such independent organizations seemed to lie in the capacity of each MTS to
serve many farms, an important advantage in view of relative scarcity in agricultural machinery and equipment. It was a kind of rationing device by which the
scarce equipment was assigned to and shared by a number of farm units. In the
beginning the MTS undertook mainly tilling work. Gradually, as more and diverse
equipment was acquired and experience gained, activities of the MTS were widened
to include sowing, weeding, harvesting, thrashing, and transportation.

Important reorganizations took place in 1960 and 1966. In the early part
of 1960 the MTS within state farms were abolished, tractors and other equipment
being divided among the work brigades.[87] This gave state farms control of the
agricultural equipment used within their confines, while the MTS was given the
responsibility of aiding solely collective farms. Another consequence of the
reorganization was that the name of the MTS was changed from Nong kikye imgyŏngso
(farm machine hire station) to Nong kikye chagŏpso (farm machine work station).
Underlying this superficial change in title was a significant break from the
prevailing relationship between the MTS and collective farms. Until the change,
the task of the MTS was simply to supply farm equipment to the collectives,

TABLE 11

MACHINE-TRACTOR STATIONS AND AGRICULTURAL MECHANIZATION, 1953-1970

	1953	1956	1960	1961	1962	1963	1964	1965	1969	1970
1. MTS (Number)	15	48	89	117	144	154	163	174		
2. Tractors, total in North Korea (Number)	372	1,542	6,318	n.a.	n.a.	n.a.	n.a.	n.a.		20,850*
3. Of which: MTS (Number) (3)/(2) (%)	347 (66.4)	1,244 (80.7)	5,214 (82.5)	n.a.	n.a.	n.a.	n.a.	n.a.		
4. Tractors, total horsepower (1,000)	11.5	38.4	187.5	209.9	235.4	270.0	300.0	459.0*		
5. Of which: MTS (1,000 HP) (5)/(4)	7.5 (65.4)	31.1 (80.9)	133.2 (71.1)	178.2 (84.9)	193.2 (82.1)	210.0 (77.8)	n.a.	n.a.		
6. Horsepower per MTS: (5)/(1) (1,000)	0.5	0.6	1.5	1.5	1.3	1.4	n.a.	n.a.		
7. Farm trucks, total in North Korea (1,000)	-	-	.8	1.6	n.a.	n.a.	3.0	4.3*		5.1*
8. Total area plowed by tractors (1,000 chŏngbo)	118	370	1,145	1,278	1,509	1,761	n.a.	n.a.		2,977*
9. Of which: by MTS (1,000 ch) (9)/(8) (%)	93 (78.8)	334 (90.3)	1,034 (90.3)	n.a.	n.a.	n.a.	n.a.	n.a.		
10. Ratio of area plowed by tractors to total cultivated land (%)	2.6	10.5	36.0	45.0	46.0	50.0	53.0	n.a.		
11. Horsepower per 100 chŏngbo of cultivated land (HP)	1	2	10	10	n.a.	14	15	n.a.	18[a]	22[b]

*Estimate based on the growth rate over 1960; [a]as of February 1969; [b]as of April 1970.

Sources: For MTS, 1953-60, ERNK, No. 79, p. 33; for 1961, "Development of People's Economy of Our Country in 1961," Kyŏngje chisik, February 1962, p. 41; for number of trucks, Idem.; for 1962, ERNK, No. 84, p. 16 and Pukhan yoram, 1968, p. 116; for 1963, Statistical Summary of DPRK, 1946-63, pp. 20-21; for 1964, Nodong sinmun, January 16, 1965, p. 1; for 1965, Kŭlloja, No. 1, January 5, 1966, pp. 11-18; for 1969-70, Nodong sinmun, November 3, 1970 and November 10, 1970, and The People's Korea, February 12, 1969 and April 29, 1970.

receiving in return for the specific service rendered a stipulated amount of fees for "hire." This arrangement caused considerable friction between the MTS and collective farms. One source of friction and complaint was that since the MTS was paid a fixed fee the workers from the MTS were said to have lacked incentives for increasing the output, thus evading any responsibility connected with the output other than nominally fulfilling the contracted work.[88] The reform assigned joint responsibility for the total output to the MTS as well as to the collectives.

By February 1966 the reform, affecting mainly the collective farms, was carried further. At that time most of the tractors directly controlled and operated by the MTS were distributed to collective farms for permanent stationing. While collective farms were given direct responsibility for the operation of the tractors, their ownership was to remain with the MTS. The MTS would still maintain one mobile tractor work brigade, one truck transportation team, and a repair shop. Tractor operators are assigned by the MTS, but they are paid by the collective farm to which they are assigned, on the basis of workday points and work standards set by the MTS,[89] thus providing incentives to the tractor operators for work done on the farm. Keeping a minimum of tractors, trucks, and other farm vehicles unassigned to a specific farm gives mobility to the MTS in terms of assisting collective farms on an emergency basis. The reorganization is an attempt to combine the flexibility and mobility of the MTS with the advantages of permanent and fixed stationing of tractors, lack of which caused friction and inefficiency.

The growth of the MTS and their role in the mechanization of agriculture in North Korea is summarized in table 11. Since their inception in 1950, the MTS grew continuously in number and came to control most of the tractors available in North Korea. The decline in the proportion of tractors held by the MTS in terms of horsepower between 1956 and 1960, in spite of an increase in the proportion of the number of tractors during the same period, indicates that on the average the tractors distributed to the state farms in the early part of 1960 were larger in size (horsepower per tractor) than those held over by the MTS for use in the collectives. Since 1960 the average size of the MTS in terms of horsepower was slightly on the decline while the number of the MTS kept increasing steadily.

In terms of the total area plowed by tractors, the role of the MTS has been preeminent. However, without taking into consideration the intensity of plowing

in different plots of land for different crops, such figures are not too reliable. All that the present figures show is the area broken or covered by the
tractors. That a given acre of land may be plowed or cultivated either intensively or extensively needs no elaboration here. According to the figures the
area plowed by the MTS increased more than tenfold between 1953 and 1960. If,
instead, horsepower per MTS was substituted, the increase was slightly less than
threefold. However, horsepower per chŏngbo as an indicator of the role of the
MTS is limited to the extent that it excludes in its measure any improvement in
the quality of tractors or of efficiency in their use, in that more acres can be
plowed with a given amount of horsepower per acre.

The North Korean regime claims accomplishment of a high degree of mechanization in agriculture. Usually such claims are based on figures showing the
relative growth in the number of tractors and the ratio of the total cultivated
area plowed by tractors—which is impressive. However, as is commonplace with
relative comparisons, this spectacular growth is explained by the fact that the
number of tractors in the base year was very small (only 372 tractors with
11,460 horsepower in 1953). Even in 1970 the number of tractors was 20,850 for
the whole of North Korea.

In its drive for what the regime calls "technical revolution" in agriculture the timetable, especially since 1960, called for concentrated effort in the
the mass production of agricultural machinery. This was to achieve the second
phase of the triple-phased rural technical revolution: irrigation, mechanization, and electrification. The first phase seems to be regarded by the regime
as already realized.[90] However, reverses in the production of tractors since
the Seven Year Plan, especially during 1962-63, must have considerably slowed
down the planned tempo of rural mechanization as seen by slower growth in the
number of horsepower per chŏngbo between 1961-70.

Available data for 1960 on the mechanical and draft power between state and
collective farms (table 12) reveal some further insight into the state of agricultural mechanization in North Korea. First, an average state farm had under
its disposition twice the horsepower per 100 chŏngbo of cultivated land and 3.5
times the horsepower per 100 workers of an average collective farm. Since the
draft power ratios are nearly equal, the discrepancy is explained mostly by the
differential mechanization. The fact that there is more discrepancy in the
capital-labor ratios than in the capital-land ratios between these two types of

farms is simply a reflection of a higher labor-land ratio in the collective farm.*

TABLE 12

ENERGY SOURCES OF STATE AND COLLECTIVE FARMS, 1960
(HORSEPOWER)

	Per 100 chŏngbo of cultivated area			Per 100 chŏngbo of sown area			Per 100 workers		
	M*	D	T	M	D	T	M	D	T
State farms	47.0	7.0	54.0	42.0	6.0	48.0	65.0	9.0	74.0
Collective farms	15.0	10.0	25.0	11.6	7.6	19.2	13.0	8.0	21.0
(1)/(2)	3.1	.7	2.2	3.6	.8	.3	5.0	1.1	3.5

*M = Mechanical; D = Draft; T = Total.

Source: Hong Tal-son, op. cit., p. 103.

Statistics of tractors and other farm machinery conceal a significant amount of defective machinery as well as ineffective utilization. For example, the complaint was made in November 1962 that a number of farm machine plants have produced defective implements and machine parts "because of inadequate heat treatment in the process of production."[91] This had the effect of shortening the life of these items. The poor quality in the products of some farm machine plants was attributed to bad labor management and shortcomings in the supply of raw materials. Also, in 1961 efficiency in the use of machinery was so low in some locations that draft animals were used to do the work all over again. Poor assignment of machinery and "sporadic rather than concentrated approaches to tasks" were blamed for the inefficiency. Wasted fuel also resulted from such practices.

---

* $\left(\dfrac{K_s}{L_s} \Big/ \dfrac{K_c}{L_c} \right) \left< \left(\dfrac{K_s}{M_s} \Big/ \dfrac{K_c}{M_c} \right)\right.$

$\dfrac{L_c}{L_s} \left< \dfrac{M_c}{M_s} \right.$

$\dfrac{M_s}{L_s} \Big/ \dfrac{M_c}{L_c}$

where s = state farms; c = collective farms; K = capital; L = land; M = labor.

Waste was further attributed to the lack of cooperation in clearing the fields of objects that hinder efficient operation of tractors and other machinery. Because of this, in some areas farm machines could not be operated and manual labor had to be applied, "resulting in a poor crop in spite of the investment of a huge amount of labor and machine power." Lack of coordination between the MTS and the collectives was reported to have resulted in tractor drivers going from one collective farm to another looking for work, thus wasting much labor and resources. Significantly, however, the principal cause underlying the inefficiency in the utilization of farm machines seemed to lie in the lack of spontaneous cooperation as well as an absence of incentives on the part of the peasants and machine operators who were accused of harboring a negative and conservative attitude toward farm mechanization.

State Investment in Agriculture

The best available indicator of the importance which the North Korean regime attaches to agriculture is the allocation of state investment (table 13).

State investment known in North Korean literature as "state basic construction investment" consists of state investment in fixed assets. As such it comprises the bulk if not all of the total agricultural investment. There have been considerable amounts of on-the-farm investment[92] in such projects as greenhouses, storehouses, workshops, stalls, and other buildings. Farm investment in fences, hedges, drainage, livestock increases, and so on should also be included in the total investment. Lack of data on the magnitude of these types of investment makes it difficult to assess their importance. Nevertheless, state investment is a good, though not complete, barometer of capital formation in agriculture.

State investment in agriculture has been on the rise since the pre-Korean War days. Agricultural investment as a proportion of the total state investment, however, showed no appreciable rise until the Seven Year Plan. The proportion actually dropped slightly during the Three Year Plan and Five Year Plan, respectively. There have been widespread complaints concerning the unbalanced growth in the different sectors of the economy, meaning essentially the lagging growth of agriculture. Annual average proportion of 20.0 percent allocated for agricultural investment during 1961-69, with a rising tendency during the latter years, reflects the regime's attempt to remedy the situation. The change in the relative emphasis of the North Korean regime is made more explicit in the rates of

41

TABLE 13

STATE BASIC CONSTRUCTION INVESTMENT, TOTAL AND AGRICULTURAL, 1949-1969
(In 1957 constant prices)

	1949	1954-56[a] (3 Y P)*	1957-60[a] (5 Y P)*	1960	1961-64[a]	1961-69[a] (7 Y P)*
A. State investment:						
1. Total state investment (million won)	89	357	500	567	672	975
2. Investment in agriculture (million won)	10[b]	32	52	70	126[b]	195
3. (2) ÷ (1)	(11.3%)	(9.2%)	(11.6%)	(12.3%)	(18.7%)	(20.0%)
4. Investment in afforestation	n.a.	6	6	5		
5. (4) ÷ (1)	–	(1.7%)	(1.2%)	(0.9%)		
6. [(2) + (4)] ÷ (1)	–	(10.6%)	(11.6%)	(13.2%)		
B. Breakdown of agricultural investment according to uses (total, 100%):						
1. Irrigation projects	n.a.	56.5	46.5	32.4		45.0
2. Farm equipment repair centers		10.1	13.9	26.3		
3. Livestock		9.4	9.1	14.2		
4. Others		24.0	30.5	26.1		

*3 Y P = Three Year Plan; 5 Y P = Five Year Plan; 7 Y P = Seven Year Plan.

[a]Annual averages; [b]estimate based on percentage data.

Sources: For 1949, Kim, Ha-myŏng, Chosŏn kyŏngje chiri: sang (Economic Geography of Korea, Vol. 1) (Pyŏngyang: State Publishing House, 1958), p. 157.

    For 1954-56, CCY, 1958, p. 202.

    For 1957-60, ibid., pp. 500-502.

    For 1961-64, CCY, 1965, p. 481.

    For 1961-69, Nodong sinmun, November 10, 1970.

    For afforestation, The 1961 North Korea Yearbook, p. 502.

    For the breakdown of agricultural investment, ibid., pp. 261-262.

expansion planned for industry and agriculture in the Seven Year Plan. The
planned growth rate of industry for the period is substantially lower than the
actual rate during the Five Year Plan, while the rate of growth planned for
agriculture in the Seven Year Plan is greater than that during the preceding
Plan period. Subsequently, the gap between growth rates of industry and agriculture has been somewhat narrowed. Although a definite upward jump was made
in the 1960s, agriculture's share of total state investment planned for the Six
Year Plan (1971-76) is slightly less (an annual average of 18 percent) than that
of the previous Plan period.[93]

Investment in afforestation has not kept pace with the growth in total
state investment or investment in agriculture; in fact, during 1954-60 it remained at about the same level as during the Three Year Plan in absolute amount,
while it declined as a ratio of total state investment.

State investment in agriculture was spent on such diverse projects as irrigation construction, farm equipment repair centers, livestock, and others, the
first continuing to be assigned the highest priority throughout the entire
period. Expenditures on irrigation include construction of reservoirs, dams,
and pumping and water-diversion stations. Expansion in investment in the category of farm equipment repair centers, which makes up a poor second, is probably
a reflection of both the drive for, and the result of, gradually increasing
rural mechanization. As mechanization spread intensively and extensively, repair centers capable of servicing a growing amount of facilities and implements
must be expanded simultaneously.

Growth and Structural Change* in Agricultural Production

Agriculture is composed predominantly of three major types of activities:
crop raising, the livestock sector, and sericulture. Crop raising, which includes fruits as well as grains and tubers, has contributed the predominant
share of the agricultural product, whereas the livestock sector has been a poor
second (table 14). Production in sericulture as a share in the total

------

*Throughout the study the phrase "structural change" refers to change in
the percentage composition of national income, industrial and agricultural production, foreign trade, and the like. It does not refer to organizational
change.

TABLE 14

AGRICULTURAL PRODUCTION: GROWTH AND STRUCTURAL CHANGE, 1946-1968

	1946	1949	1953
I. Growth in Gross Agricultural Product total (%)	100	151	115
a. Crops (%)	100	146	113
1. Grains[a]	100	140	123
b. Livestock (%)	100	185	133
c. Sericulture (%)	100	293	177
II. Composition of Gross Agricultural Product, total=100%			
a. Crops	90.8	88.2	89.0
1. Grains[a]	(56.4)	(52.8)	(61.3)
b. Livestock	8.4	10.4	9.7
c. Sericulture	0.6	1.1	0.9
d. Others	0.2	0.3	0.4
III. Gross Agricultural Product per capita (%)	100	145	125

*Author's estimates.

[a]Includes rice, corn, barley, wheat, miller, and pulses.

[b]Percentage increment over the preceding year.

Sources: For grains, 1946-1956, CCY, 1958, p. 192; for 1958, Haebanghu urinara ŭi inmin kyŏngje palchŏn, p. 245; for 1963, DPRK Statistical Summary, 1946-63, p. 19; for 1967-68, The People's Korea, February 12, 1969; for the rest, The 1961 North Korean Yearbook, pp. 470, 483-484.

agricultural output is negligible. Grain production constitutes the most important component of crops.

Intertemporal analysis indicates that there has been a gradual change in the composition of the total product in favor of the livestock branch. This trend will no doubt continue in the future as emphasis on the development of livestock production constitutes part of North Korea's long-run agricultural policy. The livestock sector has been traditionally weak in Korea. In 1938 before the outbreak of World War II, only 6 percent of the total agricultural product in the whole of Korea originated in this branch; 1.3 percent in sericulture; and the rest, 92.7 percent, in crops.[94] The economic reason for this relative insignificance of the livestock branch is easy to understand. Owing to the expanding population and the limited amount of arable land available because of the mountainous nature of Korea's topography, agriculture in Korea has been concentrated on producing food for human consumption. Unless new and effective

1956	1958	1960	1961	1962	1963	1964	1965	1967	1968
160	n.a.	224			268				
154	n.a.	205			242				
151	n.a.	200	254	264	274	274	238	(16%)[b]	(11%)[b]
208	n.a.	301			369				
299	n.a.	543			420				
87.0	72.8	77.2			76.0*				
(53.4)	(n.a.)	(n.a.)							
11.4	23.4	17.3			18.0*				
1.1	1.9	2.3			1.0*				
0.5	1.9	3.2			5.0*				
159	n.a.	191			214				

methods of breeding domesticated animals and of raising the yield of fodder, such as corn, are introduced, it would be uneconomical to expand the livestock population which competes with the human population for scarce land. To be sure, the low development in the livestock sector during the Japanese occupation was partly a result of the deliberate Japanese policy to turn Korea into a chief rice supplier to Japan.

Several factors give North Korea comparative advantages over South Korea in the livestock sector. First, population pressure is much less in the North. Second, the North is more mountainous than the South and as a result grazing land, mountain plateaus, and hills that are unsuitable for crop raising are relatively more abundant. Third, such important feed items as corn and oats are produced predominantly in North Korea.

The won value of the total output in agriculture (Gross Agricultural Product) grew at an annual average rate of 6.0 percent between 1946-63 (table 14).

The growth rate of 5.3 percent in crops lagged slightly behind the total output, while the rate for the livestock and sericultural sectors was, respectively, 8.0 and 8.8 percent. The change in the relative importance of the three branches is the consequence of the differential rates of growth. Growth rate of the agricultural product per capita between 1946-63 amounts to 4.6 percent per annum. There are reasons to believe that not only do official agricultural statistics for the years covered contain marked exaggeration but that the actual growth rate in agriculture slowed down considerably from 1963 to the end of the decade. To begin with, figures for the post-1963 total agricultural production indices remain conspicuously missing in official publications while, in contrast, the same for total industrial production has been published for every year up to 1970. Obviously, the regime is attempting to conceal or downplay poor performance. Then there are evidences to point to substantial statistical inflation during 1956-61 and a disappointing performance for most years of the 1960s.

The damaging effects of the Korean War on agriculture are evident in the index of the gross agricultural product which declined from the prewar level of 151 (1949) to 115 in 1953, the year of the armistice. It is reported officially that during the war 370,000 chŏngbo of farm land was damaged along with a loss of 250,000 head of cattle, 330,000 pigs, and 90,000 fruit trees.[95] By 1956 all branches of agriculture recovered to the prewar level of 1949 except fruit production, which had been declining since 1946. The effect of war was also felt in the composition of the agricultural product. In spite of an overall trend of slowly declining importance of crops, their (crops) relative position improved temporarily during the Korean War at the expense of livestock and sericulture. The relative importance of grains also increased. This must have been partly because of the increased importance and urgency placed on the production of basic food items (rice being the most important) to feed the army and carry out war efforts and partly because of the different degrees of damage incurred by war.

Some Strategic Indicators of Agricultural Development

Various physical data on agricultural development are presented in table 15, followed by rates of growth of each series in table 16. It is clear that there has not been any significant increase in the area of cultivated land during the period, although there were year-to-year fluctuations. A near-upper limit seems

46

to have been reached in the cultivable land available at the level of 2 million chŏngbo. This means that any increase in agricultural production in North Korea must largely come from factors other than expansion in the supply of arable land. Thus, it has been an integral part of the North Korean agricultural policy to emphasize intensive cultivation so as to raise the yield per unit of the limited land available.[96] As an extension and specific application of this policy the regime has been making constant efforts to raise the rate of land utilization,* apply increasing amounts of fertilizers, extend irrigated areas, and generally introduce and disseminate advanced agricultural know-how. Raising agricultural productivity via highly intensive cultivation has become a major goal of the agricultural sector during the current Six Year Plan.

The intensity of the use of cultivated land has been increasing significantly, as indicated by the rate of land utilization calculated for each year. In 1946 the rate was 1.04 and in 1961 it rose to 1.49. This means that on the average about half of the total cultivated land is being cropped twice a year. Because of climatic conditions prevailing in North Korea, double cropping of rice is nearly impossible. Hence, the rate reflects solely the intensity of dry land use. If, for this reason, the acreage for rice is excluded in the calculation, the rate of dry land utilization would be much higher. Since the area of cultivated land has not increased appreciably, the multiple cropping index largely reflects expansion in the sown area, which was growing at an annual rate of 2.8 percent for 1947-1961. In 1961 there was 54.4 percent more sown area than in 1946. However, compared to 1944, a year before the end of Japanese rule, the increase in 1961 was 28.6 percent. Sown area for corn shows the highest rate of growth while sown area for cotton has actually declined (from 60,000 chŏngbo in 1946 to only 29,000 chŏngbo in 1960). Sown area for rice also increased at an annual rate of 2.0 percent for 1947-61, which, given the near impossibility of double cropping of rice, must reflect an increase in the supply of paddy fields.

Production of important crops has been steadily growing except during the Korean War. The only exception is the production of cotton, which, after reaching a peak in 1949, has never recovered the pre-Korean War level. By 1960 the

---

*Rate of land utilization is simply derived by dividing the acreage of sown (cropped) land by that of cultivated land. It is sometimes called multiple cropping index. It shows an average number of times a given land is sown for crops in a given year.

TABLE 15

SOME PHYSICAL INDICATORS OF AGRICULTURAL DEVELOPMENT, 1944-1970

Indicators	Units	1944	1946
I. Crop Production:			
A. Grains	1,000 tons	2417	1898
a. Rice	1,000 tons	1008	1052
b. Corn	1,000 tons	116	156
B. Cotton	1,000 tons	n.a.	15
C. Potatoes (Irish and Sweet)	1,000 tons	775	492
II. Land Utilization:			
A. Sown area, total	1,000 chŏngbo	2321	1934
Grains	1,000 chŏngbo	1996	1670
Rice	1,000 chŏngbo	400	388
Corn	1,000 chŏngbo	173	174
Cotton	1,000 chŏngbo	n.a.	60
Potatoes	1,000 chŏngbo	139	189
B. Cultivated area, total	1,000 chŏngbo		1860
C. Rate of land utilization			1.04
D. Yield per chŏngbo (of sown area)			
Grains	Kilogram	1211	1137
Rice	Kilogram	2520	2711
Corn	Kilogram	671	897
Cotton	Kilogram	n.a.	250
Potatoes	Kilogram	5576	2603
III. Domestic Animal (as of the end of the year):			
A. Cattle	1,000 head	756	472
B. Dairy cattle		1391	766
C. Horses	1,000 head	16	10
D. Sheep and goats	1,000 head	30	7
E. Pigs	1,000 head	385	220
IV. Sericulture:			
A. Cocoons (production)	tons		1881
V. Irrigation:			
A. Total irrigated area	1,000 chŏngbo		119
B. Percent of paddy field under irrigation	percent		30.7
VI. Chemical Fertilizers:			
A. Total applied	1,000 tons		
B. Per chŏngbo of cultivated land	Kilogram		
C. Per chŏngbo of sown (crop) land	Kilogram		
VII. Rural Electrification:			
A. Proportion of rural villages using electricity	percent		
B. Proportion of farm households using electricity	percent		

Sources: For 1944, CCY, 1958, pp. 193-194, 196, 199-200; for potatoes, ERNK, No. 79, pp. 36-37, 41, 47; for 1967-70, Nodong sinmun, November 3, 1970 and November 10, 1970 and The People's Korea, February 12, 1969; for the rest, Kyŏngje chisik, February 1962, pp. 40-41; ERNK, No. 79, pp. 41, 46; Statistical Summary of DPRK, 1946-63, pp. 19-23; Korea News, No. 1, 1965, p. 2; Korea News, No. 2, 1965, p. 14; Hama Takeo, op. cit., p. 56; Nodong sinmun, October 11, 1966; Sakurai Hiroshi, Ajia keizai (Asian Economy), November 1964, Tokyo, pp. 51-59; U.S. Dept. of State, "The Role of Agriculture in North Korea's Development," Research Memorandum, RSB-105, June 21, 1962 (Unclassified), p. 8; CCY, various issues.

1949	1953	1956	1960	1961	1962	1963	1964	1965	1967	1968	1969	1970	7YPT*	6YPT*
2654	2327	2873	3803	4830	5000	5210	5210	4526	(16%)[a]	(11%)[a]			6600	7000~ 7500
1158	1229	1392	1535	1919	2560	3040		2103		(13%)[a]			3000	3500
375	224	760	950	1616						(16%)[a]				
78	18	5	7	15										
782	412	948	851											
2386	2296	2413	2765	2986										
2112	2103	2165	2279	2302										
382	432	493	500	520										
282	241	608	784	933										
81	40	15	29											
120	86	122	133											
1983	1965	1899	1913	2009		1996								
1.20	1.17	1.27	1.45	1.49										
1257	1107	1327	1669	2098										
3031	2845	2824	3070	3690										
1330	929	1250	1212	1721										
963	450	333	241											
6517	4791	7770	6398											
788	504	485	672	665		685	706							
959	637	1205	48214											
9	6	15	8											
13	25	87	184	218		298	344							
660	543	710	1123	1393		1135	1441							
5582	3270	4186	8134											
157	228	361	473			545	601		797					
33.6		73.5	92.7			94.1						100		
260		215	307			599	640				982			
131	16	113	160	249		300								
109	14	89	110	166										
	47.2					93.3	95.5					100		
	41.0					70.8	81.1					91.2		

*7YPT = Seven Year Plan Target; 6YPT = Six Year Plan Target.

[a] Percent increment over the preceding year.

cotton output barely recovered the 1946 level. Although it is known that climatic conditions in North Korea do not favor cultivation of cotton, it is not certain at this point to what extent the failure in cotton production is attributable to unfavorable natural conditions or to other factors. It seems unlikely that external conditions such as weather alone have been responsible for the steady downward trend in production since the Korean War. To be sure, there has been a decline in the sown area of cotton. However, the decline in production has been more than proportionate and this fact is reflected in a drastic decline in the yield per chŏngbo.* The decline in the sown area of cotton points to a deliberate government policy to transform part of the marginal cotton fields for raising other crops, especially food crops, in view of the government emphasis on the increase in food production. As long as North Korea can import cotton the decline in cotton production will not impose any limits on the growth of industries that use cotton as raw materials. North Korea has been continuously importing cotton from both Communist China and the U.S.S.R.

According to official claims, production of grains has been growing at an annual rate of 4.7 percent for 1947-65 (7.2 percent for 1957-60) so that it more than doubled between 1947-65. As to specific components, production of corn has been growing the fastest while rice has been trailing behind that for grains as a whole. Many evidences, some circumstantial, lead to the conclusion that these official statistics have to be substantially discounted, especially since 1957. They also point to disappointingly slow growth all through the 1960s. First, an independent estimate (table 17) shows that the official figures include substantial inflation between 1956-61. It is significant that the exaggeration of output became more pronounced starting from 1959, coinciding with the completion of collectivization and the introduction of the Chŏllima movement. Both of these factors tend to have built-in biases toward statistical overreporting of output. The revised estimates, based on internal consistency and crop yields, have been tested with observed food supply availabilities. These adjusted output figures show that there has been no appreciable improvement in the production of grains since the Five Year Plan was initiated, while there were year-to-year fluctuations. Second, according to one Soviet source, total grain production during 1961-68 increased only by 10 percent (an annual rate of 1.2 percent).[97] Third, North Korea has been a consistent net importer of cereals of substantial amounts

---

*Yield is based on the cropped area.

TABLE 16

AGRICULTURAL DEVELOPMENT: ANNUAL GROWTH RATES AND PER CAPITA

	Annual Rate of Growth (Percent)				Per Capita				
	1954-56	1957-60	1961-63	1947-63	1944	1946	1960	1963	1965
I. Agricultural production:									
A. Total	11.6	8.4	6.3	6.0	(282.4	205.0	352.5	450.4	364.8
1. Crops	10.8	7.4	5.7	5.3					
a. Grains*	7.1	7.2	3.5a	4.7b	(117.8	113.6	142.3	262.8	169.5
(1) Rice*	4.2	2.4	6.5a	3.7b					
(2) Corn	50.2	5.7	69.0d	16.8c	kg(13.6	16.9	88.1	145.4d	
b. Cotton	-34.7	8.8	14.0d	0.0c	(1.6	1.6	0.6	1.4d	
c. Potatoes	23.1	-2.6		4.0e	(90.5	53.1	78.9		
2. Livestock	16.0	9.7	7.1	8.0					
3. Sericulture	19.1	16.1	-8.3	8.8					
B. Per capita (total agri-cultural production)	8.3	4.7	3.8	4.6					
II. Land utilization:					chŏngbo				
A. Total area cultivated	-1.0	0.3	1.3	0.4		(0.20	0.18	0.17	
B. Total sown area	1.6	3.6	8.0d	2.8c		(0.21	0.26	0.27	
III. Irrigation:									
A. Total irrigated area	16.5	7.0	6.2g	9.4f					
IV. Chemical fertilizers:									
A. Total applied		9.4	20.1g	6.2g		27.0j	28.5	53.1i	

*Annual rate of increase of grain production for 1967 and 1968 is reported to be 16% and 11%, respectively, while rice production increased by 13% in 1968 over 1967 (see table 17).

a1961-65; b1947-65; c1947-61; d1961; e1946-60; f1947-64; g1961-64; h1949-64; i1964; j1949.

Source: Based on tables 14 and 15.

for all the years between 1960-68 with a peak trade deficit (in cereals alone) of $22.77 million in 1966. If trade deficits are any indication 1961, 1966, and 1967 stand out as bad years as far as cereals are concerned. Fourth, statistics for grain production for the years since 1966 have not been made public, unlike those for some major industrial products. Finally, the 1976 (Six Year Plan) target for grains shows an increase of only 6.1 to 11.4 percent (depending on the minimum or maximum target figure used) of that originally planned for 1967. The same is true for rice.

TABLE 17

ADJUSTMENTS IN THE OFFICIAL GRAIN PRODUCTION CLAIMS, 1956-1961

	Production (1,000 tons)						Rates of Growth
	1956	1957	1958	1959	1960	1961	5 Year Plan (1957-1960)
Grains:							
Official State Dept.	2,873	3,201	3,700	3,400	3,803	4,830	7.2
Estimate	2,782	2,982	3,240	2,278	2,781	3,378	0.0
Difference	91	219	460	1,122	1,022	1,452	
Rice							
Official State Dept.	1,392	1,459	n.a.	1,515	1,535	1,919	2.4
Estimate	1,392	1,459	1,512	1,392	1,400	1,615	0.3
Difference	0	0	-	123	135	304	
Corn							
Official State Dept.	760	1,130	n.a.	566	950	1,606	5.7
Estimate	669	911	1,074	483	784	1,215	4.0
Difference	91	219	-	83	166	391	

Sources: Table 15; U.S. Department of State, "The Role of Agriculture in North Korea's Development," pp. 9-13.

It is clear that at this rate grain output would fall far short of the planned target of the Seven Year Plan by 1970, not to speak of its fulfillment by the original target year of 1967. The poor performance in this most important segment of agriculture has been in spite of the regime's all-out efforts through increased multiple cropping, irrigation, fertilizers, and mechanization. All these input-related factors have been growing faster than output (tables 15 and 16).

Understandably, the basic line of agricultural policy has been to give priority to the production of grains while facilitating the development of industrial

crops, livestock, sericulture, and fruit growing.[98] In an effort to increase
rice production, North Korea has been experimenting with growing rice in dry
fields which give high yields and are far more favorable for the introduction
of mechanization and require less labor than paddy field rice. Rice culture by
the dry bed method is expected to give an average yield of 4 tons per chŏngbo[99]
under the cropping conditions of 1962. The future direction in agricultural
production, especially rice and corn, was clearly set in a speech by Kim Il-song
at a collective farm in August 1962. He said:

> Hitherto corn has been the king of dry field crops, but in the future it
> must give way to dry field rice. Next year...the total acreage under dry
> field rice should be expanded to 150,000 hectares throughout the country.
> In 1964 the acreage should be further increased to 300,000 and in 1965 to
> 400,000 hectares....When we can insure sufficient rice for feeding the en-
> tire population by expanding the acreage under paddy and dry field rice,
> corn will be largely directed to feeding domestic animals so as to produce
> meat....[100]

It may be anticipated that the yield of the existing paddy field will not
rise sufficiently even if irrigation facilities and fertilizer applications are
expanded unless greatly improved seeds are introduced.[101] Rice culture in the
paddy fields does require extensive use of labor and is difficult to mechanize.
Successful cultivation of rice in dry fields will raise the yield and the productivity of labor and for this reason may appreciably contribute toward growth
in rice production. Compared to the South, North Korea enjoys a relative abundance of dry fields while paddy fields are predominantly located in the South.
Expansion in the dry field cultivation of rice, however, must largely come at
the expense of other crops, in this case probably corn. Although North Korea
has a long way to go before it can produce an adequate supply of rice to feed
the population, a successful expansion in rice production is of utmost importance
to the government and the ruling party in view of its impact on the incentives
of the peasants as well as industrial workers.

The growth rate of the production of potatoes was 4 percent for 1946-60 and
10.9 percent for 1953-60. Although output in 1960 showed considerable improvement over 1946, as compared to 1944 it constituted less than a 10 percent increase. Per capita output of potatoes has actually declined since the Japanese
era. In 1944 per capita production of potatoes was 90.5 kilograms whereas in
1960 it declined to 78.9 kilograms. Sown area for potatoes in 1960 showed a decline over both 1944 and 1946. This is partly offset by a rise in the yield.

Since output figures are those at the places of harvest, the net amount of
crops available will be somewhat smaller, owing to the inevitable reductions

incurred through losses, damages, handling, transporting, and storing. In this connection the government extended (around 1963) its control over threshing and grain-processing plants run directly by collectives by means of a single city or Kun grain administration office. The extension of state control to grain mills is attributed to lower rates of recovery of grains at collective-operated mills, an average of 3 to 4 percent lower than that of state-operated mills. The backwardness of milling machines, a shortage of machine parts, and lack of skills on the part of workers are blamed for this.[102] There seems to be a general lack of technicians competent enough to operate and repair milling machines, and the low recovery rate, no doubt, is partly due to this state of affairs. Moreover, lack of incentives and cooperation on the part of the workers at the mills operated by the collectives may also account for the inefficiency in grain milling.

Development in the livestock sector is generally more favorable. Impressive growth has taken place in the dairy industry as measured by the increase in the number of dairy cattle at a rate of 34.4 and 85.6 percent, respectively, for 1947-60 and 1954-60. No doubt these high rates are partially accounted for by the near insignificance of the dairy industry during the Japanese days and the destruction during the Korean War. This growth in dairy products seems to have come at the expense of beef production, as the number of nondairy cattle has not increased appreciably. This trend, to a certain degree, reflects the diminishing need and role of cattle as a source of draft power as rural mechanization spreads. Population of horses is on the decline as is the trend elsewhere in the world. Usefulness of horses other than for such luxurious purposes as racing has been diminishing as machines take over as sources for draft power. Growth in sheep, goats, and pigs is quite rapid even in per capita terms and in comparison to the level under the Japanese. Aside from increased availability of meat such as pork and mutton, increasing amounts of raw materials for leather, textile, and other related industries are provided through such expansion.

The Korean War devastated the mulberry fields and seriously damaged sericulture. But cocoon production had recovered the prewar level in the beginning of the Five Year Plan, and in 1960 it was more than 4 times that in 1944 and about 2.5 times that in 1953. Increase in cocoon production seems due, inter alia, to an improved technique of raising silkworms. It is reported, for instance, that a strain of silkworms which feed on castor beans is being cultivated now and that this has the effect of markedly increasing the yield of cocoons. Also, a method of cultivating silkworms more than twice a year is being popularized.[103] In the past silkworms could be cultivated only twice a year, in the spring and in the autumn.

Summary and Outlook

There has been a drastic change in the land tenure system and in the organization of agricultural production since the communists took over North Korea in 1945. Private farming, after a brief period of encouragement through land reform, disappeared from the North Korean scene altogether with the completion of socialized agriculture by 1958. Of the two types of farm organizations—state farms and collectives—into which all the private farms have been transformed, the latter is the predominating form.

Commitment to collectivized farming along the lines of Marxist-Leninist ideologies has been a central theme in the North Korean agricultural policy with all its trappings. Collectivization, however, has brought no discernible improvement in agricultural production. Collectivization has been accompanied by a substantial increase in inputs and technological improvements such as mechanization, chemical fertilizers, irrigation, land utilization rate, and farm labor. Availability of arable land has been the only exception to the increasing trend. Yet production has not responded correspondingly. The law of diminishing returns owing to the inevitably fixed supply of land undoubtedly offers partial explanation for the poor performance. The major blame, however, must be assigned to factors related to the nature of the agricultural organization, ownership, and distribution arrangements associated with collectivization. Perhaps the same factors that usually explain the Soviet failure in agriculture will apply here as well. These factors are generally centered around the lack of incentives on the part of the peasants and the coercive nature of the entire farm operation. The situation has not been helped by the assignment of low priority to agriculture as reflected in the allocation of state investment expenditure, the regime's reaction to the adverse trend through stronger central control, or intensified exhortations and indoctrination as substitutes for material incentives.

To be sure, several measures have been introduced since the Seven Year Plan to furnish material incentives among the peasants in order to mollify them and to stimulate productivity as well as to reduce the industry-agriculture income gap. These measures have included raising the prices of some farm products while

55

lowering those of farm implements, machinery, and other input items. In addition, it is claimed that other benefits (social and cultural services) amounting to 50 percent of cash incomes were granted to the peasants during 1961-69.[104] Most far-reaching in this respect was the gradual reduction and eventual abolition of agricultural tax-in-kind. Tax-in-kind had been admittedly a chief avenue for extracting the forced savings necessary to finance the Korean War and industrialization. However, in actuality apart from its window-dressing effect, abolition of the tax would have no significant effects on the incentives of the peasants or on government efforts to secure necessary grains. Since the government's need for grains has not lessened and since the pricing and marketing of farm products are all under its strict control, other indirect and more subtle avenues could be used. A series of measures, in fact, was introduced by the government coinciding with the tax relief in order for the government to secure grains.

Understandably and inevitably, North Korea has sought foreign markets for alleviating domestic food shortages. In spite of the claim by the North Korean leadership that the nation has "completely solved the problem of food"[105] the country has been a substantial and chronic net food importer during 1960-69 with the exception of 1969 when it accumulated a trade surplus in cereals. In the peak year of 1966 trade deficit in cereals amounted to $22.77 million.

Lack of room for expansion in arable land, especially in paddy fields, underinvestment, an ideological commitment to a collectivized method of farming, emphasis on nonpecuniary incentive systems, and excess central control and decision making will remain for North Korea major stumbling blocks in its efforts to raise agricultural production sufficiently to ensure viability in food and to meet the increasing raw material requirements of industry. It is evident that the North Korean leadership itself realizes the problem and does not view future prospects with optimism. For the first time since North Korea instituted economic plans, the planned growth rate for agriculture was suppressed in its official announcement for the current Six Year Plan: the leadership does not have to account for targets which have not been made public.

CHAPTER
3

The Industrial Sector

Heritage of Japanese Occupation

At the beginning of the communist takeover of North Korea in 1945, the North Korean industry was in a state of chaos and disrepair. The industrial plants that North Korea inherited from the Japanese were not in good operational condition: in their last-ditch efforts to maximize war-related industrial products toward the end of World War II, the Japanese neglected to maintain and replace the machinery as it wore out. To make matters worse, the fleeing Japanese had, in the face of the advancing Soviet Army, inflicted considerable destruction and sabotage. It was reported, for instance, that 64 mines were totally flooded, 178 partially flooded, 6 enterprises—including the Chŏngjin Iron Works, Sup'ung Hydroelectric Plant, and Pyŏngyang Aircraft Plant—were completely destroyed, and 47 enterprises partially destroyed; in addition, 19 hydroelectric plants were put out of operation.[1] Furthermore, withdrawal of trained Japanese personnel who used to occupy all key managerial and technical positions created an extreme shortage of skilled manpower and managerial know-how.

Nevertheless, the Japanese left behind a modestly developed industrial base concentrated in heavy industry, especially the metal and chemical industries, with concomitant development in hydroelectric power production, railroad transportation, and communication. Japan introduced modern mining methods, up-to-date and large-scale chemical and hydroelectric plants, and a railroad system second to none in Asia at that time.[2] Significantly for industrialization, the North was the chief producer of electricity in Korea, providing the bulk of electricity generated (80 percent in 1942) and possessing an overwhelming share of the generating capacity (92 percent of the annual average capacity around 1944)[3] owing to the North's natural endowment for hydroelectric potential. Being relatively well-endowed in their deposits, the North's level of production of strategic minerals (coals, iron cores, and zinc) was relatively high, especially toward the end of the Japanese rule.[4]

However, there were serious defects in the industrial structure and location. The Korean industry, geared primarily to the benefits of the Japanese, was dependent on Japan for final processing and finished products: heavy industry was limited to the production of mainly raw materials, semifinished goods, and war supplies, which were shipped to Japan proper for final processing and consumption. This dependence on Japan was especially pronounced in the machine-building (engineering) industry, which Japan did not allow Korea to develop. In a classical pattern of a colony, Korea acted as a supplier of important raw materials, semifinished products, and rice, as well as a market for Japan's manufactured goods. Industrial location under the Japanese eloquently testifies to its primary goal: most industrial centers were strategically located on the eastern or western coastal areas near ports so as to connect them efficiently with Japan proper. The railroad network, though by far the most developed system then existing in Asia, was mainly developed along north-south lines, thus lacking lateral lines connecting various points in the east with those of the west. The main purpose behind the building of the railroad system by the Japanese was to link the southern part of Korea with the northern section and, more important, for the purpose of a long-term war and territorial expansion in mainland Asia.

Severance of the North Korean economy from Japan and South Korea meant that North Korea's traditional market for raw materials and semifinished goods as well as its sources of food and manufactured goods were cut off, not to speak of the withdrawal of the entrepreneurial and engineering skills supplied mainly by Japanese personnel. Links between industry and agriculture, between heavy and light industry, and between raw materials and finished products were disrupted. Thus the problem facing the communist regime in North Korea as it began to gain foothold and solidify its power was to develop a viable economy through industrialization reoriented toward other communist bloc countries while at the same time rectify the "malformation" in the "colonial" industrial structure. Subsequently, the problem was compounded further by the requirements for reconstructing the economy, particularly industry, nearly devastated by the Korean War. The strategy that the North Korean leadership followed through various economic plans was the priority development of heavy industry. In the pursuit of this policy, the strategic importance of the machine-making industry, which was the

58

weakest link in heavy industry under the Japanese, was early recognized as the "kingpin" of heavy industry. Indeed, North Korea has subsequently made rapid progress in industrialization, laying a firm foundation in heavy industry. In its new structure the machine-building industry has come to assume a key importance.

Nationalization of Industry[5]

Elimination of Private Industry

The formal process of transferring private ownership of industry to state and collective ownership was set into motion with the proclamation of the nationalization decree[6] by the Provisional People's Committee on October 10, 1946. Even before the formal decree, however, key industrial enterprises were already controlled by the people's committees under the leadership and assistance of the Soviet occupation force.[7] Thus the decree simply legalized what had been de facto nationalization up to that time.

With the decree, 1,034 key industrial enterprises comprising 90 percent of all North Korean industry[8] were confiscated. The takeover was made easier by the withdrawal of the Japanese, who formally owned and controlled almost all the key industrial enterprises.

Since the initial sweeping measure toward nationalization in 1946, there was a lull in the regime's campaign against private enterprise. During the period immediately following the nationalization decree, private enterprises were not only tolerated but even officially encouraged, as evidenced in the Provisional People's Committee decision of October 4, 1946,[9] announced, significantly, a few days before the nationalization decree. The decision guaranteed enterprises and commercial houses owned by Korean citizens (which were small in size) against nationalization. Further, it authorized the provisional government to sell or make available to Koreans Japanese-owned small consumer-goods factories employing less than 50 workers. This conciliatory strategy was obviously motivated by expediency under conditions of transition and economic disarray. Safeguarding the property rights of owners of handicraft and small industries would stimulate private capital in this sector and thus permit the government to concentrate its scarce financial resources on other sectors considered strategic, such as heavy industry.[10] Encouraging the private sector would also prove useful to the regime since that sector supplied entrepreneurial and technical skill which would otherwise have been in short supply after the Japanese withdrawal.

However, in spite of the ostensibly tolerant attitude on the part of the regime toward private enterprise, private entrepreneurs had to overcome numerous obstacles and handicaps in the course of production. The regime's labor, rationing, and price policies and its control of raw materials placed the private industry at a competitive disadvantage. The government set ceilings on wage rates with the result that private manufacturers were not able to attract needed labor. Private manufacturers also found it difficult to attract labor from state enterprises, as workers would lose ration privileges which only workers at state enterprises enjoyed. Further, workers were required to obtain discharges from the state enterprises for the transfer. Other than operating from inventories and obtaining occasional supplies from the free market, private manufacturers depended on the government for allocations of raw materials. The government allocation policy, however, discriminated against private industry. When they received allocation, private manufacturers were placed on a contract to furnish the government with a corresponding amount of final products at government-fixed prices.[11] Moreover, private firms required government permission to operate or to expand.[12] Under such conditions it is not surprising that by 1950 private manufacturers were typically operating at about one-fourth of the plant capacity,[13] and that the contribution of the private sector to the gross industrial product declined substantially (table 18). The trend continued during and after the Korean War and by 1958 private enterprise as a form of business ceased to exist.

From the very beginning the private sector was largely confined to small-scale manufacturing such as food processing, weaving and spinning, metal-working, manufacture of stationery, paper, and cosmetics, and cottage handicrafts. As late as 1957 (the first quarter), one year before complete socialization, almost 30 percent of the food processing and 14 percent of metal-working were performed by the private manufacturing establishments (table 19). The scale of operation of private manufacturing firms was extremely small: in May 1957, the average number of workers per establishment was only 2.5.[14] Only 14 percent of a total of 633 private firms employed more than 5 workers and the rest—86 percent—were operating with an average of 1.4 workers per establishment.[15]

TABLE 18

CHANGE IN THE RELATIVE IMPORTANCE OF STATE, COOPERATIVE,
AND PRIVATE ENTERPRISES, 1946-1963

	1946	1949	1953	1954	1956	1957	1958	1960	1962	1963
I. Number of enterprises:										
1. State enterprises	n.a.	n.a.	n.a.	743	744	n.a.	1795	2254	2205	2295
Of which: locally managed				184	160		1254	1752	1594	n.a.
2. Producers' cooperatives		567	581	556	551	824	819	489	385	642 }
Fisheries' cooperatives				165	162	n.a.	176	155	171	→
3. Private enterprises	n.a.	n.a.	n.a.	n.a.	n.a.	633	n.a.	-	-	-
II. Gross Industrial Product according to ownership (%):										
1. State owned	72.4	85.5	86.2	88.9	89.9	90.6	87.7	89.7	n.a.	91.2
2. Cooperatives	-	5.2	9.9	7.3	8.1	8.1	12.2	10.3	n.a.	8.8
3. Private	27.6	9.3	3.9	3.8	2.0	2.0	0.1	-	-	-
Of which: small merchandise industry	(4.4)	(1.5)	(1.0)	(1.1)	(0.7)	(0.5)	(0.1)	-	-	-
III. % of former private entrepreneurs, handicraft workers and merchants transferred into socialized sectors (as of December):										
1. Socialized		22.5	33.7	39.5	62.7	77.2	100.0	100.0	100.0	100.0
Of which:										
Joined cooperatives		(11.0)	(16.7)	(18.7)	(39.8)	(54.2)	(76.6)			
Turned workers, clerks, etc.		(11.5)	(17.0)	(10.8)	(22.9)	(23.1)	(23.4)			
2. Not socialized		77.5	66.3	60.5	37.3	22.8	-			

Sources: I, For 1954, 1956, 1958, and 1960, ERNK, No. 79, p. 21; for 1949, 1953, and 1957, "Our Country's Cooperative Management," Kyŏngje kŏnsŏl, (Economic Construction) February 1958, p. 65; and for 1963, Statistical Summary of DPRK, 1946-63, p. 13.—II, For 1954, "Our Country's Cooperative Management," loc. cit.; for 1957, CCY, 1958, p. 180; for the rest, Statistical Summary of DPRK, 1946-63, p. 14.—III, Kim Il, "Concerning Further Development of Local Industries," Chŏnguk chibang sanŏp mit sŏngsan hyŏpdong chohap yŏlsŏngja taewhae munhŏnjip (Documents for Nationwide Local Industries and Producers Cooperatives Enthusiasts Meeting) (Pyŏngyang: Korean Labor Party Publishing House, 1959), p. 34; for number of private enterprises, Haebanghu uri nara ŭi inmin kyŏngje palchŏn, p. 179.

State Enterprises

With the elimination of private industry all the industrial establishments in North Korea today fall under two categories in terms of ownership-control arrangements. The first form is state enterprises which are state-owned and state-managed. The second and the only other form is industrial cooperatives. From the very beginning of the regime, starting from the nationalization decree, state enterprises played a dominant role (table 18). By 1963, five years after private enterprise disappeared from the North Korean scene (and the last year for which such information is available), state enterprises contributed an overwhelming portion of the total industrial output (91.2 percent with 2,295 enterprises), the rest originating from the cooperative sector.

TABLE 19

CONTRIBUTION OF THE PRIVATE SECTOR
TO THE GROSS INDUSTRIAL PRODUCT, 1957
(Data for First Quarter Only)

Item	Contribution as % to the Gross Output in the Respective Industry
Food processing.	29.6
Oil paper.	12.6
Stationery	10.0
Metal-working.	13.6
Paper.	6.2
Textiles	5.2
Cosmetics.	9.0
Cultural goods	7.7

Source: Cho Chae-sŏn, Kwadogie issŏsŏ ŭi chosŏn nodongdang ŭi kyŏngje chŏngchaek (Economic Policy of the Korean Labor Party during the Period of Transition) (Pyŏngyang: Korean Labor Party Publishing House, 1958), p. 114.

Though the North Korean industrial enterprise is an administrative arm of the central government, it is an independent and autonomous unit of production insofar as it is deemed solely responsible for fulfilling the assigned tasks. The state-appointed manager assumes responsibility for the productive activities of the enterprise and is assisted in his task by the chief engineer, vice-manager(s), second engineer, and supervisors. The chief engineer, acting as the "chief of staff" for the enterprise, is the principal representative of the manager and shares the responsibility on matters of production with him.[16] With the introduction of the Taean industrial management system in 1961, control and management of each industrial enterprise was explicitly and formally placed under the collective leadership of the in-plant (communist) party committee which has become the highest decision-making unit (chart 1); this is clear in Kim Il-song's own definition of tha Taean system (so named because the system saw its birth with Kim Il-song's personal "guidance-tour" at Taean Electric Plant in December 1960). According to Kim, under the Taean system (Taean saŏp ch'aegye):

CHART 1

ORGANIZATIONAL CHART OF LARGE-SCALE INDUSTRIAL ENTERPRISES

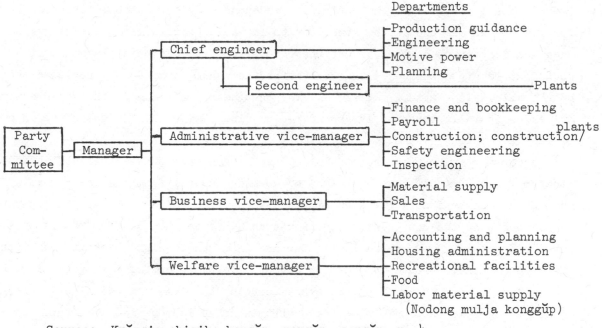

Source: Kyŏngje chisik: kongŏp, nongŏp, sangŏp, p. 4.

...factories and enterprises conduct all their management activities under the collective leadership of the Party committees and carry out their economic tasks by giving precedence to political work and rousing the producer masses to activity, under which the superiors help inferiors in a responsible manner....

Our Party put an end to one-man management by the director, the outdated way of enterprise management, defined the Party committee as the highest leading organ at each economic unit and set up the system of collective leadership by the Party committee in enterprise management. Thus, the Party committee was made to steer economic activities by collectively discussing and deciding upon the orientations and ways and means for the settlement of important matters arising in the economic work in each period and directing and supervising their satisfactory implementation and, at the same time, to scrupulously attend to Party organization work and ideological education so as to actively organize and mobilize all the working people to the execution of revolutionary tasks.[17]

Initially, the financing of state enterprises was based on budget allocation. Under the budget allocation system the enterprise receives a given budget from the government to cover the operating expenses during a fiscal period. If, at the end of the period, the enterprise accumulates any surplus of revenues over expenditures, this is turned over to the government. In case of deficit an additional budget is allocated to make up for the loss.[18] Thus the enterprise under this system is not directly responsible for its financial condition and hence its efficiency.

In an effort to make the enterprise independently accountable financially for its operations and at the same time to infuse a certain measure of independence and initiative on the part of the enterprise, the system of independent accounting (Toknip ch'aesanje) has been introduced and has gradually replaced the budget allocation system. It is believed that nearly all the North Korean enterprises, especially those of large and medium size, are currently under the independent accounting system.

Under the independent accounting system[19] each enterprise receives, in addition to fixed capital, only a minimum of working capital from the government through the central bank. The enterprise is required to meet the various operating expenses in the course of production such as those incurred for raw materials, wages and salaries, and depreciation for machinery and equipment on its own with the fund obtained through sale of its output. In the event of a shortage in working capital it can borrow from the bank according to plan. An additional supply of state funds is made only when the government plan is modified to expand its output goals. The central bank has the responsibility of making sure that the government funds are utilized properly by the enterprise. Before March 1964 interest was charged on loans, but since then the enterprise is provided with interest-free (loan) funds necessary to carry out the planned output. Difficulties in the operation of enterprises owing to scarcity of working capital must have been the major reason for the reform. Under the independent accounting system a portion of the surplus (or profit) is retained by the enterprise for its own use, unlike the budget allocation system under which any surplus is turned over to the government in its entirety. Thus the independent accounting system provides some built-in incentives to the enterprise since it is rewarded or

64

penalized financially depending on how efficiently it performs the government-
assigned task of delivering production quotas. This is the government's way of
ensuring the economic and maximum utilization of scarce resources on the part of
the enterprises.

In the mid-1960s (simultaneously with the introduction of the subteam contract system in the collective farms), the independent accounting system began
to be applied to various small production units (shops, work brigades) within
the enterprise and is referred to as the internal accounting system (Naebu
ch'aesanje). This is an intraenterprise incentive system whereby a record is
kept of various factors of production used by each working group. Those units
which show reduction and economic utilization of inputs are rewarded by bonuses.
This is an attempt to narrow the work-reward gap among industrial workers by
making the work more directly and immediately responsible and rewardable.

Fulfilling the quota, while the most important, is not the only success indicator of the management of the state enterprise. The enterprise is not only
asked to fulfill the "quantitative indices" such as the quantity of output but
also the "qualitative indices." The latter include effectiveness in the utilization of equipment and productive capacity, labor, productivity, cost reduction,
profit, and so on.[20] Profit, for instance, plays an important role in that it
is used as a barometer of how efficient the enterprise is in minimizing the cost
of producing the planned target. This means that the North Korean enterprise is
not encouraged to meet the production quota at any cost. Rather, it is asked to
fulfill the quota while at the same time minimizing the cost.

Not only does profit influence managerial behavior as a success indicator
but it also has built-in material incentives for the manager and the workers of
the enterprise. This is achieved by allowing the enterprise to retain a portion
of the profit for various purposes. Up to 50 percent of the profit is taxed and
paid to the government treasury; the remaining half is kept by the enterprise
for accumulation in the "enterprise fund." Of the "enterprise fund," 30 percent
is earmarked for the introduction of new technology, improvement in existing
equipment, expansion in production and product diversification, and quality improvement. Of the remaining, 30 percent is allocated to improve the cultural
and welfare facilities of the workers and 40 percent for rewards and temporary
subsidies to workers. Where the internal accounting system has been introduced,
20 percent of the fund can be earmarked as bonuses for the work teams under the
system, presumably out of the 40 percent general reward pool.[21]

Unlimited maximization of profit, as well as unlimited overfulfillment of
targets, however, is not encouraged, especially when a firm produces multiple
products, for it may tempt the enterprise to overfulfill the target of more
profitable commodities at the expense of less profitable products. In such
cases, a balance of profit and plan fulfillment in each individual product rather
than an overall profit seems to be emphasized. Kim Il-song, deploring such practices, was quoted to have said that "a considerable number of our enterprises and
their leaders are producing easily processable and/or expensive products in an
unnecessarily large quantity, and, by long storage or idle stockpiling of these
products, they are failing to assure a prompt currency circulation as well as a
return to the state and are even jeopardizing the commodity circulation plans."[22]

There has been a marked increase in the size of state enterprises in terms
of the number of employed workers (table 20). Of all the size classes, the highest growth has occurred in the largest size enterprises (over 3,000 workers),
followed by the next size class (2,001 to 3,000 workers). This is reflected by
an increase in the relative frequency of these large state enterprises (hiring
more than 2,000) between 1954-63. In an economy where the development of heavy
industry has been assigned priority, the emergence of a number of giant-sized enterprises is not surprising. (For instance, with 11,500 workers Pyŏngyang Cotton
Textile was the largest enterprise in North Korea [in 1963] followed by Kangsŏn
Steel Plant which hired 11,000 workers.)[23] As a result, there is a substantial
degree of concentration of workers in a small number of large-scale enterprises.

State enterprises are classified into central and local enterprises depending on their size, sphere of influence, and utilization of output. Accordingly,
central enterprises are those which operate on a larger scale than do local enterprises and whose products possess nationwide significance, utilized throughout the economy. Local enterprises, in contrast, are small in size and their
products are mainly for local consumption, typically utilizing locally available
resources. Central state enterprises are controlled by the appropriate ministries of the central government through the respective bureaus concerned, whereas
local state enterprises are under the control of the appropriate agencies of the
provincial or municipal people's committee.

Local industries have come to play an increasingly important role in industrial production, particularly since 1958, as a result of a deliberate government campaign. Before 1958, all local state enterprises were under the control
of the provincial authorities. Since then, at the suggestion of Kim Il-song and

TABLE 20

SIZE DISTRIBUTION OF STATE ENTERPRISES ACCORDING TO NUMBER OF WORKERS, 1954-1963

Workers	Number of Enterprises				Number of Workers (Percent)			
	1954	1957	1960	1963	1954	1957	1960	1963
Total number	742 (100.0%)	(100.0%)	2254 (100.0%)	2295 (100.0%)	100.0	100.0	100.0	100.0
Under 100	319 (43.0)	(36.2)	1274 (56.5)	1018 (44.4)	6.2	3.5	9.0	5.9
From 101-500	287 (38.7)	(41.3)	645 (28.6)	897 (39.1)	29.4	28.2	27.0	30.7
" 501-1000	89 (12.0)	(13.4)	182 (8.1)	186 (8.1)	29.7	26.1	19.0	15.9
" 1000-2000	38 (5.1)	(7.5)	92 (4.1)	114 (5.0)	23.3	27.1	19.2	19.5
" 2001-3000	6 (0.8)	(0.7)	29 (1.3)	34 (1.5)	6.8	4.7	10.1	9.7
3001 & over	3 (0.4)	(0.9)	32 (1.4)	46 (2.0)	4.6	10.4	15.6	18.3

Sources: For 1954 and 1957, Academy of Science, Uri nara inmin kyŏngje essŏ saengsannyŏk kwa saengsan kwangye ŭi hosang chagyong (Inter-relationship Between the Productivity and the Relations of Production in the People's Economy of Our Country) (Pyŏngyang: Academy of Science Publishing House, 1960), p. 26.

For 1960 and 1963, Statistical Summary of DPRK, 1946-63, p. 13.

the Party, enterprises managed at the municipal and county level sprang up like "bamboo shoots after the rain" throughout North Korea. It was claimed that the mass movement initiated by Kim for the purpose of expanding the food-processing industry and the production of daily necessities resulted in the construction of more than 1,000 new factories within two to three months and that more than 85 percent of these factories immediately began production.[24] Judging from the hastiness and the number involved, they must have been small, with little mechanization.

Several reasons can be advanced as factors that influenced the North Korean policy-makers toward emphasizing the local industries and instituting some measure of decentralization. Since local industries are typically consumer-goods producers and processors of agricultural products for food, the move, first of all, reflects the regime's attempt to rectify the unbalanced growth between heavy and light industry by boosting the latter.

Second, extensive central control of industry has brought with it excessive expansion, complexity, and compartmentalization in the central controlling organs. The resulting bureaucratic inefficiency, lethargy, and corruption—coupled with a sort of interministry and interoffice rivalry—produced a waste of resources owing to the lack of flexibility in the supply of materials and correct estimation of the needs of various sectors of industry. Concentration of administrative personnel and technicians in central industries meant that there was a dearth of able managerial and skilled workers in local industries.[25] Economic waste arising from an imbalance in the allocation of high-echelon man-power between central and local industries had to be eliminated.

Third, the development of local factories would lead to fuller and better utilization of local resources to meet local requirements. Any seasonal labor surplus that may arise in a particular locality at a particular time can be more effectively estimated and mobilized locally to suit the local needs. Also, locating plants near the source of raw materials or consuming points would reduce transportation costs for those industries that use local raw materials or serve the local market. Kim Il-song, speaking in October 1959 at the national convention of the local enterprises and cooperatives, pleaded emphatically for more effective and expanded exploitation of local raw materials, encouraging local industries to find ways to use local materials as inputs.[26] There has been some success in the movement, in that the proportion of raw materials originating from local sources in the gross output of local industries rose from

58.8 percent in 1958 to 60.5 and 62.5 percent, respectively, in 1959 and 1960. Reportedly, the successful trend continued into subsequent years. In addition to increased dependence on local raw materials, new and better use of agricultural by-products and waste industrial materials is also being urged.[27]

Fourth, the development of local industries based on local resources stimulates heavy industry by enabling the government to concentrate its investment funds on central and heavy industrial projects. Also, since local industries use as raw materials the products of collective farms, they stimulate agricultural production. In addition, local industries are expected to spur agriculture through increased production of, and providing increased repair services for, various farm implements.[28] Furthermore, local industries are urged and empowered to set up medium-sized enterprises, such as iron works with an annual capacity of 10 to 20 thousand tons, and cement manufacturing plants with an annual capacity of 30 to 50 thousand tons, whose products are to be supplied to local industries. This is part of the renovation in industrial management introduced in October 1959.[29]

The growing importance of local industries is shown by various indicators. First of all, the proportion of the total state revenue contributed by local industries (through profit deductions and turnover taxes) increased (from 9.2 percent in 1958 to 16.5 and 21.2 percent, respectively, in 1959 and 1960).[30] Also, there has been a substantial increase in the share of local industries in the gross industrial output (from 13.3 in 1956 to 37.8 percent in 1963). Relative growth was more pronounced in the role of local industries in the production of consumer goods (table 21).

Among the consumer goods the main domain of local industries is in food items such as soy sauce, bean paste, and processed vegetables (table 21). These items are generally characterized by low capital and technical requirements for production and can be easily produced with primitive tools and equipment on a small scale. Judging from the number of trained and skilled workers and machinery available in local industry, the level of mechanization was still very low in 1962. In that year, there were reportedly 4,000 technicians and skilled workers, 2,150 sets of lathes, and 350 sets of shapers in local industries.[31] The production of textile goods, on the contrary, was dominated by central industries. This is explained by the fact that the textile industry is dominated by a few large modernized factories located in major cities. Containing the Pyŏngyang Cotton Textile Plant and other large textile plants, Pyŏngyang City

TABLE 21

PROPORTION OF MAJOR CONSUMER GOODS PRODUCED BY LOCAL INDUSTRY,
1956, 1961, 1963, AND 1969

Items	Proportion (Percent)			
	1956	1961	1963	1969
Total consumer goods	18.2	56.0	59.0	50.0*
Textiles		19.4	n.a.	
Confectionaries		85.0	n.a.	
Bean paste		100.0	99.2	
Underwear		65.6	n.a.	
Processed vegetables		98.5	n.a.	
Processed alcoholic beverages		86.2	n.a.	
Socks		58.5	95.5	
Soy sauce		100.0	95.5	
Vegetable oil		66.8	57.9	
Shoes		34.0	31.1	

*Approximate.

Sources: For 1961, Pak Yong-song, loc. cit.; for 1963, "Statistical Material on the Development of the 1963 People's Economic Plan," Kyŏngje chisik, February 1964, pp. 42-46, translated in JPRS, ERNK, No. 123, p. 22; for 1969, Nodong sinmun, February 25, 1970.

stands out as the largest textile center. Other major textile plants are the Sinŭiju Textile Plant, the Kaesŏng Textile Plant, and the Kusŏng Textile Plant, all of which are reported to be highly modernized. Local textile plants are chiefly confined to the use of inferior and low-quality materials, industrial wastes, and locally available raw materials, such as rags, fabrics produced from wild plants, hemp and flax, and fabric remnants.[32]

The share of local industries in the total consumer-goods production has declined somewhat in recent years to 50 percent in 1969 from 56 and 59 percent, respectively, in 1961 and 1963. This must reflect faster growth in the large-scale central enterprises in the production of consumer goods toward the end of the 1960s. In spite of the slight relative decline in the production of total consumer goods, the gross value of local industry has grown rapidly so that in 1969 it was three times that in 1958.[33] Appeals for innovation and mechanization in local industry within local means have continued in recent years as evidenced by official North Korean literature and speeches.

Industrial Cooperatives

The decline and the eventual elimination of the private industrial establishments were due mainly to the absorption of the private manufacturers and
their workers into the cooperatives. September 1947 marked the beginning of the
cooperative form of industrial production with the emergence of producers' cooperatives which were initially placed under the supervision of the already existing consumers' cooperatives formed the previous year. By the end of that year,
28 producers' cooperatives were in operation, made possible by the "conversion"
of former handicraft cottage industry and "free lance" workers. By 1953, producers' and fisheries' cooperatives became separate and distinct organizations
independent of the consumers' cooperatives.[34]

Besides the producers'cooperatives, there sprang up in 1956 what are called
production-marketing (saengsan p'anmae) cooperatives, a kind of semiproducers'
and semimarketing cooperative. The primary purpose behind their formation was
that of converting small and medium private merchants into "socialistic" industrial workers. Tax incentives were introduced in 1956 to make the conversion
economically advantageous by granting reduction in tax rates or outright tax exemption.[35] It is expected that in time they will be eventually absorbed by producers' cooperatives, consumers' cooperatives, or state commercial institutions.

Further modification in the organization of the industrial cooperatives
took place in 1957 when producers' cooperatives were divided and classified into
three forms or types according to the nature of the organization, property arrangements, and settlement of incomes earned. Thus in the case of Type I, private ownership of means of production is permitted and for this reason is considered "primitive." In Type II, cooperatives which are considered "intermediate"
and "transitional," private ownership of the means of production is still permitted while an attempt is made to absorb gradually the privately owned portion
of the property into collective ownership. Control and management of the means
of production apart from ownership, however, are made collectively. In Type III,
there is complete communal ownership of all the means of production, and distribution of income is based solely on labor contribution. This form is considered
"superior" and most "advanced," since it is completely "socialistic." Type I industrial cooperatives no longer exist in North Korea. The proportion of Type III
increased rapidly (from 23.6 percent in 1956 to 75 percent in 1960, the remaining
25 percent belonging to Type II) and has become the dominating form of cooperative.[36]

The highest managing and administrative body of a producers' or fisheries' (marine) cooperative is elected by the general assembly of the members of the respective cooperatives and is under the direct supervision of the governing body of the provincial or municipal association of cooperatives. The central committee of the nationwide association of cooperative industries assumes the responsibility of setting up the general guidelines concerning the goals and activities of all the industrial cooperatives in the country. The governing body of each association is in turn elected by the general assembly, which is made up of the representatives from each member cooperative.[37]

The number of producers' cooperatives, after a steady rise up to 1958, when socialization of industry was completed, has declined (table 18). The number of fisheries' cooperatives, on the other hand, has remained relatively stable. The reduction in the number of producers' cooperatives was the result of a large-scale transformation of these cooperatives and their workers into state enterprises, particularly those managed locally. It was, for example, reported that 347 producers' cooperatives with over 53,000 workers were absorbed into state industrial enterprises in 1960,[38] making the average size of the absorbed cooperative about 153 workers. Those selected for absorption tend to be larger-than-average cooperatives. For instance, compared to the average size of 153 workers per absorbed cooperatives in 1960, the average number of workers in the remaining cooperatives was 119 workers (66,000 workers in a combined total of 556 producers' and fisheries' cooperatives) in 1962.[39]

Cooperatives are engaged mostly in small-scale production, such as food processing, handicrafts, and cottage-type industries. Collectively, the cooperative form of production is relatively unimportant, contributing only a small share (8.8 percent in 1963) of the gross industrial output.

State Industrial Investment

Perhaps the best indicator of the importance that the North Korean planners assign to industry in their development plans is the allocation of state industrial investment. Examination of the growth and allocation of the state industrial investment for 1949-70 (table 22) leads to the following observations. First, state investment in industry in absolute amount has been rising rapidly throughout the period. This trend is certain to continue into the 1970s as the

Six Year Plan calls for expending in six years more than the amount spent in 10 years of the Seven Year Plan.[40]

Second, North Korea's commitment to economic development through rapid industrialization, especially through fast growth in heavy industry, is apparent. More than one-half of the total state investment has been allocated to the industrial sector throughout the period, the allocation registering its peak during the Seven Year Plan (two-thirds in 1965, for example).

Third, as a single sector, heavy industry has consistently received the largest amounts of state investment throughout the entire period of North Korean existence. Upward of 40 percent of the total state investment was spent on heavy industry during the Three Year Plan and Five Year Plan. The share dipped a little during the early years of the Seven Year Plan but began to rise shortly thereafter. For the current Six Year Plan an average of 41 percent of the total state investment is planned to be allocated to heavy industry. This points to the continued North Korean developmental strategy of assigning highest priority to heavy industry.

Fourth, investment in heavy industry has occupied an overwhelming portion (more than 80 percent) of total state industrial investment on the average, at the expense of investment in light industry. The share of light industry in total state industrial investment has not only remained at a low level but has not improved appreciably. Heavy industrial investment is concentrated on the electric, coal, mining, metallurgical, and machine-building industries with prime importance increasingly given to extractive industries during the 1960s and the Six Year Plan, while the textile industry is the area of concentration for light industrial investment.

Based on the statistical evidence presented here, a strong case could be made to refute the North Korean official policy of balanced growth between light and heavy industry, except for the early 1960s. It appears quite evident that the policy of parallel development between heavy and light industry, motivated perhaps to mollify the populace, was discarded at least for the time being in favor of the former. Planning an average of only 17 percent for light industry for the Six Year Plan is the newest evidence of adherence to the old policy, in spite of the lip service the regime pays for improving the lot of the people via faster growth in the consumer-goods sector.

TABLE 22

STATE INDUSTRIAL INVESTMENT, 1949-1970
(In Constant Prices of April 1, 1957)

	1949	1956	1960	1961
Total State Investment (million won)	89.0	351.0	567.0	593.0
A. Investment in industry (million won)	39.4	188.1	260.3	344.5
B. (A) as percent of total state investment	44.3	53.6	45.9	58.1
C. Composition (percent) of industrial investment				
1. Heavy industry		(93.3)	(80.6)	(69.7)
Electrical industry		14.8	11.1	11.1
Coal industry		6.7	11.4	9.9
Mining industry		8.6	23.9	16.3
Metallurgy industry		7.7	5.7	6.2
Machine industry		6.3	11.7	9.1
2. Light industry		(16.7)	(19.4)	(30.3)
Textiles		4.0	4.6	3.7

*3 Y P = Three Year Plan; 5 Y P = Five Year Plan; 7 Y P = Seven Year Plan;
6 Y P = Six Year Plan.

[a]Reported as two-thirds.

Sources: CCY (various issues); Nodong sinmun, November 10, 1970; The
People's Korea, April 29, 1970; Joseph S. Chung, "The Six Year Plan (1971-76)
of North Korea: Targets, Problems and Prospects," Journal of Korean Affairs,
July 1971, pp. 17-18.

74

TABLE 22, Continued

1962	1963	1964	1965	1969	1970	3 Y P* (1954-56) Annual Average	5 Y P* (1957-60) Annual Average	7 Y P* (1961-70) Annual Average (1961-68)	6 Y P* (1971-76) Annual Average
652.0	860.0	760.0				356.9	501.0	975.0	
363.8	481.6	494.0				177.0	257.0	555.6	
55.8	56.0	65.0	66.7[a]	56.6		49.6	51.3	57.0	49.0
(63.7)	(68.2)	(73.8)	(87.3)		(80.7)	(81.1)	(82.6)	(80.0)	(83.0)
12.9	14.6	11.5				14.4	11.9		
9.9	12.6	14.7				5.3	9.6		
15.7	17.5	19.4				8.2	16.3		
5.0	5.8	6.1				7.0	10.5		
7.4	10.1	11.1				7.7	12.4		
(36.3)	(32.8)	(26.2)	(12.7)		(19.3)	(18.9)	(17.4)	(20.0)	(17.0)
7.2	8.7	5.5				5.4	5.8		

Industrial Growth and Structural Change

Overall Industrial Growth

After the departure of the Japanese, the North Korean economy made significant inroads toward industrialization. In spite of the Korean War, which nearly
crippled the economy, the rate of North Korea's industrial growth has been phenomenal (tables 23 and 24). The gross industrial product (defined in "Notes to
Tables 23 and 24") in 1970 was 69 times that in 1946, registering an average
growth per annum of 19.3 percent. In per capita terms the growth rate of industry for 1947-70 was 17.3 percent per year. These official growth statistics contain elements of exaggeration owing to various factors (see Appendix B and "Notes
to Tables 23 and 24"). A Western estimate of the indices of North Korea's industrial growth for 1946-63 is consistently lower than official rates. The following is a comparison of official and recalculated indices of industrial growth for
various periods:

	1949-56	1956-59	1960-63	1949-63	1956-63
Official index (%)	9.0	45.2	15.1	17.4	26.5
Recalculated index (%)	6.6	36.0	7.8	15.6	25.3

Source: Pong S. Lee, "Overstatement of North Korean Industrial Growth,
1946-63," Journal of Korean Affairs, July 1971, p. 8.

Discounting the official growth rates because of statistical inflation would
leave the pace of North Korea's progress toward industrialization still impressive and place her among the world's high growth economies.

While the overall industrial growth rate is high, North Korea's speed of
industrialization slowed down considerably in the 1960s (table 24). The slowdown
was climaxed by a decline of 3 percent in industrial output in 1966, marking the
first time since the beginning of the regime that industrial output ever declined.
Under the circumstances it was clear that the planned rate of industrial growth
of 18 percent a year during the original Seven Year Plan (1961-67) was impossible
to fulfill. Inevitably, the target year of the Seven Year Plan was extended to
1970, and it is no coincidence that the official announcement for extending the
target year of the Plan was made in 1966. As it turned out, even by the end of
the extended target year, total industrial output barely fulfilled the original
target.

Structural Change in Industry

Concomitant with rapid industrial development, the structure of North Korea's industry has undergone a marked change since 1945 (table 23). This change is a reflection of North Korea's all-out campaign to industrialize her backward, predominantly agricultural economy and, at the same time, to rectify the imbalance in industrial structure inherited from the Japanese. A dramatic case in point is the change in the role of the machine-building and metal-processing industry whose relative share of the gross industrial product rose from a mere 1.6 percent in 1944 to nearly one-third (31.4 percent) in 1967. The rising importance of the machinery sector and the resultant structural change is evident within heavy industry itself. Output contribution of this sector rose from an insignificant proportion (2.3 percent) in 1944 to occupy more than half (56.7 percent) of the total heavy industrial output.

The rising importance of the machinery and metal-working industry in the composition of the industrial output came at the expense of the metallurgical, ore-mining, forest products, marine products, fuel and electric-power industries. The textile industry has improved its relative position significantly since 1944 but its importance remained relatively stable during 1957-65. Thus, North Korean industry progressed from a predominantly extractive-industry-oriented stage to one with the predominant role played by the machine-building industry.

The relative importance of producer goods and consumer goods in the composition of the total industrial output has remained comparatively stable although there were some fluctuations over the years. During the pre-Korean War period, the relative importance of the former was steadily increasing. However, the upward tendency was interrupted during the war when the trend reversed itself. This must have been due to the severe war damage incurred upon the heavy and large-scale industrial plants which were prime targets for bombing because of their strategic significance. In the early post-Korean War years, the relative position of producer goods was regaining its former position until 1960 when the trend again reversed itself. To be sure, stability in the relative composition of producer goods and consumer goods is not the same thing as stability in the relative output composition between heavy and light industry. Producer goods in the North Korean classification include products of industries which are not generally considered as heavy industry, such as leather goods, seasoning materials, cotton textile, dye materials, brick, flax and hemp, rubber, plate glass and glass materials, and the like.[41] North Korean emphasis has been in such heavy

TABLE 23

INDUSTRIAL OUTPUT: GROWTH AND STRUCTURAL CHANGE, 1944-1970

	1944	1946	1949
I. Growth in Total and Per Capita Industrial Output:			
A. Gross Industrial Product (GIP)			
1946 = 100%		100	337
1960 = 100%			
B. GIP as annual increment (percent)			
C. GIP per capita (1960 = 100%)			
II. Composition of GIP:			
Total	100.0%	100.0%	100.0%
Electric power industry	1.4	3.4	1.6
Fuel	3.8	4.6	4.1
Ore-mining	15.7	6.7	8.1
Metallurgical	13.3	9.5	11.0
Machinery manufacture and metal processing industry	1.6	5.1	8.1
Chemical industry	10.1	10.1	9.5
Pharmaceutical industry	0.2	0.3	1.0
Building materials industry	2.5	1.0	2.5
Textile industry	6.0	5.5	11.4
Glass and ceramics industry	0.7	0.8	0.4
Forest products and lumber	20.0	12.4	6.4
Pulp and paper-manufacturing industry	1.5	3.2	2.2
Printing and publication industry	0.2	1.9	1.2
Stationery and magazines industry	0.9	0.9	1.6
Tanning and shoemaking industry	0.8	0.2	1.4
Rubber industry	1.8	0.3	2.3
Marine products industry	11.0	2.7	6.2
Food and luxuries industry	7.8	27.2	19.4
Oil and fat industry	0.7	0.4	0.2
III. Relative Importance of Producer and Consumer Goods:			
1. Production of means of production (A)		52.1	58.6
2. Production of consumer goods (B)		47.9	41.4

Sources: I. CCY (various issues); Nodong sinmun, October 11, 1966; People's Korea, April 29, 1970; Nodong sinmun, November 10, 1970; Korea News (Pyŏngyang), No. 2, 1965, pp. 12-15; P. H. M. Jones, "Poor Results in Pyŏngyang," Far Eastern Economic Review (Hong Kong), March 26, 1964, pp. 668-669.

II and III. For 1944-60, Joint Publications Research Service (JPRS), The 1961 North Korean Yearbook, pp. 477-78; for 1961, Kyŏngje chisik (Economic Knowledge), February 1962, p. 39; for 1962, JPRS, ERNK, No. 106, pp. 3-4; for 1963, ERNK, No. 123, pp. 19-22; for 1965, Korea Today, No. 11, 1966, p. 15, and Nodong sinmun, October 11, 1966; for 1967, Nodong sinmun, September 8, 1968.

See "Notes to Tables 23 and 24."

1953	1956	1960	1961	1962	1963**	1964	1965	1966	1967	1968	1970***
216	615	2100	2400	2900	3100	3600	4100	4000	4600	5300	6900
		100	114	137	148	173	195	189	221	254	330
			14	20	8	17	14	−3	17	15	
		100	112	130	138	156	171	162	184	207	254
100.0%	100.0%	100.0%	100.0%	100.0%	100.0%		100.0%		100.0%		
0.6	0.7	0.3	0.3	0.3	0.2		n.a.				
0.7	1.8	1.3	1.2	1.1	1.2		n.a.				
9.3	6.1	4.0	3.9	3.1	3.2		n.a.				
1.8	8.6	6.8	3.9	6.1	7.4		n.a.				
15.3	17.3	21.3	22.7	22.0	25.6		29.0		31.4		
3.1	4.7	5.4	6.1	7.0	8.3		n.a.				
2.3	1.5	4.0	n.a.	n.a.	n.a.		n.a.				
1.4	4.8	5.9	n.a.	n.a.	5.7		n.a.				
25.7	18.4	16.8	n.a.	16.8	18.6		17.2**				
0.9	1.2	1.7	n.a.	n.a.	n.a.		n.a.				
7.7	6.1	2.9	n.a.	n.a.	2.9		n.a.				
0.9	2.5	2.6	n.a.	n.a.	2.2		n.a.				
1.4	2.1	1.8	n.a.	n.a.	n.a.		n.a.				
2.2	3.1	5.8	n.a.	n.a.	6.6		n.a.				
3.0	2.4	1.5	n.a.	n.a.	1.3		n.a.				
1.5	1.4	1.2	n.a.	n.a.	n.a.		n.a.				
2.3	3.1	2.1	n.a.	n.a.	n.a.		n.a.				
18.5	13.2	14.4	n.a.	15.5	13.7		9.1**				
0.5	0.7	0.2	n.a.	n.a.	0.2		n.a.				
37.7	53.9	55.0*	53.0*	53.0*	53.0*						
62.3	46.1	45.0*	47.0*	47.0*	47.0*						

*Rounded off.

**Author's estimate.

***Official estimate made around November 1970.

(1) The gross industrial product in North Korea is defined as "the total value, in monetary terms, of goods produced and technical services rendered by industrial enterprises during a given period of time." The value of technical services refers to "the value of operations involving processing of goods produced by other enterprises, preparing materials discarded by industrial plants for sale to the people, packing goods, assembling parts of machines manufactured by other enterprises, and repair services for other enterprises on request. (See "Explanation of Terms," Kyŏngje chisik, December 1962, pp. 32-33). These definitions imply that the gross industrial product as computed in North Korea, as in other Soviet-type economies, contains elements of doublecounting, such as counting purchases for interenterprise production more than once. This adds to the usual problems involved in measuring the industrial output due to "grossness." Absorption and merger of small industrial plants into larger state plants tend to reduce the extent of doublecounting while addition of new plants, new processes, increased specialization and decentralization tend to increase it. Both of these have taken place in North Korea but it cannot be determined which of these opposing forces was stronger. Other potential causes of overestimate, but not necessarily of doublecounting, include the "new product effect," and the extension of nationalization and cooperatization as they took place in North Korea, which must have increased the coverage of statistical reports (see Appendix B). As would be expected, the degree of grossness is larger for the gross industrial output than for the gross agricultural output due to greater interdependence among industrial enterprises.

(2) A little detective work shows that these official percentage figures are internally consistent; that is, the relationship between rates of growth in the total output, rates of growth in each of the industrial branches, and the change in the relative composition are algebraically consistent. If we represent

T = total industrial output in absolute value
B_i = output of the ith industrial sector in absolute value
b_i = output of the ith industrial sector as a share of the total industrial output
0 = time subscript indicating the base year (first subscript)
1 = time subscript indicating another (given) year (first subscript)
t = index of total industrial output of a given year to that of the base year
k_i = index of output of the ith sector for a given year to that of the base year

it is clear, in spite of the lack of absolute output figures, that

$$t = \frac{T_1}{T_0} = \frac{\Sigma B_{1i}}{\Sigma B_{0i}}; \quad b_{0i} = \frac{B_{0i}}{T_0} = \frac{B_{0i}}{\Sigma B_{0i}}; \quad b_{1j} = \frac{B_{1j}}{\Sigma B_{1j}}; \quad k_i = \frac{B_{1i}}{B_{0i}}$$

Since it holds algebraically, for instance, that

$$b_{1i} = \frac{B_{1i}}{\Sigma B_{1i}} = \frac{k_i}{t} \frac{B_{0i}}{\Sigma B_{0i}} = \frac{k_i b_{0i}}{t}; \text{ where, to be sure,}$$

$$\Sigma \left(\frac{k_1 b_{0i}}{t} \right) = \Sigma \left(\frac{T_0}{T_1} \cdot \frac{B_{1i}}{B_{0i}} \cdot \frac{B_{0i}}{T_0} \right) = \Sigma \frac{B_{1i}}{\Sigma B_{1i}} = 1.$$

These official figures and computed figures from the algebraic relationship are so close as to pass the internal consistency test. Some divergencies are expected due to rounding errors. This method is used to estimate percentage composition of industry for 1963 and 1965 for which no official data have been forthcoming.

TABLE 24

GROWTH RATES IN TOTAL INDUSTRIAL OUTPUT AND IN VARIOUS INDUSTRIAL BRANCHES, 1953-1970

	Ratio (%) of Output[a]					Annual Average Rate of Growth (Percent)			Seven Year Plan	
	1956/1953	1960/1956	1963/1960	1965/1960	1970/1960	3 Yr.Plan (1954-56)	5 Yr.Plan (1957-60)	(1961-63)	(1961-65)	(1961-70)
A. Gross Industrial Product	285	348	148	195	330	41.8	36.6	14.0	14.3	12.8
B. Electric power industry	325	179	123			48.5*	15.7	7.2		
Fuel industry	706	275	130			91.9*	28.7	9.1		
Ore-mining	186	255	107			22.9	26.4	2.3		
Metallurgical	1383	303	147	265		40.1	31.9	13.7		
Machine-making and metal-processing	317	466	163			46.9*	46.9*	17.7*	21.5**	
Chemical	430	448	203			62.6*	45.5*	26.6*		
Pharmaceutical	193	1000	n.a.			24.6	77.8*	n.a.		
Building materials	981	479	129			14.1	47.9*	8.8		
Textiles	210	345	150	200		28.0	36.3*	14.3*	14.9	
Glass and ceramics	370	542	n.a.			54.6*	52.6*	n.a.		
Forest products and lumber	224	184	133			30.8*	16.5	10.1		
Pulp and paper manufacture	810	413	111			100.8*	42.6*	3.5		
Printing and publication	424	323	n.a.			61.8*	34.1*	17.1*		
Stationery and magazines	396	683	161			58.2*	61.6*	6.5		
Tanning and shoemaking	221	241	121			30.3	24.6	n.a.		
Rubber	275	303	n.a.			40.1	31.9	n.a.		
Marine products	385	260	n.a.			56.8*	27.0	n.a.		
Food and luxuries	202	416	128	124		26.4	42.9*	8.6	4.4	
Oil and fat	396	105	206			58.2*	1.3	23.3*		
C. Producer goods	405	361	141			29.4*	37.8*	12.1		
Consumer goods	209	332	156			27.8	35.0	16.0*		

*Represents rates of growth faster than that of the gross industrial output during the same period.

**Estimates.

[a]Ratio (%) of output for the year of the numerator to that for the year of the denominator.

Sources: "Development of the People's Economy of Our Country in 1961," Kyŏngje chisik, February 1962; p. 38; ERNK, No. 79, pp. 23-24; JPRS, 1963 North Korean Central Yearbook, p. 264; ERNK, No. 123, pp. 19-22; Nodong sinmun, November 3 and November 10, 1970. See "Notes to Tables 23 and 24."

industrial branches as fuel, metallurgical, machine-making and metal processing, chemical, building materials, and so on.

The change in industrial structure is a function of the differential rates of growth in each branch of industry over the years (table 24). Examination of growth rates of various industrial sectors shows, first of all, substantially diminished growth rates in the 1960s as compared to those in the previous years. Next, the machine-building and metal-processing sector, the key branch of heavy industry, has registered higher rates of growth, significantly higher than those of the gross industrial output during all three periods. This sector had been growing at a phenomenally high rate of nearly 47 percent per year in the post-Korean War years of 1954-60. The speed, however, slacked off considerably during the first five years of the 1960s. There are some statistical evidences to point to a substantial exaggeration in the official growth rate of this sector during the Five Year Plan period. Specifically, North Korea claims that this sector in 1959 more than doubled its 1958 output, an unbelievably high growth rate of 102 percent. Such high rate of growth over a year remains unconvincing without some corroborating performance in other sectors. One would expect, on technical grounds, that a certain percentage increase in machinery output would be supported by a corresponding increase in steel output which is used as raw material for the former. Input-output relationship between steel (input) and machinery (output) based on data between 1957-63 (chart 2) shows that the machinery output for 1959 is ridiculously out of line. (The trend line is computed without the 1959 figures.) There were special circumstances which partly contributed to the phenomenon. These were the Chŏllima movement and the Machine-tool-beget-machine-tool movement which had the effect of producing more quantity at the expense of quality. A fairly good linear relationship exists between the percentage increase in the coal output and fuel output for 1957-63 (chart 3). For 1957, and for the three years between 1960-62, an increase in fuel output is accompanied by a nearly equal percentage increase in coal. The chart points to an allegation that the output of fuel in 1959 and 1963 and the output of coal in 1958 are slightly overreported. Here again the years in which possible exaggeration occurred include 1958 and 1959.

The glass and ceramics industry and the stationery and magazines industry both show consistently high rates of growth but they are relatively unimportant in the composition of the total output. Postwar rates of growth of such key sectors as fuel, metallurgical, chemical, and building materials are significantly

CHART 2

RELATIONSHIP BETWEEN MACHINERY OUTPUT AND STEEL OUTPUT,
1957-1963

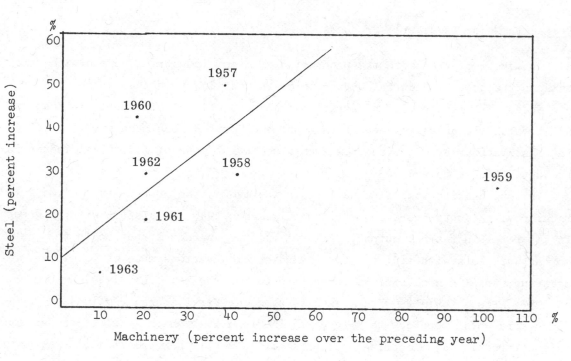

Machinery (percent increase over the preceding year)

CHART 3

RELATIONSHIP BETWEEN FUEL OUTPUT AND COAL OUTPUT,
1957-1963

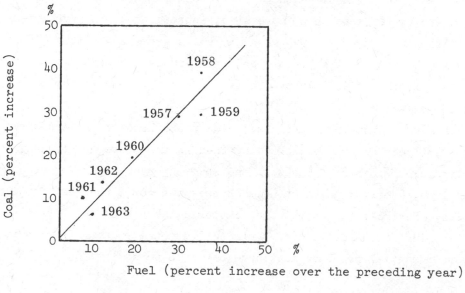

Fuel (percent increase over the preceding year)

83

high with declining tendencies in the early 1960s. Of these, only the chemical industry has been still growing faster than the total industrial output since the 1960s.

Trends in Major Industrial Products

Analysis of trends in the production of major industrial commodities which make up the total industrial output throw further light on the nature, extent, and speed of North Korean industrial progress as well as offer some indicators of strengths, weaknesses, and problems of the North Korean economy. The following observations are derived from examining output data of individual industrial products (tables 25 and 26).

First, despite some fluctuations in the 1960s, the output level of major industrial products increased very rapidly since 1946, consistent with progress in the total industrial output. All-out efforts at reconstruction in the post-Korean War years with aid from the communist bloc nations made it possible for most industrial commodities to recover to the prewar level (of 1949) by the end of 1957, except for a few items such as chemical fertilizers, carbide, and sulfuric acid whose recovery took longer. The relatively high level of production of such products as electrical power, steel, cement, chemical fertilizers, and the like by 1970 must be regarded as achievements of the North Korean industry as well as evidence of its potential. The level of per capita output of selected industrial products makes the picture even more favorable. Also, many new products have been introduced such as electric motors, transformers, lathes, tractors, automobiles, and plate glass. Although the absolute quantities produced of these products are as yet less than impressive, increasing use of such products as lathes (first introduced in 1954 when 150 units were manufactured domestically) can be expected to exert secondary and tertiary spread effects which should stimulate the further development of heavy industry in particular and industrialization in general.

Second, North Korean industry experienced widespread production setbacks and reverses (current year output falling below that in the previous years) in the 1960s affecting all segments of industry and covering such important products as iron ore, pig iron, steel, metal-cutting machines, tractors, chemical fertilizers, and textiles. Reverses in output were scattered throughout the period between 1961-66. Judging from a decline of 3 percent in total industrial output, reverses in major industrial products must have been the worst in 1966.

84

Third, even by the end of the extended target year, original Seven Year Plan quotas were not fulfilled for many of the important industrial products. Of those products for which official estimated production data for 1970 were made public, only coal shows plan fulfillment. Production of electricity, steel, chemical fertilizers, cement, and textiles had not reached the plan targets by 1970. That being the case, records for other products whose output figures have not been made public must be judged even worse. One must question, in the face of failure in meeting the targets for most of the important products which make up the total, the official claim that the total industrial output target has been fulfilled.

Fourth, physical production data have been marked by their conspicuous absence in official reports since the early years of the 1960s except those on a handful of commodities for some years. Output figures on only a few products have been made public for 1964, 1965, and 1970 while there is a complete lack of information on physical data on production for all the years between 1966-69. Gradual withholding of output data began in 1961 and the number of reported products suddenly dwindled to a few after 1964. A quick comparison of the statistical section of North Korean Central Yearbooks—say 1965 with that, for example, of 1961—will bring home this point. Furthermore, the timing of official production reports adds another dimension to the picture, reinforcing North Korean official behavior concerning the publication of data. In the past, official announcements of national output data for a given year were made public by the Central Bureau of Statistics of the State Planning Commission, predictably around the middle of the first month in the succeeding year. Not only was the date of public announcement of the 1964 figures postponed until toward the end of 1965 but they came in the form of a report by Kim Il, the First Vice-Premier, at the Second Conference of the Workers' Party of Korea held in October (5-12) 1966.[42] Also, unlike the preceding years, the 1965 figures were made public only in terms of percentage indexes over 1964 which tend to show relatively high growth for 1965. After a complete black-out on production data between 1966-69, what little information was published for 1970 came in the form of Kim Il-song's report to the Fifth Congress of the Workers' Party. Current drastic reduction in the number of published output figures had its beginning in 1964, immediately after the year of major reverses in the production of important industrial products and slowdowns in industrial output. Significantly, every one of the products whose figures were made known for 1964 had shown production gains over the

TABLE 25

PRODUCTION OF THE MAJOR INDUSTRIAL PRODUCTS, 1944-1970

Item	Unit	1944	1946	1949	1953	1956	1960
Electric power	Million KWH	8137	3934	5924	1017	5120	9139
Coal	1,000 ton	5740	1270	4005	7.08	3908	10620
Graphite	1,000 ton	24	16	46	-a	19	62
Iron ore	1,000 ton	n.a.	-	680	-	678	3108
Pig iron (includes granulated iron)	1,000 ton	481	3	166	-	1231	853
Ferroalloy	ton	5348	835	8011	32	6521	16972
Steel	1,000 ton	147	5	144	4	190	641
Rolled steel	1,000 ton	105	10	116	4	133	474
Electric motors	each	-	-	668	-	8817	40588
Electric transformers	each	-	-	1637	233	5527	5971
Metal cutting machines (lathes)	each	-	-	-	-	1010	2904
Tractors	each	-	-	-	-	-	3002
Automotive	each	-	-	-	-	-	3111
Sulfuric acid	1,000 ton	393	108	304	-	109	255
Chemical fertilizers	1,000 ton	512	156	401	-	195	561
Caustic soda	1,000 ton	12	3	9	(0.3)	6	25
Cement	1,000 ton	894	103	537	27	597	2285
Carbide	1,000 ton	152	42	136	6	99	125
Plate glass	1,000 m^2	-	-	-	-	1960	5070
Lumber	1,000 m^3	670	304	536	285	1068	1321
Paper products	1,000 ton	10	4	17	4	26	47
Textiles	1,000 km	1	3	13	22	77	190
Cotton yarn	1,000 ton	1	(0.5)	2	2	10	21
Marine products	1,000 ton	362	--c	273	122	365	465
Salt	1,000 ton	140	97	280	42	157	324
Vegetable oil	1,000 ton	5	1	8	7	9	14
Soy sauce	1,000 k.litre	5	1	18	18	28	86
Bean paste	1,000 ton	3	(.045)	--c	27	55	101

Sources: For 1944, JPRS, Development of the National Economy and Culture of the People's Democratic Republic of Korea: 1946-57 (English Translation of the Russian-language material of the same title) (Washington, D.C.: JPRS, 1959), pp. 27-36; for 1946-61, ERNK, No. 79, pp. 26-29; for 1962-63, Tŏitsu chosen nenkan 1964 (One Korea Yearbook) (Tokyo: Tŏitsu chosen shinbunsha, 1964), p. 733; Chŏsen benran (Korea Handbook) (Tokyo: nihon kokusai mondai kenkyujo, 1964), p. 116; Far Eastern Economic Review 1965 Yearbook, pp. 232-233; The People's Korea, January 23, 1963, p. 1; for 1946-64, Hama Takeo, op. cit., pp. 50-57; "Report of Central Statistical Board, DPRK State Planning Commission," Korea News, No. 2, 1965, pp. 12-15; Nodong sinmun, January 19, 1966, p. 1; for the Seven Year Plan targets for major industrial commodities, Tŏitsu chosen nenkan, 1964, p. 733; Chŏsen benran, pp. 113-118; for 1968, 1970, and Six Year Plan targets, Nodong sinmun, November 3 and November 10, 1970. See "Notes to Table 25."

TABLE 25, continued

1961	1962	1963	1964	1965	1968	1970[f]	Seven Year Plan Target	Six Year Plan Target-1976
10418	11445	11766	12393	13261[d]		16500	17000	28,000-30,000
11682	13209	14040	14403[d]	17860	(2500)[g]	27500	25000	50,000-53,000
n.a.	n.a.	n.a.	n.a.				n.a.	
3543	3336	3860	n.a.	(24%)[e]			7200	
930	1213	1159	1339	n.a.			2300	3,500-3,800
n.a.	n.a.	n.a.	n.a.	n.a.			n.a.	
776	1050	1022	1132	1234[d]		2200	2300	3,800-4,000
536	633	762	n.a.	(14%)[e]			1700	2,800-3,000
43429	48879	50040	n.a.	(8%)[e]			n.a.	
n.a.	b	5617	n.a.	n.a.			n.a.	
2625	3360	3327	n.a.	(49%)[e]			7500	27,000
3993	2500	3033	n.a.	(101%)[e]			17100	
3267	n.a.	4022	n.a.	(76%)[e]			10000	
273	316	321	n.a.	n.a.			650	
662	779	853	n.a.	(-5%)[e]		1500	1700	2,800-3,000
26	32	43	n.a.	n.a.			100	
2263	2376	2530	2610	2401[a]		4000	4300	7,500-8,000
141	179	191	n.a.	n.a.			530	
4193	5537	5230	n.a.	(9%)[e]			10000	
n.a.	n.a.	3740	4050	n.a.			n.a.	
59	65	71	n.a.	n.a.			250	
187	256	227	n.a.	(0%)[e]		400	500	500-600
n.a.	n.a.	n.a.	n.a.	n.a.			n.a.	
591	840	640	770	785[d]			1200	1,600-1,800
392	421	421	n.a.	n.a.			n.a.	
n.a.	27	n.a.	n.a.	n.a.			n.a.	
103	116	130	n.a.	(13)[e]			183	
121	134	143	n.a.				173	

[a]Indicates no (zero) output.

[b]715,000 kva.

[c]Presumed to indicate negligible output.

[d]Based on % figures.

[e]Percentage increment over 1964; lack of absolute output figures for 1964 prevents estimation of the same for 1965 based on percentage increase.

[f]North Korean official estimate announced in November 1970.

[g]The Seven Year Plan target for coal was claimed to have been attained in 1968; the source does not indicate the exact output figure for that year.

Notes to Table 25

Unlike the data for 1944, the last complete year under the Japanese occupation, production data for all other years are those by the state and cooperative
industries, that is, output by the private sector is not included. Private enterprises were completely absorbed by or transformed into either the cooperative
form or into state enterprises by 1958. Therefore, starting from 1959 output by
state and cooperative enterprises coincides with the total industrial output of
the entire economy. Even before the completion of the "socialization" process
in 1958, the share of the private sector in the composition of total output had
been small and it has become almost negligible since the Korean War: it declined
from 27.6 percent in 1946 to 9.3 percent in 1949, and between 1953 and 1957 it
dropped from 3.9 percent to a mere 1.3 percent. In addition, the private sector
largely concentrated on the small-scale, handicraft type of manufacturing,
whereas production of the important industrial products had been nearly completely nationalized from the beginning of the regime.

TABLE 26

PRODUCTION OF MAJOR INDUSTRIAL PRODUCTS
Per Capita and Growth Rates, 1957-1970

		Per capita output			Annual average growth rates (percent)			
					Five Year Plan	Seven Year Plan		
	Unit	1960	1963	1970a	(1957-60)	(1961-63)	(1961-65)	(1961-70)
Electric power	KWH	847.8	1068.7***	1,184	15.5	8.8	7.7	6.1
Coal	Kg	985.2	1439.4***	1,975	28.4	9.7	10.9	10.0
Iron ore	Kg	288.3	329.5		46.3	7.5		
Pig iron	Kg	79.1	111.2*		38.7	11.9b		
Steel	Kg	59.5	99.5**	158	35.5	15.3*	13.9	13.0
Rolled steel	Kg	40.0	65.0		37.4	17.1		
Electric motors	each	0.0038	0.0043		46.5	7.3		
Electric transformers	each	0.0006	0.0005		2.0	-2.0		
Metal cutting machines	each	0.0003	0.0003		30.2	4.7		
Tractors	each	0.0003	0.0003		--	0.3		
Automotive	each	0.0003	0.0003		--	8.9		
Sulfuric acid	Kg	23.7	27.4		23.7	8.0		
Chemical fertilizers	Kg	52.0	72.8	108	30.2	15.0		10.3
Caustic soda	Kg	2.3	3.7		42.9	19.8		
Cement	Kg	212.0	193.5**	287	39.6	3.4	1.0	5.8
Carbide	Kg	11.6	16.3		6.0	16.1		
Plate glass	m²	470.3	446.4		26.7	1.0		
Lumber	m³	122.5	366.3*		5.4	32.3*		
Paper products	Kg	4.4	6.1		16.0	14.8		
Textiles	m	17.6	25.0**		25.2	6.2	11.0	
Marine products	Kg	43.1	63.3***		6.3	11.2		7.7
Salt	Kg	30.1	35.9		19.9	9.1		
Soy sauce	Litre	7.9	11.1		32.1	14.9		
Bean paste	Kg	9.3	12.2		16.2	12.4		

a North Korean official estimate announced in November 1970; b during 1961-64; *1964; **1965.

Sources: Based on Table 25; Kim Il-song, Biography III, Tokyo: Miraisha, 1970, p. 47; Nodong sinmun, November 3, 1970.

previous years; information on other products was withheld. The implication of omission seems to carry over to subsequent years as well. A complete blackout of information started with 1966 when the gross industrial output actually declined. All this points to a positive correlation between the amount of official published data and the economic performance.

Some Contributing Factors to Growth and Slowdown

North Korea's industrialization has been characterized by continuing and all-round high performance during the 1940s (between 1945-50) and 1950s (except during the Korean War) on one hand and slowdowns and reverses in the 1960s on the other. Setbacks in the 1960s resulted in the failure and eventual extension of the Seven Year Plan. The following[43] is an attempt to analyze some important factors contributing to differential paces of industrial growth in these periods.

There are economic and noneconomic reasons why North Korea's "Stalinistic command economy"* has been well suited to the goals of its economic planners in the early stage of the country's development, which may partially explain the phenomenally high growth during the late 1940s and during the reconstruction period following the Korean War in the 1950s. Many Western economists share the view that the Stalinistic command economy was not merely less harmful but positively advantageous during the early period of economic development.[44] These advantages tend to be gradually and increasingly dwarfed by shortcomings as the economy grows.

---

*Soviet-type economies are called command economies since the government's command, rather than market forces, regulates the operation of the economy on the basis of one comprehensive central plan. The term "Stalinistic command economy" applies to the type of command economies characterized by the Soviet economic system in operation from the time of the introduction of the first Five Year Plan in 1928 until about twelve years after Stalin's death in 1952, during which the central planning authorities attempted to plan and control nearly every aspect of the economy, be it microlevel economic decisions or macroaggregates and proportions. Since the early 1960s, a new economic reform movement began to spread throughout the Soviet Union and the communist nations of Eastern Europe (except Albania) which has affected a partial relaxation and decentralization in central planning. A certain measure of autonomy over microeconomic decisions has been delegated and some pecuniary incentives have been provided to individual producing units and their workers with a greater role assigned to the market and market forces.

At the beginning stage of development, with a single goal of industrialization in a relatively small and simple economy, less rigor is required of planners in terms of their choice of priorities and technique of planning. As the size of the economy grows the mathematical and physical complexity of planning and choice-making multiplies, making the slapdash nature of the centralized decision-making process more inefficient and wasteful than in the formative and reconstruction period. Sooner or later, as development progresses, opportunities for extensive economic growth—growth attained by expansion in the utilization of unemployed or underemployed labor force and natural resources—diminish. At the same time, the difficulty of the command economy, "exceedingly well adapted to marshalling such unutilized resources at a time when augmentation of efficiency is of relatively less importance in achieving rapid growth,"[45] increases.

As reconstruction was completed in the post-Korean War years the North Korean economy had to shift from extensive resource exploitation to the intensive margin in which diminishing returns from bottlenecked sectors began to increase inefficiencies throughout the economy. Further growth had to come largely from raising the productivity through expanded technology and efficiency at the micro level. Since the 1960s, "Let's Raise the Rate of Utilization of Existing Facilities" and its variant have become familiar slogans in North Korea. Priority given to the mining industry about the end of the Five Year Plan, and through the Seven and Six Year Plans, as evidenced by the state investment policy and the sense of urgency conveyed in nationwide "Let's Raise the Productivity in Extractive Industries" campaigns, points to power and fuel industries as sectors with the major bottlenecks. These sectors were clearly identified by Kim Il-song in his report[46] to the Fifth Congress of the Workers' Party. He stated:

> However, because the power industry and extractive industry have not developed firmly ahead of processing industries they [power and extracting industries] were unable to provide power, fuel and raw materials in ample supply... which explains why our industry is not able to exercise its full might. For this reason, during the Six Year Plan new construction will be kept at a minimum in the industrial sector whose primary efforts will be directed toward developing power and extractive industries ahead [of other industrial branches] in order to provide enough power and fuel to various industrial sectors on one hand, and toward the work of putting flesh on all branches of industry as well as toward full utilization of existing industrial potential.

Fulfillment of the Seven Year Plan target for coal by 1970, the only known major industrial product to achieve this, must be regarded as an indication of the partial success of the campaign. Although North Korea's industrial strategy for the Six Year Plan calls for a frontal attack at developing the fuel and power

91

industries, her reliance on external sources for crude oil and coking coal (as compared to anthracite coal with which North Korea is relatively well endowed) along with rubber and light metals will continue to strain industrial development for some time to come, as the North Korean leadership realizes.[47]

Labor is another serious shortage area. Relative lack of population pressure may have certain long-run advantages but North Korea's (relatively) small population imposes a short-run bottleneck with the present conjunction of technology and available resources. The country has experienced severe drains on its labor force through sizable population loss before and during the Korean War both from the war dead and the outflow of refugees into South Korea. (For instance, total population in 1953 was 1.13 million short of that in 1949.) Refugees and war dead are likely to be largely composed of males of productive ages. This situation coupled with the initial lower population density made North Korea a labor-scarce economy, a rarity among Asian countries. Problems of labor shortage are of such magnitude and persistence that the North Korean leadership considers:

> Whether or not we can continually assure the high tempo of socialist construction and fulfill the present Six Year Plan successfully depends decisively upon solution of the real situation through improving the work of labor administration.[48]

Two major solutions are advanced by the North Korean planners to alleviate the labor shortage. The first concerns better utilization of existing labor through improved allocation and regulation of labor. An example of such a policy is to increase the use of female labor in such "light-labor" industries as light industry while reallocating the male youth from these industries to "heavy-labor" industries. Saving labor through technical improvement is the other major solution. In this connection increased mechanization and introduction of automation are emphasized, especially in heavy industrial sectors such as the extractive industries.[49]

Another principal factor in the rapid industrial growth during the time when North Korea was reconstructing the war-torn industry was the injection of a substantial amount of foreign aid from the communist nations headed by the Soviet Union and Communist China during the years following the conclusion of the Korean War. As a matter of record, imported capital and technology from the communist countries dwindled after the beginning of the 1960s. Obviously, one reason for the decline in foreign aid stems from the fact that the case and appeal for aid are stronger when the need concerns reconstruction rather than assisting normal growth requirements. As important, undoubtedly, was North Korea's tight-rope position in the Sino-Soviet rift and her insistence on establishing an "independent" and "self-reliant" economy, probably as a way to survive the rift between the two communist giants,[50] which might have been an additional factor contributing to this trend. Or, just as plausibly, disappointing external assistance could have simply forced her to resort to a policy of self-reliance and the concept of Chuch'e (national identity) adopted and introduced toward the end of the 1950s.[51] Whatever the long-run merits of an independent and self-sufficient economy and no matter what the motivation behind North Korea's adoption of this policy, a decline in foreign aid has imposed a severe bottleneck in the supply of foreign capital and technology, notwithstanding North Korea's frantic efforts to supply part of them domestically. Many experts believe that the shifting of closer ties with the Soviet Union since 1965 in the constantly swinging pendulum between Communist China and the Soviet Union was chiefly motivated by the greater possibilities of extracting economic and military aid from the latter than from the former. As one student of North Korea put it:

> To be blunt about the whole changing attitude, Pyongyang needed more and new military equipment, scientific knowledges and, above all, oil from the Soviet Union. From China, they had little to gain or "study." In addition to these, the American bombings of North Vietnam since the beginning of February last year (1965) made themselves increasingly felt in North Korea. Pyongyang's desire for a new defense guarantee from Moscow increased....Important factors that contributed to the warming of relations between Moscow and Pyongyang, I believe, included Moscow's successful psychological manipulation of North Korean leaders, Pyongyang's urgent need for modern military equipment partly caused by the worsening development of the Vietnamese War and finally, Kim's (Kim Il-song's) own desire to acquire more practical economic and technical "interests" from the Soviet Union.[52]

Expansion and increasing self-shouldering of the defense burdens have been North Korea's official justification for the economic slowdown in the 1960s. Kim Il-song, in his 1965 New Year's Message, stated that "it is true that the economic development of our country has been delayed somewhat compared with what was expected, because we had to direct great strength to further increase the defense capacity in the last two or three years to meet the changing turn of events."[53] This was, also, the first official admission that all was not going well with the Seven Year Plan. The same theme was repeated by Kim in his report at the Fifth Congress of the Workers' Party in November 1970.[54] The turn of events which compelled North Korea to accelerate the diversion of resources to defense was necessitated by the real, imagined, or alleged threat to North Korea arising from the military revolution in South Korea, increased involvement of the United States in Vietnam, and the weakening solidarity among the communist bloc nations.[55] Accordingly, a series of policy measures was taken by North Korea beginning in 1962 to pursue a parallel development between defense and non-defense sectors. As a result, the share of national defense to the total national budget rose from an average of 4.3 percent during 1956-66 to an average of 31.2 percent between 1967-70. In the same period the share of defense expenditure to national income leaped from an average of 3.1 percent to 20.0 percent. The big jump occurred in 1967 when defense expenditures increased to 30.4 and 17.7 percent from 10.0 and 5.6 percent, respectively, in 1966 as a share of national budget and national income.[56]

Tied in with dwindling and reluctantly given foreign aid and North Korea's policy of self-reliance and independence, increased military spending must have had a depressing effect on the economy and played a major role in shaping the course of economic development. However, the poor performance cannot be attributed to defense alone. First, since the current build-up in defense did not start until around the mid-1960s, it cannot explain slowdowns and production reverses that occurred before that time. Second, since defense-related goods constitute part and parcel of total output, slowdown in growth in such products as steel, lathes, pig iron, and iron ore cannot be blamed on the increased military budget. If anything, output in these sectors would tend to increase at the expense of others. Third, increased military spending must come at the expense of nonmilitary investment and not of consumption in order to produce a negative output effect. Even here the detrimental effect, if any, will work itself out in the long run, not in such a short time-period. State investment in all industrial (and agricultural) sectors was consistently and substantially higher in the 1960s than before. Fourth, even if expansion in military spending had been accompanied by an increase in military manpower the alternative cost of this action does not seem to be too great. True, the economic pressure of maintaining a large army is perhaps higher in North Korea than in South Korea because of a relative labor shortage in the former. However, in order to alleviate the high opportunity cost, the army in North Korea had long ago adopted a plan of self-support by which it could either produce its own foodstuffs or earn purchasing power by assisting irrigation and other projects under the auspices of the ministries of national defense and agriculture as well as the State Planning Commission.[57]

For a planned economy like that of North Korea, economic performance must be judged in terms of its own expectations (plan targets) as well as a more or less objective norm. North Korea's economic performance during the 1960s was a failure in both terms—too low growth rates to fulfill Plan targets as well as production reverses and negative growth rates. Failure of the North Korean economy to fulfill the Seven Year Plan within the original timetable, and the resultant readjustment, stems from a divergence between the actual and perceived (by the planners) production possibility frontier. The following discussions will advance the thesis that there were factors during the early post-Korean War period which contributed to the setting up of unrealistic production targets beyond possible production capabilities. Overconfidence and the consequent planning errors arose basically from high growth during the reconstruction period, statistical inflation, and excessive zeal on the part of the planners.

First, high growth during the reconstruction period made the planners overconfident in North Korea's industrial capacity. There were many factors which raised the actual growth rates during the rehabilitation period. To begin with, there was the relative ease of rehabilitation as compared to "normal" development. Such inputs as technical know-how and organizational skill cannot be totally destroyed by war, which obviously puts a war-devastated economy like North Korea's at an advantage relative to one starting from scratch. In addition, foreign aid was readily available for North Korea during the reconstruction. In this connection, according to some observers, planning of very high growth rates in the 1960s seems to lead to the probability that the North Korean leadership counted heavily on continued economic aid at the time the Seven Year Plan was constructed, thus committing the sin of miscalculation.[58] Another potential source for high growth during the reconstruction may be related to the so-called advantage of latecomers in economic development in the availability and employment of up-to-date technology. Specifically, inflow of more advanced and up-dated capital and technology into North Korea from the communist nations must have been a factor giving rise to unusually rapid growth during 1954-60. Apart from the absolute magnitude of growth, the size of relative development (rates of growth) would be very high during a reconstruction period in which the industrial output starts from a small base, owing simply to the statistical nature of the growth indexes.

Overconfidence also resulted from overestimation, deliberate or not, of the actual growth and, hence, of the actual potential during the latter part of the 1950s. Substantial overreporting in the official output figures in the machinery and, to a lesser extent, in the fuel and coal industry (as well as in agriculture) were especially centered around 1958-59. There were special circumstances which made statistical inflation concentrated during the last three years of the 1950s. Complete socialization of industry by 1958 undoubtedly widened the statistical coverage on one hand and intensified the tendency for deliberate overreporting on the other (see Appendix B). Upward bias would be more pronounced around 1959, the first whole year of operation under complete socialization.

It was also in 1959 that the Chŏllima Movement* was first introduced, obviously inspired by China's Great Leap Forward Movement of 1958. Such a movement—which places emphasis on exhortations and "socialist competition" among the individual workers and among different groups of workers (work teams, plants, and enterprises) in vying for the "coveted" titles of Chŏllima "heroes"—would have built-in tendencies for exaggerating output and causing disproportionate growth among different sectors. Cumulative disruptions in the input-output relationships and sectoral imbalances would be the end results. The Chŏllima and like movements through their secondary repercussions turned the North Korean economy into near chaos around 1959.[59] It is no wonder that 1960 was officially designated a "buffer year," a year of adjustment to restore balance among sectors and in growth.

Such movements would also tend to tempt the workers and the managers to sacrifice quality for larger quantity and to increase current production at the expense of future output. Defaulting quality is another source for statistical inflation. Although production of "shoddy" and "wrong" goods is a familiar problem of Soviet-type economies, one notices unusually large production claims made in 1958-59 along with frequent official warnings and campaigns to upgrade the product quality. Improving product quality is such an economy-wide problem that it is listed as one of the major tasks of the Six Year Plan.[60] The so-called Kongjak kigye sekki chigi undong (literally the machine-tool-beget-machine-tool movement) is a dramatic example of statistical overestimation of output via defaulting of quality. Under this campaign, workers are encouraged to reproduce

---

*The Chŏllima (literally, thousand mile horse) movement was inspired by a legendary horse in the Chinese novel Shan-kuo-chih (Tales of the Three Kingdoms) which galloped a thousand miles a day. It is frequently known in English as the Flying Horse movement. The moral of the movement is clearly to induce the workers and their leaders to work harder and try to fulfill government production targets at the speed of a thousand miles a day in order to accelerate the "construction of socialism in the country." Under the movement those work teams, plants or enterprises that successfully overfulfill the assigned targets of production are given the title of Chŏllima "heroes."

the machines they operate. Starting in March 1959 with Kim Il-song's visit to the Chuŭl Flax Factory, the nationwide movement was claimed a huge success. It was reported that within a year since the movement, a total of 13,000 machine tools were built at plants throughout North Korea.[61] The quality of machinery, especially those of precision, made in such a haphazard manner, must have been extremely low, not to mention the additional problem of parts, maintenance, and short life. No doubt the defaulting of quality resulting from such campaigns partly explains the unusually large claim and statistical inflation of the machinery output in 1959. Long-run effects would be even worse. Output of these low-quality machines, whether producer or consumer goods, would continue to be equally shoddy for years to come. Such a movement is in direct violation of the most elementary economic principles: economies of mass production arising from specialization and division of labor, and the law of comparative advantages. It is inevitable that future plans for output made on the basis of the availability of such shoddy capital goods become frustrated. Here, then, lies another important explanation for the below-Plan performance in the Seven Year Plan years. North Korea's own claim of an unusually high proportion (94.3 percent in 1964) of domestically supplied machinery is an indirect admission of the low level of quality, technology, and precision connected with machinery products. No doubt North Korea's quest for autonomy along with diminishing foreign aid have provided added impetus for such uneconomic movements.

The influence of Communist China also indirectly contributed to planning errors through overzealousness on the part of the North Korean leadership. While North Korea initially patterned its economy closely after the Soviet model, China's influence became significant about 1958, although a beginning of Chinese influence coincided with her intervention during the Korean War. North Korea was at first greatly impressed and influenced by China's Great Leap Forward of 1958. It is significant that the completion of socialization in all sectors of the economy was achieved immediately in the wake of the Great Leap Forward movement. It was in 1959, also, when the Chŏllima movement was first introduced in North Korea, affecting every aspect of the life of peasants and workers. The Chinese movement and the Chŏllima movement, its Korean version, inspired the North Korean leaders and economic planners to be bold, overzealous, and overly optimistic.[62] Interestingly, the 1967 targets set in 1961 were generally lower than those planned in 1958 for the target years of 1964-65 (table 27). Peking's humiliating backward leap and subsequent reassessment of production claims must have been factors in the decision of the North Korean planners to adjust the targets downward. However, as it turned out, even the revised targets proved beyond reach.

Inaccurate statistical reporting, reluctance to admit failure, and delay in communications are additional factors which would postpone timely downward adjustment of the planned growth.

TABLE 27

OUTPUT TARGETS FOR MAJOR COMMODITIES DURING THE SEVEN YEAR PLAN:
EARLY AND FINAL PLANS COMPARED

Commodity	Units	Final Target for 1967	Targets for 1964-65 Planned in 1958
Electricity	Kwh (millions)	17,000	20,000
Coal	1,000 ton	25,000	25,000
Pig iron	1,000 ton	2,300	4,000
Steel	1,000 ton	2,300	3,000-3,500
Cement	1,000 ton	4,300	5,000
Chemical fertilizers	1,000 ton	1,700	1,500-2,000
Textiles	Kilometer	500,000	500,000
Marine products	1,000 ton	1,200	1,000
Grains	1,000 ton	6,600	7,000

Sources: Terao Goro, op. cit., p. 122, for targets for 1964-65 planned in 1958; final target for 1967, table 25.

Summary and Conclusion

This chapter shows that North Korea has built a solid foundation for industrialization since the communist takeover in 1945. Its industry has undergone rapid growth and structural change in spite of a war that shook the economy to its foundations. The greatest growth has been in heavy industry, especially the machine-building industry, in contrast to the announced policy of parallel development between light and heavy industry. Discriminatory allocation of state investment funds was one major cause for the differential growth.

While North Korea's overall industrial gain has been both rapid and substantial, it began to experience slowdowns and reverses in its industrial growth after the 1960s. The discrepancies between the planned and actual output were so immense and diffused that substantial improvement in performance during the

98

last years of the Seven Year Plan would hardly have modified her failure to carry out the planned pace of industrialization. Under the circumstances, modification of the plan in the way of extending it three more years to 1970 was inevitable. In a way, the very success of the economy during the reconstruction period bred the germinal causes for the slowdown in the 1960s.[63] Factors existed which on one hand raised the actual growth rates during the reconstruction period: relative lack of bottlenecks and opportunities for extensive economic growth; large inflow of external aid; relative ease of rehabilitation as compared to "normal" development; advantage of being a latecomer; possible efficiency of central command planning for a small and simple economy in the beginning stage of development, and so on. There were, on the other hand, factors that exaggerated real growth in the form of statistical inflation, as well as influenced the leadership to set up goals too ambitious to attain.

All these elements combined to produce lower actual growth and overambitious and unattainable plan targets for the Seven Year Plan. The net result was that not only was North Korea's performance during the Seven Year Plan a failure in terms of low growth rates but also in terms of its own highly publicized expectations which forced it to lose face by extending the plan. The latter could have been avoided had the planners been more realistic.

For all its dislocations the North Korean industry seemed to have shown some degree of flexibility and resilience and its disruptions did not reach the magnitude of those in Communist China. According to the words of an economic observer on North Korea:

> ...nothing shows that North Korea's economy has suffered the disasters and dislocations that have afflicted that of China since 1958. For one thing, North Korean industry is long established and fairly highly developed, while the population presses much less heavily on all the means of subsistence. For another, North Korea is apparently...much better placed than China to evoke increased production from the countryside by offering more of the good things of life.[64]

From all indications, the recent dislocations seem to have been contained by now and the output level of some industrial products, especially in terms of per capita, around 1970 is quite impressive. Relative to other developing nations the per capita output level compares favorably though it is still far behind other industrialized economies. With a relatively small population, North Korea is free from the kind of population pressure that plagues South Korea, Japan, and other Asian countries. For this reason, it may be predicted that per capita output of some major industrial commodities such as electric power, cement, plate glass, steel and iron ores of North Korea may, in a not too distant future, reach a level comparable to that of Japan and a few other developed nations, even though the total output of the former may lag far behind those advanced countries.

A very high degree of nationalization characterized North Korean industry from the beginning of the regime, with private industry relegated to a minor and declining role. Since 1958, when "socialization" of industry was completed and the last remnants of private enterprise in industry disappeared, all industrial enterprises became either state enterprises or cooperatives, the former playing an overwhelming role in the share of total industrial output and total industrial labor force.

The control, management, and incentive systems of North Korean industry have not deviated fundamentally from the Stalinistic central command system which North Korea patterned after the Soviet Union. While economic slowdowns in the Soviet Union and East European communist countries toward the end of the 1950s and in the early 1960s opened up a new era in which economic reforms liberalizing the central planning system swept throughout these countries, North Korea has shown no inclination to change the basic tenets of industrial control in spite of its greatly reduced pace of industrialization in recent years. To be sure, there have been some scattered measures which, to a limited degree, relaxed the central control and infused industrial operations with some pecuniary incentives. These measures include decentralization of industrial management by emphasizing local industries and the introduction of the independent accounting system along with the internal accounting system. But these have been more than offset by such developments as the Chŏllima movement and the Taean system, which put politics before economics and emphasized exhortations and nonpecuniary incentives rather than material incentives.

North Korea's dogmatic adherence to ideological, administrative, and bureaucratic control of industry in the day-to-day decision making of individual productive units will prove a major depressant in its quest for rapid industrialization in the years to come, as exemplified by its recent slowdowns. The declining efficiency of the central command industrial control system must somehow be dealt with through reforms of one kind or another. Analysis of the motivations and circumstances behind North Korea's lack of flexibility and readiness to liberalize her prereform Soviet-type central planning system will be deferred to chapter 5, where an overall analysis of North Korea as an economic system will be attempted.

4

Foreign Trade

Introduction

North Korea, like other developing countries, has depended on external trade and assistance as a means of procuring the resources and technology necessary for her economic development. Imports of industrial and consumer goods and technical assistance from the communist countries facilitated the initial undertaking of development projects before the Korean War, the maintenance of the economy during the war, and subsequent major reconstruction and industrialization projects. Rapid expansion in exports made possible by North Korea's all-out drive and her growing economy earned the foreign exchange necessary to pay for the imports. In addition to exports, foreign economic aid in the form of outright gifts and long-term credits was an important instrument for obtaining imports. This dependence on economic assistance as well as on military aid of all forms was at its height during the war and the following reconstruction period. Rapid growth in North Korea's foreign trade brought with it a drastic change in the commodity composition of both imports and exports and a slow change in the direction of the trade.

This chapter will begin with a description of various institutional aspects of North Korea's international trade, followed by an analysis of the changing trend in the total magnitude and commodity structure of the trade. North Korea's trade will then be treated geographically: North Korean trade with the Soviet Union, Communist China, East European countries, and the noncommunist world.

Administration of Foreign Trade

In communist countries foreign trade is the monopoly of the state, and North Korea is no exception. State trading in these economies has proved to be an important tool both economically and politically. Economically, it is geared to the long-term needs of national economic plans as well as to the adjustment of unplanned short-run bottlenecks and surpluses.

Administratively, foreign trade in North Korea has been under several jurisdictions. When the North Korean Provisional People's Committee was established on September 20, 1946, it came under an independent Foreign Trade Commission; this was subsequently absorbed by the Bureau of Commerce in January 1947 and eventually was transferred to the Ministry of Commerce in September 1948 when the People's Republic was formed. It remained under that ministry until October 1952 when the Ministry of Foreign Trade was created to meet the changing needs of the time. The primary reason behind the transfer seems to lie in the increasing amount of economic aid that poured in from the communist bloc countries during the Korean War, which necessitated expansion of the agency in charge of this most vital wartime source of supply.[1] Subsequently, control was placed under the Ministry of Internal and External Commerce until September 1958 when the ministry was reorganized into two ministries as a part of the accelerated drive for expanding exports. Since that time the Ministry of Foreign Trade has been administering external trade while the Ministry of Commerce has handled domestic trade.

In the prewar period when private enterprise was still permitted, a certain amount of private foreign trading was allowed although it was under the tight control of the government. During and immediately after the Korean War the government took over completely and since that time the state has monopolized foreign trade. Actual transactions have been delegated to state-managed or cooperative trading firms which negotiate trading details and generally carry out government directives. Each firm specializes in a few basic lines such as machinery, mineral ores, marine products, and daily necessities and some of them maintain branch offices abroad.[2] Since they operate under strict government direction, no competition is allowed among them. In February 1962, in an effort to promote exchange of complete plants and related technology, the government placed trading firms specializing in "plants" under the direct control of the Bureau-General for International Economy, an organization independent of the Ministry of Foreign Trade. In addition, the Commission for the Promotion of Foreign Trade was formed in 1952 for the specific purpose of initiating and promoting trade with those countries with which either no diplomatic relations had been established or no trade agreements had been negotiated.

As the post-Korean War reconstruction was completed, North Korea launched a full-scale drive for industrialization starting from the Five Year Plan (1957-60) which increased the demand for foreign exchange to finance development projects. The problem of foreign exchange became acute as foreign aid began to be gradually withdrawn with progress toward rehabilitation. In order to cope with the problem a series of measures was introduced to expand and encourage export industries along with a campaign to conserve foreign exchange. A preliminary measure was a decision at the June 1958 Plenary Meeting of the Party[3] to create a bureau to organize nationwide programs to study and mobilize export possibilities, specifically in agricultural products and in ore, metal, chemical, and other industrial products. The Party also adopted measures to improve quality, standardization, and packaging of exported goods and set up regulations and credit organs relating to export trade. Further, a joint order of December 13, 1960, by the Ministries of Foreign Trade and Finance introduced a system of export subsidies.[4] In addition, North Korea began to expand its participation in international trade fairs as a part of its export drive. As early as 1955, North Korea spent about U.S. $20,000 for displaying its export products at the international trade fair hosted in East Germany.[5]

Economizing scarce foreign exchange in North Korea took the form of allocating it largely for importing capital goods at the expense of consumer goods. For example, during the Five Year Plan 73 percent of foreign exchange was assigned to pay for imports of capital goods and raw materials while the remaining 27 percent was allocated to purchase essential consumer goods from abroad.[6]

One of the means by which the government offers protection to industry and at the same time attempts to conserve foreign exchange is by taxation on imports. Tax rates based on the ad valorem principle are set to equate prices of foreign goods to those of domestically produced goods in order to boost domestic production of what the regime considers essential. Also, tax rates favor imports of machinery and scientific equipment but discriminate against consumer-related goods. No duties, however, are imposed on commodities imported in accordance with trade agreements. Since in actuality North Korean foreign trade is predominantly instrumented through some form of trade agreement, except with a few partners of the noncommunist world such as Japan and Hong Kong, the economic effects of such a tariff is probably minimal.[7]

Payments for transactions with Communist China are carried out in the currencies of both countries, but the Russian ruble is used for establishing prices and making payments in North Korean trade with other communist bloc countries. Payments with noncommunist nations are settled through letters of credit mostly by pound sterling, franc, and dollar.[8] For the purpose of international trade an exchange rate of 2.57 won per U.S. dollar has been applied since 1967. For example, an official exchange rate of 6.17 per British pound, the currency of transaction in North Korea-Japan trade, has been used since the devaluation of the pound in November 1967. Using the official exchange rates, this translates to an exchange rate of 140 yen or 38.9 cents per won.[9] Previous to the pound devaluation, the exchange rate was 7.2 won per pound, that is, 150 yen or 41.7 cents per won (2.4 won per dollar).[10]

Trend in the Total Value and Commodity Composition of North Korea's Trade

The total value of North Korea's foreign trade has expanded at a rapid pace since 1946 (table 28). The only significant interruption in the upward trend in both exports and imports occurred during the Korean War when normal foreign trade activities either nearly ceased or slowed down considerably, particularly toward the end of 1950 and at the beginning of 1951 when the war was fought within the North Korean territory. A rough positive correlation between on one hand the total trade volume and on the other the size and health of the economy and the intensity of North Korea's economic relationship with her largest trade partner—the Soviet Union—seems warranted here. Growth of imports has been much more volatile from year to year than that of exports. This is undoubtedly due to North Korea's reliance on imports to relieve unplanned short-term shortages in material which by their nature fluctuate yearly. This can be readily seen by the accumulation of sizable trade deficits in 1959 and 1969 in spite of a marked increase in exports during these years. Significantly and understandably, each of the years (1959 and 1969) with the largest trade deficits occurred toward the end of the Five and (extended) Seven Year Plan, respectively. In addition, a general rising trend in imports reflects the increased demand for imports necessary to carry out long-term development programs and to meet the requirements of a growing economy. Unfavorable trade balances have been characteristic of North Korea's trade throughout its existence. It is presumed that the unexpected surplus for 1966-67 partly arose from North Korea's trade surplus with Communist China, whose exports to North Korea declined drastically due to

TABLE 28

TOTAL VALUE OF FOREIGN TRADE, 1946-1969 (Estimates)*
(Million U.S. Dollars)

Year	Total Value (X+M)	Total Index 1949= 100%	Total Annual Incre- ment(%)	Exports (X)	Exports Index 1949= 100%	Imports (M)	Imports Index 1949= 100%	Trade Balance (X-M)
1946	22.8	12.6		n.a.	-	n.a.	-	n.a.
1949	182.3	100.0		76.3	100.0	106.0	100.0	- 29.7
1953	73.0	40.0		31.0	40.6	42.0	39.6	- 11.0
1954	68.3	37.5	-6.4	n.a.	-	n.a.	-	n.a.
1955	105.3	57.8	54.1	45.0	59.0	60.3	56.9	- 15.3
1956	140.3	77.0	33.2	65.8	86.2	74.5	70.3	- 8.7
1957	214.8	117.8	53.1	100.0	131.1	114.8	108.3	- 14.8
1958	290.0	159.1	35.0	135.0	176.9	155.0	146.2	- 20.0
1959	348.0	191.2	20.0	113.0	148.1	235.0	221.7	-122.0
1960	320.0	175.5	-8.2	154.0	201.8	166.0	156.6	- 12.0
1961	326.4	179.0	2.0	160.0	209.7	166.4	157.0	- 6.4
1962	352.5	193.4	8.0	224.0	293.6	128.5	121.2	+ 95.5
1963	420.8	230.8	19.4	190.7	249.9	230.1	217.1	- 39.4
1964	415.6	228.0	-1.2	193.4	253.5	222.2	209.6	- 28.8
1965	441.1	242.0	6.1	208.3	273.0	232.8	219.6	- 24.5
1966	463.4	254.2	5.0	244.2	320.1	219.2	206.8	+ 25.0
1967	500.0	274.3	7.9	260.2	354.1	239.8	226.2	+ 30.4
1969	696.1	381.8		306.7	402.0	389.4	367.4	- 82.7

Sources: _Chukoku seiji keizai soran, 1962_ (Political and Economic Survey of China, 1962), Tokyo: Ajia Seikei Gakkai, 1962, p. 939; Ministry of Foreign Affairs, _Chōsen benran_ (Handbook of Korea), Tokyo: Institute of International Affairs, 1961, p. 65; _Ajia boeki_ (Asian Trade), Tokyo, No. 19, August 1962; _Nitcho boeki_ (Japan-Korea Trade), Tokyo, November and December 1966; _CCY_, various issues; _Nodong sinmun_, August 10, 1966; _Democratic People's Republic of Korea_ (DPRK), Pyŏngyang: Foreign Languages Publishing House, pp. 244-245; _People's Korea_, May 24, 1972; _Area Handbook for North Korea_ (DA Pam. No. 550-81), Washington, D.C.: U.S. Government Printing Office, 1969, pp. 373-374; Ch'a Byŏn-kŏn, "North Korea's Foreign Trade and Its Characteristics," _Kukje munje_ (Journal of International Studies), Seoul, October 1972, p. 24.

*Derived, when such information is available, from secondary sources based on trade partner's data. Russian ruble figures are converted into dollars at the official exchange rate. When such data are missing, North Korea's official foreign trade index is used to estimate the absolute amount. Some discrepancies between the two series (North Korean official trade index and data from trade partners) are expected due to handling of the transportation costs (insurance and freight); that is, whether trade values are expressed c.i.f. or f.o.b.

the upheaval during the Cultural Revolution. In the 1960s (1961-67) foreign
trade (total value) grew faster than national income (11.4 percent per annum as
compared to 8.9 percent), thus raising foreign trade as a ratio of total national
output. Analysis of the direction of trade will throw some light on the factors
affecting the general movements of the volume and balance of trade.

North Korea's commodity structure of foreign trade underwent a phenomenal
shift after 1953 (table 29). The predominance of mineral exports gave way to
metals, while in imports the relative importance of machinery and equipment declined and that of fuels increased significantly.

In 1953 the importation of machinery and equipment constituted one-third of
total imports which were overwhelmingly paid for by minerals. This fact may
dramatize effectively the nature of the North Korean economy after three years
of war and at the beginning of her reconstruction and drive for industrialization. Since then the relative importance of mineral exports declined drastically
(from 81.8 percent in 1953 to 7.2 percent in 1969) whereas that of the ferrous
and nonferrous metals, which significantly include steel, rose sharply (from
9 percent in 1953) to constitute the largest category of exports (nearly one-half
in 1964 and about 40 percent in 1969). However, 1953 is hardly a normal year
for most commodities, especially those of heavy industry. Production of steel,
for instance, was especially hard hit by war so that it virtually ceased to exist
during 1951. In 1953 the output of steel and rolled steel was only 2.5 and 3.0
percent, respectively, that of 1949. For this reason, growth in the relative
importance of the steel exports since 1953 is not merely an indication of the
long-run and fundamental structural change but also of the abnormally low production in 1953 due to the war damage.

Machinery and equipment continue to be the most important class of items
for which North Korea relies on external sources (30.2 percent of the total imports in 1969). During 1959-68, imports of machinery and equipment, including
complete plants, ran at an annual average of about $42.7 million (a cumulative
total of $427.2 million).[11] Fuels and fuel oil had been rapidly gaining in im-
portance to assume the position of the second largest import category. Lack of
domestic sources for good coking coal and oil, the increasing requirements for
energy sources in the face of industrial progress, and the stepped up pace of
military preparedness in recent years will necessitate continued imports of
these items, although fuller utilization of the hydroelectric potentials with
which North Korea is generously endowed may partly restrain this trend in the
future.

TABLE 29

CHANGE IN THE COMPOSITION OF FOREIGN TRADE, 1953-1969

	Percent							(+) (-)*
	1953	1956	1959	1960	1963	1964	1969	
A. Exports, total	100.0	100.0	100.0	100.0	100.0	100.0	100.0	
Machinery and equipment	0.4	0.3	0.9	5.3	4.6	3.9	5.2	+
Electrical products	2.2	0.1	2.4	–	2.3	1.6	**	
Fuels and fuel oil	–	0.4	4.8	3.2	3.1	3.8	**	+
Minerals	81.8	54.3	14.5	12.8	12.4	11.5	7.2	–
Ferrous & nonferrous metals	9.0	30.9	33.4	43.7	46.3	49.9	39.6	+
Chemical products	0.05	5.9	13.4	12.1	7.2	6.0	8.0	
Construction materials	–	–	1.9	3.3	**	**	10.0	+
Fibers and textile products	0.7	0.3	–	0.6	**	**	**	
Agricultural by-products	3.9	3.6	13.7	10.2	8.8	11.0	12.2	+
Perishables and luxuries	0.1	1.3	12.2	6.3	**	**	**	
Marine products	1.8	2.9	2.8	1.8	**	**	**	
Others	0.05	–	0.4	0.7	**	**	**	
B. Imports, total	100.0	100.0	100.0	100.0	100.0	100.0	100.0	
Machinery and equipment	34.3	32.7	34.8	22.5	23.6	21.2	30.2	
Electrical products	8.6	7.7	5.4	1.6	1.9	2.2	***	–
Fuels and fuel oil	9.8	8.4	12.4	18.3	22.3	22.1	19.3	+
Minerals	0.2	0.5	0.8	1.0	6.0	4.6	***	+
Ferrous and nonferrous metals	7.2	11.8	10.1	7.0	9.5	9.8	8.7	
Chemical and rubber products	9.8	7.5	6.2	6.2	11.5	11.8	8.2	
Construction materials	1.4	0.02	0.1	0.1	***	***	***	
Pulp and paper products	3.2	0.8	1.0	0.9	***	***	10.4	
Fibers and textile products	3.9	13.0	5.2	7.6	***	***	***	
Cultural items and daily necessities	1.0	0.9	0.4	0.6	***	***	***	
Agricultural by-products	0.2	6.3	7.7	19.9	9.1	2.1	10.0	
Perishables and luxuries	0.2	1.2	1.2	5.8	***	***	***	
Others	19.2	9.2	14.7	8.5	***	***	***	

* + = rising; - = declining.

**These items when lumped together constitute 15.3%, 12.3%, and 17.8% of total exports in 1963, 1964, and 1969, respectively.

***These items when lumped together constitute 16.1%, 26.2%, and 13.2% of total imports in 1963, 1964, and 1969, respectively.

Sources: For 1964, CCY, 1965, p. 483.

For 1953-60, ERNK, No. 79, pp. 73-74.

For 1969 (estimates), Ch'a Byŏn-kŏn, op. cit., p. 25.

North Korea has been a net importer of cereals (mostly wheat and its preparations) in spite of the regime's claim that the country is self-sufficient in
food. For example, during 1960-69, its cumulative net imports of cereals
amounted to $102.61 million (with an annual average of $10.261 million). Cereal
imports (net) fluctuated widely to meet the demand of domestic food needs.
Years of bad harvest (such as 1961 and 1966) were accompanied by imports (net)
which exceeded $20 million ($30.58 million in 1961 and $22.77 million in 1966).
The only exception in the unfavorable balance of cereal trade occurred in 1969
when a surplus of $1.7 million was made. Imports of wheat and wheat flour have
been mainly paid for by exports of rice which constituted the main cereal category for exports (constituting 94.5 percent of total exports of cereals with an
annual average of $63.96 million and 43.95 million metric tons for 1960-69).
Next to cereals, apples and silk have been the two most important agricultural
products for export, bringing in an average foreign exchange earning of $6.1
million per year during 1960-69 and $2.2 million between 1964-69.[12]

Direction of North Korea's Trade

From the beginning of the regime the trade partners of North Korea have
largely been confined to communist bloc countries, predominantly the U.S.S.R.
and Communist China (table 30). The percentage of North Korean trade with the
communist bloc during the post-Korean War years up to 1963 was above 90 percent.
At times, especially during the years immediately following the Korean War, the
figure was nearly 100 percent. Since the mid-1960s the proportion has been
gradually declining owing to expanding North Korean trade with the noncommunist
world, especially with Japan and Western Europe. By 1969 the relative share of
North Korean trade with the noncommunist world passed the one-fourth mark.

North Korea's heavy reliance on communist bloc countries for its external
trade out of the seventy or so nations with which it maintains economic relations is derived from several factors, some of which are interrelated. First,
there is the political and ideological affinity for the bloc. Second, related
to the first is the advantage of a planned economy like North Korea to trade
with other planned economies according to trade agreements, geared to the
national plans of each of the partners. Third, rehabilitation from the destruction of the Korean War required a large injection of aid and trade. Because of

the nature of the war and given North Korea's international position, the communist bloc was the only source for assistance and trade. This must explain North Korea's near complete trade dependence on the bloc during the post-Korean War reconstruction period. The fourth factor is the availability of aid, credit, market, and trade opportunities with the bloc. Fifth, the trade embargo imposed by the United States and other Western nations which went into effect during the Korean War had severely curtailed North Korean trade with some of the important potential trade nations of the noncommunist world including Japan. According to a study showing the importance of the communist bloc to the total trade value of each of the communist nations for 1955 and 1958, the share of interbloc trade to the total trade was the highest for North Korea and Albania. The percentage share ran in the upper nineties for both countries.[13]

Trade with the U.S.S.R.

By country, the Soviet Union has been the single largest trade partner throughout the period of the North Korean regime (table 31), the proportion of the North Korea-U.S.S.R. trade at times reaching more than 80 percent of the total North Korean trade. Understandably, North Korean dependence on the Soviet Union was the highest in the immediate post-Korean War years. Since 1956, the last year of the Three Year Reconstruction Plan, the relative share began to decline and in the 1960s it became relatively stable at around 40 percent.

The value of North Korean trade with the Soviet Union has been steadily increasing since 1946 despite mild year-to-year fluctuations (from a mere $18.5 million in 1946 to $328.2 million in 1969). It is presumed that normal trade activities were severely curtailed during the Korean War period, especially during the early stage of the war, and that what trade existed was largely made up of imports from the Soviet Union in the form of such relief materials as food, clothing, medical supplies, and other daily necessities as well as industrial materials geared especially to the munitions industry. This, of course, was in addition to the imports of military hardware and other war-related supplies. By 1955, the total trade volume was recovered to the prewar level of 1949. The Seven Year Plan saw a definite upward trend in Soviet-North Korea trade as compared to the previous plan periods. During the Five Year Plan the total value stayed close to an annual average of $116.7 million, while during 1961-69 it maintained an average of $206.0 million per year, with a discernible upward jump

TABLE 30

DIRECTION OF NORTH KOREA'S TOTAL TRADE, 1946-1969
(Million U.S. Dollars)

Year	(1) Trade with USSR	(2) (1) as % of Total	(3) Trade with Comm. China	(4) (3) as % of Total	(5) Trade with Other Comm. Countries
1946	18.5	81.1%			
1947	37.1				
1948	66.2	(b)			
1949	85.1	46.7%			
1953					
1954					
1955	84.9	80.6%	9.5	9.0%	10.5
1956	105.0	74.8%	14.5	10.3%	20.3
1957	122.5	57.0%	58.6	27.2%	27.0
1958	105.1	36.2%			
1959	125.7	36.1%			
1960	114.1	35.7%			
1961	156.1	47.8%			
1962	168.9	47.9%	92.4	26.2%	77.9[c]
1963	170.2	40.4%			
1964	163.6	39.4%	(f)	(f)	
1965	178.1	40.4%	(f)	(f)	
1966	177.9	38.4%	(f)	(f)	
1967	218.3	43.7%			
1968	293.1	n.a.			
1969	328.2	47.1%	110.0[g]	15.9%[g]	

Sources: For noncommunist world, based on files at the U.S. Department of Commerce.

For the rest, Kim Il-song sonjip (Collected Works of Kim Il-song), Vol. 2, p. 533; Chosen no keizai, p. 126; Chosen benran, p. 65; Chugoku seiji keizai soran, loc. cit.; Dairiku Junpo (Continental Ten-Day Reports), Tokyo, Middle-of-the-month issue, November 1963; U.N., Yearbook of International Trade Statistics, various issues; O Hyŏn-sang, op. cit., p. 245; N. Samsonov, "Economic Progress and Development of Foreign Economic Relations of North Korea," Moscow, September 1958, translated in JPRS, No. 878-D, pp. 7-10; Shinn Rinn-Sup et al., Area Handbook for North Korea, Washington, D.C.: U.S. Government Printing Office, 1969, pp. 373-374; Ch'a Byŏn-kŏn, op. cit., p. 24.

TABLE 30, continued

(6) (5) as % of Total	(7) Trade with Communist Bloc (2)+(4)+(6) (%)	(8) Trade with Noncommunist World	(9) (8) as % of Total	(10) Total Trade
				22.8
	83.4%e		16.6%e	182.3
				73.0
	95.0%e		5.0%e	68.3
10.0%	99.6%	(a)	(d)	105.3
14.5%	99.6%	(a)	(d)	140.3
12.6%	96.8%	(a)	(d)	214.8
		(a)	(d)	290.0
	97.5%c	8.3	2.4%	348.0
	96.3%c	11.8	3.7%	320.0
	93.5%c	21.3	6.5%	326.4
22.1%c	96.2%c	13.4	3.8%	352.5
	93.8%c	25.9	6.2%	420.8
	89.1%c	45.1	10.9%	415.6
	88.9%c	59.4	13.5%	441.1
	86.0%c	65.3	14.0%	463.4
	86.3%c	68.5	13.7%	500.0
	n.a.	n.a.	n.a.	n.a.
	72.7%c	190.2	27.3%	696.1

[a]Less than $300,000.

[b]Share of total value not known but exports and imports constitute 78.5 and 69.2 percent, respectively, according to the official North Korean source.

[c]Derived by subtracting the share of trade with the free world from the total value. Due to the fact that the trade with the free world and the communist bloc nations do not add up to 100%, these are approximate figures. See explanation in (d).

[d]Negligible. Components do not add up to the total value. Discrepancy is due to rounding errors and the distortion effect of the various exchange rates used by the communist nations as well as other free-world countries. Free-world trade figures are based on U.S. Department of Commerce dollar figures while other components appear in rubles in the source.

[e]Official North Korean percentage figures.

[f]Total value of trade with Communist China during 1964-66 is presumed to be roughly equal to that between North Korea and the Soviet Union.

[g]Estimate.

TABLE 31

NORTH KOREA'S TRADE WITH THE U.S.S.R., 1946-1968
(Million U.S. Dollars)

Year	(1) Exports to USSR (X)	(2) Imports from USSR (M)	(3) Total Value with USSR (X+M)	Total Value with USSR 1949= 100%	Trade Bal- ance (X-M)	(1) as % of Total N.Korean Exports	(2) as % of Total N.Korean Imports	(3) as % of Total N.Korean Trade Volume
1946	n.a.	n.a.	18.5	21.7%	n.a.	n.a.	n.a.	81.1%
1947	n.a.	n.a.	37.1	43.6	n.a.	n.a.	n.a.	n.a.
1948	n.a.	n.a.	66.2	77.8	n.a.	78.5%	69.2%	n.a.
1949	n.a.	n.a.	85.1	100.0	n.a.	n.a.	n.a.	46.7%
1955	40.8	44.1	84.9	99.7	-3.3	90.7%	73.1%	80.6
1956	51.2	53.8	105.0	123.4	-2.6	77.8	72.2	74.8
1957	62.5	60.0	122.5	143.9	2.5	62.5	52.3	57.0
1958	47.0	58.1	105.1	123.5	-11.1	34.8	37.5	36.2
1959	51.6	74.1	125.7	147.7	-22.5	45.7	31.5	36.1
1960	74.7	39.4	114.1	134.1	35.3	48.5	46.4	35.7
1961	79.1	77.0	156.1	183.4	2.1	49.4	48.5	47.8
1962	88.2	80.7	168.9	198.5	7.5	39.4	63.9	47.9
1963	88.1	82.1	170.2	200.0	6.0	46.2	36.0	40.4
1964	80.7	82.9	163.6	192.2	-2.2	41.7	40.4	39.4
1965	88.3	89.8	178.1	209.3	-1.5	42.4	38.6	40.4
1966	92.3	85.6	177.9	209.0	6.7	38.8	39.1	38.4
1967	108.0	110.3	218.3	256.5	-2.3	41.5	46.0	43.7
1968	120.9	172.2	293.1	344.4	-51.3	n.a.	n.a.	n.a.
1969	126.6	201.6	328.2	385.7	-75.0	41.3	51.8	47.1

Sources: For total trade value with the U.S.S.R. between 1946-49, Kim Il-song sŏnjip, vol. 2, p. 535; for share of North Korea's exports to, and imports from, the U.S.S.R. for 1948, Chosen no keizai, p. 126; for the rest, U.N., Year-book of International Trade Statistics, various issues.

since 1967, perhaps coinciding with the improved North Korea-Soviet relationship around that time.

Although the overall balance of trade has been characteristically unfavor-able to North Korea (a deficit of $111.7 million between 1955-69), there seems to be a definite cyclical pattern. First, the period between 1955-59 (the ini-tial date possibly extending as far back as the pre-Korean War years) was marked by unfavorable trade balances ($37 million) except for 1957. This period coin-cides with the reconstruction stage. The second period covering the years be-tween 1960-66 enjoyed a favorable balance ($53.9 million). This gradual im-provement in the trade balance, of course, is the result of faster growth in North Korea's exports than in imports during the period. Some observers speculated that the North Korean trade surplus with the U.S.S.R. during this period might probably be a reflection of North Korean repayments of development loans from the latter.[14] The period of unfavorable balance returned in 1967. The following years saw the largest trade deficits ever made with the U.S.S.R. ($51.3 million and $75.0 million, respectively, in 1968 and 1969). This must represent increased importation of necessary capital, raw materials and others required to finish successfully the Seven Year Plan before the extended target year of 1970 as well as an extension of sizable credit by the U.S.S.R. The cyclical nature of the trade balance generally coincides with the fluctuating relationship between the two countries, positing a correlation between political and economic relationships. Understandably, North Korea's trade deficit with the U.S.S.R. occurred during periods when an amicable relationship existed. These are the times when aid, whether grant-type or loans, could be easily negotiated. The importance of the Soviet Union as North Korea's primary source of credit and capital goods can be surmised, for example, by the fact that in 1969, the year of the largest trade deficit for North Korea, her deficit with the Soviet Union constituted 90.7 percent of total North Korean deficits with the world.

Available information on the composition of the Soviet-North Korean trade for 1949 reveals that North Korea's exports to the Soviet Union were primarily made up of iron and steel, minerals, chemical fertilizers, and carbide (table 32). In addition, 6.5 tons of gold were exported in 1949 with 9 tons of refined gold being planned for export in 1950.[15] For many commodities, the amount exported to the Soviet Union constituted a significant proportion (headed by 71 percent for zinc) of the total production. Principal Soviet interest and impact on the North Korean economy are clear from these data. For all the commodities listed in the table a much larger amount was planned to be exported to the Soviet Union in 1950.

In the same year about two-thirds of North Korea's imports from the Soviet Union were made up of coking coal, crude oil, industrial and agricultural machinery, locomotives, rolling stock, chemicals, and parts while daily necessities accounted for slightly less than one-third. It is speculated that North Korea paid for most, if not all, military supplies from the Soviet Union. According to one report, the reliability of which cannot be determined, military goods constituted more than one-third of North Korean total imports (including military supplies) during the period between June 1949 and May 1950.[16]

Examination of the commodity composition of the Soviet-North Korean trade for 1955-65[17] reveals that the export trade in the early stage of the period was

TABLE 32

COMMODITY COMPOSITION OF NORTH KOREA'S TRADE
WITH THE SOVIET UNION, 1949-1950

(1,000 tons)

| | 1949 | | | 1950 | |
	Exports (A)	Total Production (B)	A/B	Planned Exports (C)	(C) as % of Total Planned Production
1. Exports:					
Copper	803	2,498*	32.1%	2.915	13.7%
Lead	4,381	9,046*	48.4	12,405	64.5
Zinc	5,400	7,600*	71.0	19,450	51.4
Tungsten	630	2,250*	28.0	2,900	46.6
Iron ore	30	680	4.4	910	5.5
Pig iron	51	166	30.7	370	27.0
Steel	29	260	11.2	186	33.3
Fertilizer	104	401	25.9	416	21.6
Carbide	18	136	13.2	143	28.0

2. Imports, Composition (Total 100.0%) for 1949:

Coking coal, locomotives, industrial and agricultural machinery, parts, etc.	67.3%
Daily necessities (textiles, etc.)	28.2
Cultural goods excluding books	4.2
Others	0.2

*In lieu of actual production figures which are not available, planned production is used.

Sources: For total production, JPRS (No. 4148), op. cit., pp. 27-36; for the rest, North Korea: A Case Study in the Technique of Takeover, p. 109; Chosen no keizai, p. 126.

predominated by metallic ores and concentrates but their importance sharply and continually declined in both absolute and relative terms: their importance as a percentage of total exports to the U.S.S.R. declined from 60.7 percent in 1955 to 19.1 percent in 1959 to a mere 1 percent in 1965. In absolute amount their exports in 1965 were only 36 percent of 1955. A sudden drop occurred between 1957-58 (from 52.8 percent in 1957 to 24.5 percent in 1958, or in absolute amount from $33.0 million to $11.5 million), suggesting that smelting capacities were expanded sharply around 1958. In contrast to this and significantly, exports of base metals and semimanufactured goods had been gaining importance, iron and steel constituting a sizable portion of this category. For example, there has been a spectacular upward surge in the exports of steel products (rolled as well as high-speed steel) in both absolute and relative terms. The

proportion of steel exports to total North Korean exports increased from a trickle
of 3.9 percent in 1955 to 49.4 and 40.2 percent, respectively, in 1964 and 1965.
During 1955-1965 the dollar value of steel exports increased from $1.6 million
to $35.48 million, making the 1965 value slightly more than 22 times that in 1955.
In terms of quantities, the exports of rolled steel grew from a small level of
700 tons in 1955 to a total of 80,900 tons in 1967. Other export items[18] include
nonferrous metals, magnesia clinker, nonmetal minerals, leaf tobacco, and fruits
(chiefly apples). One item of special interest is the fact that North Korea now
and then exported rice to the Soviet Union, which amounted to $6.1 million in
1965. However, the value of rice exports in the previous years remained small
($1.7 and $2.4 million, respectively, in 1960 and 1961).

On the import side, preponderance of machinery and equipment (including complete plants) has been the overwhelming characteristic as it had been before the
Korean War and there was no indication up to 1965 that this trend was changing.
With the exception of years between 1960-62, the proportion of this group to the
total imports stayed well above the one-third level (37.3 percent in 1955, 39.8
percent in 1959, 25.1 percent in 1961, and 32.5 percent in 1965). This group includes metal-cutting machines, power equipment, ball-bearing rollers, motor
vehicles, and complete plants. At least based on data throughout 1959-65, imports
of some machinery were either stopped or dwindled to small quantities. The first
group includes construction equipment (since 1960), road construction equipment
(since 1963), and tractors (since 1964), while the second group includes metal-
cutting machines, equipment for light industry, food industry, and chemical industry, railroad rolling stock, and motor vehicles. Since North Korea began to
turn to the noncommunist world for some of this machinery and equipment, the
above trend may imply both some import substitution and geographical redistribution of import sources. The tendency seems to be clear that the U.S.S.R. has
been the primary source for importing complete plants while the noncommunist
countries have supplied light machinery and equipment. From a low of $2.0 million
in 1959 the imports of complete plants increased to $16.8 and $11.8 million, respectively, for 1964 and 1965. Since 1962 complete plants have constituted the
largest single item in the category of machines, equipment, and complete plants
(constituting 66.7 and 45.1 percent, respectively, of the total imports in this
category for 1964 and 1965). The next most important group of imports has been
mineral fuels, lubricants, and related materials, of which gasoline and diesel
fuels make up the bulk. Up to 1960 gasoline had been the largest single item but

imports of diesel fuels increased sharply in 1961 and since then have maintained
about the same level as that of gasoline in metric tons (172.9 million metric
tons of gasoline and 175.0 million metric tons of diesel fuels in 1965). Entire
domestic consumption of petroleum products is nearly completely dependent upon
imports from the Soviet Union. With the completion of two oil refineries imports of crude oil would be expected to increase at the expense of refined oil
in the future. Construction of North Korea's first oil refinery (with a daily
capacity of 40,000 barrels) began in 1967 with Soviet assistance under the
1967-70 trade and technical-assistance agreement between the two countries.[19] A
second refinery (with an annual capacity of 2 million tons) is to be constructed
in Unggi (located less than fifteen miles from the Soviet border) between 1968
and 1973.[20] Reportedly, the project was already under way in August 1968. Besides the commodities discussed so far, North Korean imports include chemicals,
automobile tires, ferrous and nonferrous rolled stock, cable and wires, pipes,
vegetables, animal oil, and other food items. Food imports include wheat, the
principal item, and rye which North Korea imported from the U.S.S.R. in all the
years between 1955-65 with the exception of 1964. Although the value of these
cereals fluctuated, probably owing to fluctuating domestic food production and
weather conditions, which at times cause bad harvests, it reached a high point
of $22 million in 1961 (from a low of around $2 million in 1955). Comparing
North Korea's rice exports to the Soviet Union with the former's imports
of wheat and rye, North Korea has been a heavy net importer of food.

As a whole, change in the commodity pattern of North Korean trade with the
U.S.S.R. generally follows that of the former's total trade with the world.

The charge that the Soviet-European satellite terms of trade have been generally unfavorable to the latter has been frequently made and publicized and the
issue has not been settled—considerable controversy exists on the subject.[21]
Some qualitative and circumstantial evidence has also been advanced to indicate
that the terms of trade were unfavorable to North Korea before the Korean War.
For example:

> ...north [sic] Korea's exports to the USSR were subject to rigid inspection
> by the Soviet technicians in the factories and by Soviet trade officials at
> ports of exit and they were reexamined by a representative of the Soviet
> Ministry of Foreign Trade on arrival in the USSR. Frequently these commod-
> ities were judged to be substandard and therefore had to be sold at greatly
> reduced prices. On the other hand, Soviet commodities were almost uncondi-
> tionally received in North Korean ports, with virtually no inspection of
> quality and therefore no adjustment in price in the event that specification
> were not met. The very fact that the details of the trade were such closely

guarded secrets may be taken as an additional indication that the USSR dictated exploitative terms. And finally, it is to be noted that the officials in the North Korean foreign trade offices appear to have been selected in particular for their loyalty to the USSR. The chief of the Trade Control Bureau of the Ministry of Commerce and the heads of the Import and Export Offices in that bureau were all Soviet-Koreans.[22]

It was also reported that before 1949 crude oil from the Soviet Sakhalin Oil Trust was sold to the Wŏnson Oil Company at world market prices, but petroleum products were purchased by the Soviet Union at artificially low prices established by the Soviet authorities.[23] North Korea made a sharp attack against Soviet high-handedness regarding terms of trade as late as September 1966. In a public statement[24] North Korea complained that:

> For equipment and stainless steel plates you gave us in the name of "aid" in connection with rehabilitation and construction of our factories for prices far higher than on international markets, you took away from us tons of gold and huge amounts of expensive ferrous metal and other raw materials for prices far cheaper than on international markets.

This unusually vituperative statement, coming as it did in the period of North Korea's siding with the hardline policies of Communist China, was most probably aimed at political and psychological targets. Nevertheless, it is a rare revelation surrounding North Korea-Soviet economic relations. A thorough analysis of the terms of trade, however, requires quantitative data on prices and quantities of goods traded. In addition, there are many theoretical difficulties involved in the measurement of the trade terms to be coped with.

North Korea's continuing and renewed interest of closer economic ties with the Soviet Union, despite her charges (if true), lead one to speculate that either the terms of trade were improving or she was in such dire need of assistance and trade with the Soviet Union that she would trade in spite of unfavorable terms. For one thing, the ever deepening Sino-Soviet rift gave North Korea a greater measure of maneuverability and a stronger bargaining power in dealing with both contenders who had been openly wooing her allegiance.

Although trade between the two countries had existed since the beginning of the North Korean regime, it was not until 1949 that a formal trade agreement was signed. Since then, three basic long-term treaties concerning economic cooperation have been in effect. Details relating to actual quantity, composition, and credit agreements of trade for each year is instrumented through annual trade agreements based on general guidelines set forth in the basic treaty covering the period. The Treaty Concerning Economic and Cultural Cooperation, the first economic treaty ever signed between the two countries, formally went into effect

on March 17, 1949. The treaty was to last ten years after which it could be renewed if so desired by both parties. The treaty provided for "most favored
nation" treatment in mutual commerce and navigation as well as toward activities
of natural and legal persons of one party while in the territory of the other.
Based on the treaty the following specific agreements were concluded. First, a
trade agreement was signed for the period 1949-50 specifying commodities to be
traded. (North Korea's imports and exports in 1949 listed above are results of
this agreement.) Second, a credit of 212 million rubles was to be extended by
the Soviet Union in annual installments between July 1949 and July 1952 for the
purpose of paying for the import surplus. Repayment of the loan was to start
from July 1952 in three annual installments with an interest rate of 2 percent
per annum.[25] Third, a technical assistance program was arranged whereby Soviet
technicians were to be sent to North Korea to assist in such areas as iron works,
zinc works, automobile assembly plants, steel pipe plants, blue print designing,
and geological surveys. North Korean technicians were to be sent to various
Soviet plants to absorb advanced production techniques. Fourth, an educational
exchange agreement was concluded in which Soviet scientists and scholars were to
be invited to North Korea which, in turn, was to send students to Russian
universities.[26]

According to an agreement concluded in September 1953, North Korea received
a grant totaling 1 billion rubles (U.S. $250 million) from the Soviet Union for
the express purpose of aiding North Korea's efforts to reconstruct. The grant
was to be used to import from the grantor mainly materials necessary to rehabilitate and develop heavy industries such as iron works, steel plants, cement
plants, chemical fertilizer plants, power stations, and mines. In addition,
North Korea was to import equipment and materials for reconstructing transportation and communication facilities as well as agricultural machinery, fertilizers,
seeds, draft horses, insecticides, medical supplies, pharmaceuticals, tractors,
buses, fishing boats, and other unspecified daily necessities.[27] The full amount
of the grant was to be received within a two-year period, two-thirds to be provided by the end of 1954 and the remainder in 1955. Imports based on the agreement began to arrive in November 1953. It was reported that North Korea received
an unspecified credit of 170 million rubles (U.S. $42.5 million) from the Soviet
Union between the calendar years 1956 and 1957.[28] This must be the 1956-57
allotment of the grant negotiated in Moscow in August 1956 by the visiting North
Korean government delegation to assist North Korea in carrying out its Five Year

Plan, the grant to be extended over the period 1956-61. According to an agreement signed in February 1960, the 1960 allotment of the grant was determined to be 85 million rubles (U.S. $21.25 million) to be used for the procurement of goods from the U.S.S.R. In October 1960 in another agreement the Soviet Union canceled North Korea's debts in the amount of 760 million rubles (U.S. $190 million) which had been extended to the latter in the form of loans. The same agreement provided for a new loan of 140 million rubles (U.S. $35 million) to be repaid in annual installments for the period of ten years starting with 1967.[29]

In December 1960 a second long-term treaty on commerce and economic cooperation between North Korea and the U.S.S.R. covering the period 1961-67 was concluded in Moscow specifying the commodities to be exchanged for trade. At the same time another agreement was signed between the two parties concerning the technical assistance to be provided by the Soviet Union for 1961-67—which coincides with North Korea's original Seven Year Plan period. Both of these agreements are geared to a long-term program of further expanding North Korean heavy industries including the electric power industry. The U.S.S.R., according to the agreement, was to assist North Korea in such specific projects as raising the annual production capacity of the Kimch'aek Iron Works to a level of 2.8 million tons of steel and 2.3 million tons of rolled iron, constructing coal-powered electric power stations in Pukch'ang and Pyŏngyang with respective output capacities of 600,000 and 400,000 kilowatts, and building a petrochemical plant with an annual production capacity of 2 million tons. The Soviet Union was also to cooperate in the construction of linen and woolen textile plants.[30] It has been hinted that the Soviet Union did not fully carry out its part of the treaty commitment. Also, the idea that the Russian aid was not a pure blessing was alluded to in the North Korean denunciation mentioned earlier in connection with the terms of trade. Most of the second treaty period was marked by a low ebb in the Russo-North Korean relationship. Significantly, North Korea disclosed openly that during this period the Soviet Union opposed North Korean assignment of priority to heavy industry as well as her pursuance of a policy of autarky.[31] A third treaty concerning technical and economic cooperation between the parties was concluded in June 1966 covering the period between 1967-70, the last year coinciding with the termination of the extended Seven Year Plan.

In the March 16, 1964, issue of Pravda, marking the fifteenth anniversary of the first economic treaty of 1949, a summary of benefits which North Korea had received from the U.S.S.R. was given. According to the summary, more than

40 industrial plants and installations—including the Sup'ung Dam, Hwanghae Iron Works, Hŭngnam Chemical Combine, and Pyŏngyang Textiles—had been either reconstructed or newly built with Russian aid. It was also reported that an atomic reactor and a combined electric-power and heat-generating plant were under construction in Pyŏngyang assisted by Russian specialists. The power plant is said to have a capacity of 400 thousand kilowatts.[32] According to another Russian source[33] in 1968, the Soviet Union has "built and restored" more than 50 industrial plants and other projects since the beginning of the North Korean regime. The source also states that 18 new projects, including the oil refinery in Unggi mentioned above and the thermal power plant at Pukch'ang, would be completed with the Soviet aid. The completion of these projects, reportedly, would increase North Korea's power output by 15 percent.

Technical assistance thus far has been characterized by unilateral movement from the Soviet Union. For instance, by 1964 the Soviet Union had handed over more than 2,000 sets of various scientific and technical data to North Korea.[34] At least in one instance, the direction has been reversed. It was reported[35] both in Russian and Korean sources that six Soviet technicians, led by the department chief of the Moscow Plastic Material Designing Institute, arrived in North Korea in December 1963. They were to study, with the assistance of Korean counterparts, the industrial production method of polyvinyl alcohol, polyvinyl acetal, vinyl acetal, and vinyl acetal compound catalyzer at the February 8 Vinalon Factory.[36] They were also interested in technical problems concerning the construction and automatic operation of a vinalon factory. Judging from the fact that the Soviet Union was sending technicians to study the North Korean technique and organization of production of vinalon and the fact that construction of such an industrial complex required supporting industries, the North Korean chemical and machinery industries must have reached a fairly high level of technical development.

Trade with Communist China

North Korea's trade with Communist China began as soon as the Chinese communists came into control of Manchuria and North China long before the complete communist takeover of Mainland China and the formal proclamation of the People's Republic on October 1, 1949. It was reported that an agreement was made as early as March 1948 between Mao Tse-tung and Kim Kwa-bong, a North Korean representative, for a "mutual exchange" of such commodities as food, gasoline, industrial

goods, and medicines as well as for a military assistance pact.[37] Also, trade
relations were reported to be in existence in October 1948 between North Korea
and the Northeast Administrative Committee (of Communist China).[38] There is
virtually no information available regarding Sino-North Korea trade immediately
before the Korean conflict. Judging from the short period of time that existed
between the establishment of Communist China in October 1949 and the outbreak
of the Korean War in June 1950, commodities traffic between the two
partners was probably small. In August 1950, two months after the hostilities started, a barter agreement was signed between the two countries. According to the agreement China was to ship to North Korea commodities worth
28,852,200 rubles whereas North Korean exports to China were to be in the amount
of 14,138,286 rubles. North Korea agreed to pay for the trade deficit
(14,713,914 rubles) by remitting electricity and others. The agreement was to
be executed before the end of 1950,[39] but it is doubtful that it was ever carried out completely. Since then the fortunes of the Korean War drastically
changed, with a brief occupation of North Korea by the United Nations Forces,
Chinese intervention, and severe allied bombing and fierce battles within North
Korea itself.

During the Korean War Communist China provided North Korea with a substantial amount of economic aid in addition to military assistance. The following
is the list of goods China supplied between 1950-52.[40] Understandably, it is
made up entirely of relief goods such as food and other daily necessities.

Commodity	Quantity
Food grains	192 railroad wagons and 11,700 tons
Meat	20 wagons and 3 million catties
Pork	20 train wagons
Blankets	110,000 pieces
Cloth	35,000 bolts
Clothing	380,000 suits and 24,000 pieces
Cotton	400,000 catties
Comfort bags	25,000
Cigarettes	300,000 cartons
Towels	150,000 pieces

The first formal economic relationship between the two parties resulted
from the signing in November 1953 in Peking of the Treaty Concerning Economic
and Cultural Cooperation. Since then trade between the two partners has been
carried out through annual commodity exchange agreements following the basic
tenets set in this and other long-term treaties. Other treaties signed include
a long-term trade agreement covering 1959-62, the Treaty Concerning Commodity

Trade Between Border Areas concluded in November 1958, the Treaty of Friendship, Cooperation and Mutual Assistance signed in July 1961, the Commerce and Navigation Treaty of November 1962,[41] and the Treaty Concerning Marine Transportation.

Sino-North Korean trade grew at a fast tempo, from $9.5 million in 1955 to $110.0 million in 1969 (table 30). As a consequence China's share in the total North Korean trade with the world increased rapidly to catch up with the Soviet Union as North Korea's principal trade partner by 1964-66.[42] However, during the years following the Cultural Revolution of 1966, Sino-North Korean trade slipped behind both in absolute value and as a share of total North Korean trade (15.9 percent in 1969 as compared to roughly 40 percent during 1964-66).

Not much is known about trade balances between the two countries except that in 1957 North Korea incurred a $6 million deficit ($32.3 million in imports and $26.3 million in exports) while in 1969 exports and imports were presumed to have been roughly equal ($55.0 million, respectively).[43]

Qualitative information (for lack of quantitative data) based on the protocols for the exchange of goods for selected years between the two governments (table 33) shows that North Korean exports are increasingly characterized by machine tools, pig iron, metal and alloy steel, and the like, which are products of heavy industry. North Korean requirements for external supplies of coking coal, oil, cotton, raw rubber, sugar, and structural steel are persistent, as reflected in the composition of her imports from Communist China as from other countries. In 1957, the only year for which such information is known, the most important export item was iron ore with a total quantity of 233,000 metric tons.[44]

Communist China's economic aid to North Korea took two forms—free aid and credit. The treaty of 1953 called for China to write off the costs of all materials supplied and to assume all expenses incurred by China during the Korean War amounting to 280 million (old) yuan (U.S. $114 million[45]). This is the first time Communist China ever extended external economic assistance to any country in the world. Communist China also agreed in the same treaty to grant North Korea 800 million (old) yuan (U.S. $325 million) as free aid for the purpose of reconstructing the war-torn North Korean economy. The grant was to be made over four years between 1954-57, 300 million yuan to be delivered in 1954 and the remainder in the next three years. The grant was to be used to pay for imports from Communist China of such commodities as coal, machinery, transport equipment, construction materials, metal products, agricultural implements,

122

TABLE 33

COMMODITIES TRADED BETWEEN COMMUNIST CHINA AND NORTH KOREA
SINCE 1954 (SELECTED YEARS)

Year	North Korean Imports	North Korean Exports
1954	Coal, fishing boats, construction materials, machinery, & industrial products.	Electric power, minerals, marine products, medical herbs, etc.
1955	Rolled steel and cotton yarn.	Electric power, minerals, marine products, & fruit.
1956	Cotton, cotton yarn, cotton cloth, coal, steel products, machinery, telecommunication equipment, chemical industry raw materials, & cultural articles.	Mineral products, marine products, fruits, and medicine.
1957	Millet, cotton, cotton yarn, cotton cloth, burlap, salt, rolled steel, paper, construction materials, & sulphur.	Iron ore, ferrosilicon, tool steel, nonferrous metals, cement, calcium, carbide, fruits, & marine products.
1958	Coal, coke, cotton, cotton yarn, cotton cloth, machinery, steel rails, soy beans, & industrial chemicals.	Pig iron, iron ore, steel ingots, high-speed steel for making tools, carbon steel, electrolytic copper, electrolytic lead, electrolytic zinc, sulphate of ammonia, marine products, and drugs.
1962	Rolled steel, coal, sulphur & other ores, various kinds of machines, tires, chemicals, indigenous products, & others.	Iron ore, tractors, automobiles, machine tools & other machines, calcium carbide, fruits, marine products, indigenous goods & others.
1964	Coking coal & other minerals, crude oil, alloy iron, seamless pipe & various kinds of structural steel, tires, raw rubber, various chemical reagents, ginned cotton, sugar, & others.	Machine tools, magnesia clinker & other mineral ores, pig iron, various kinds of metal & alloy steel, cement, carbide & other chemical products, red ginseng, fiber goods, & indigenous products.

Source: Survey of the China Mainland Press (SCMP), Hong Kong, various issues.

fishing boats, grains, textiles, papers, stationery, cotton, and others. Specifically, the list of aid goods for 1954 included approximately 100,000 tons of food grains, 30,000 tons of peas, tens of million meters of textile fabrics, tens of fishing vessels, and an unspecified quantity of coal, locomotives, and passenger and freight cars. Communist China also agreed to extend technical assistance to North Korea in the form of inviting Korean technicians to China to be trained in various fields of industry as well as sending Chinese technicians to Korea. In particular, Communist China promised to assist in the reconstruction of the railroad network which had been severely damaged during the hostilities.[46]

Communist China's economic and technical assistance seems to have been concentrated in reconstructing and developing North Korean light industry, with the exception of transportation—in contrast to the Soviet Union which was called to assist mainly in heavy industrial projects. The North Korean textile industry received from China various machine parts, cotton yarn, and dye materials, as well as technicians. Leather processing machines were imported to replace to some extent the traditional handicraft method of production. The rubber processing industry was boosted by imports of raw rubber. Industries producing daily necessities were assisted through imports of machines to manufacture matches, pencils, buttons, zippers, toothpastes, and needles. Various chemicals required for the paper manufacturing industry as well as materials for the construction industry such as construction equipment, cement, plate glass, lumber, and other related items were imported. In addition, the Chinese provided labor for reconstructing some of the major bridges.[47] It is assumed that Chinese troops stationed in North Korea were the main source for such labor. In some cases it is possible that technicians who were assigned to various North Korean enterprises were drawn from the army. The form of subsequent Chinese aid to North Korea changed to that of providing long-term credits. Published information shows that Communist China extended three loans to North Korea. In an agreement of September 27, 1958, an interest-free loan of 40 million rubles (U.S. $10 million) was made for the purpose of constructing the Unbong Electric Power Plant. The principal was to be repaid in commodities over a period of ten years starting in 1963. In the same agreement another loan of 170 million rubles (U.S. $42.5 million) was provided for the construction of three plants. The interest charge was 1 percent and the principal was to be repaid in commodities over a period of ten years starting in 1961. The last known loan was made on October 13, 1960,[48] when China agreed to a loan of 420 million rubles (U.S. $105 million) over 1961-64 to be used in the construction of a tire factory, a radio equipment plant, and light industry factories producing daily necessities. China agreed to provide both industrial equipment and technical assistance for the purpose. According to the agreement North Korea would also receive cotton manufacturing and radio communications equipment. Information on interest and method of repayment is not known.

According to published information on what appears to be the first economic contact between North Korea and Mongolia, the latter provided aid goods during and after the war; these include 21 carloads of meat, cotton cloth, leather goods, and overcoats during the Korean War; 6,054 horses, 39,760 sheep, 446 dairy cows, and 18,693 goats sent between 1954-56; and 5,000 tons of wheat and 2,000 head of cattle sent since 1956.[49] The Treaty of Economic and Cultural Cooperation between the two countries was signed on November 2, 1956, and was to last for ten years. Examination of annual trade agreements during 1956-69 show that North Korean exports to Mongolia consist mainly of chemical products, various machines and tools, fiber products, rolled steel, cement, textiles, and processed food commodities in exchange for wool, glue, furs, leathers, processed sheepskin, sheep, wheat, meat, and wax.[50] North Korean exports are principally industrial products while her imports from Mongolia are agricultural and handicraft products.

North Korea's trade with Cuba, the only communist nation in the Western Hemisphere, began in 1959, a year before any formal diplomatic relationship was established. (See table 34.) Trade volume remained small, never reaching the

TABLE 34

NORTH KOREA-CUBA TRADE, 1959-1968
(Million dollars)

Year	North Korean Exports	North Korean Imports	Total Value	Trade Balance
1959	0.00	0.74	0.74	-0.74
1960	0.00	1.03	1.03	-1.03
1961	0.72	1.60	2.32	-0.88
1962	2.38	2.03	4.41	0.35
1963	2.78	2.40	5.18	0.38
1964	5.00	3.27	8.27	1.73
1965	2.70	2.49	5.19	0.21
1966	2.00	2.10	4.10	-0.10
1967	9.60	7.70	17.30	1.90
1968	9.70	7.00	16.70	2.70

Source: U.N., Yearbook of International Trade Statistics, various issues.

$9 million mark until 1967 when it more than quadrupled (as compared to 1966). In 1967 and 1968 the total value of North Korea-Cuba trade ($17.3 million and $16.7 million, respectively) was larger than that of North Korea's trade with every one of the East European communist countries for these years, except

Poland in 1968. In the beginning (1959-61) North Korea accumulated a small trade deficit, but later years, except 1966, show favorable balances. North Korean exports include electric motors, machine tools, steel, accessory parts for locomotives, ploughs, light industry products, and porcelains. Cuban exports to North Korea are mainly sugar and rope;[51] in 1961, 82.5 percent of exports were made up of sugar.[52] Besides trade, North Korea extended economic aid to Cuba in the form of relief goods, which were sent in a North Korean cargo vessel, leaving Nampo on November 26, 1963. The goods comprised 5,000 tons of polished rice, 10 tractors, 5 concrete mixers, 10,000 square meters of sheet glass, 1,000 saws, 10,000 files, 1,000 whetstones, 100,000 items of glass and ceramicware, 10,000 items of hardware for daily use, and 10,000 won worth of medicaments.[53]

At least two long-term trade agreements have been concluded between North Korea and North Vietnam: a commercial agreement in November 1960 covering the 1961-64 period and the Trade and Navigation Agreement of 1963. No details are available on either of the two. Evaluation of the published information on the annual commodity exchange agreements between the two countries since 1962 to 1967[54] reveals that North Korea supplied North Vietnam with machinery, wheel accessories, rolled steel, nonferrous metal, copper wires, plate glass, chemical fertilizers, fiber and chemical products, textiles, and others to be exchanged for apatite, chrome ore, tin, bamboo, crude drugs, glycerine, canned fruit, perfumery, and others. Here, too, North Korean exports tend to be industrial products while North Vietnamese exports are primary commodities. North Vietnam has also been the recipient of North Korean economic aid. For example, an agreement on grant-type aid was made on September 3, 1966,[55] and another providing free military and economic aid concluded on August 6, 1967.[52]

North Korea-Eastern Europe Trade

North Korea's economic relations with the communist nations of Eastern Europe probably had their beginning in the post-Korean War era when these countries joined the U.S.S.R. and Communist China in providing free economic aid to help reconstruct the war-ravaged North Korean economy through a series of separate agreements concluded within months following the ceasefire in 1953. In general, according to the contents of the agreements, and breakdown by country (summarized in table 35), the aid goods were primarily made up of those related to relief (hospitals, medical aid, daily necessities) and reconstruction of basic

126

transportation facilities and public utilities. In ruble value, East Germany
extended the largest amount, with 100 million rubles.

TABLE 35

CONTENTS OF PRINCIPAL AID GOODS TO NORTH KOREA
FROM THE EASTERN EUROPEAN COMMUNIST BLOC

Country	Date of Agreement	Contents of Principal Aid Goods
Czecho- slovakia	Sept.1953	Construction and reconstruction of machinery factories; furnishing equipment for automobile repairing, machine tool, precision instrument plants, and a hospital; recon- struction of cement factories and electric power stations; furnishing a medical team, construction materials, and daily necessities.
East Germany	Oct. 1953	Construction of electric instrument and printing plants; technical and material assistance in reconstructing the city of Hamhung; furnishing hospital equipment and medical team. Total aid amounts to 100 million rubles.
Hungary	Sept.1953	Construction of organic chemistry, measuring instruments, and machine tool factories; furnishing electrical machines, communications equipment, construction machinery, medi- cines, fabrics, shoemaking machines, and daily necessities.
Poland	Sept.1953	Construction of locomotive, passenger, and freight car re- pair shop; technical assistance in reconstructing and ex- panding a mine; furnishing mining equipment, hospital facilities, medical team, and daily necessities.
Rumania	Oct. 1953	Construction of aspirin, cement, and tile factories; fur- nishing passenger cars, fishing boats, hospital equipment, and medical teams. Total aid amounts to 65 million rubles.
Bulgaria	Nov. 1953	Construction of wood container factory; furnishing equip- ment for tile factories, yarn, fabrics, glass, hospital facilities, and medical team. Total aid amounts to 20 million rubles.
Albania	No treaty	10,000 tons of pitch for paving streets; daily necessities.

Sources: Terao Koro, Chosen sono kitato minami (Korea: North and South),
pp. 85-89; Chosen no keizai, p. 128; Yang, Key P., The North Korean Regime:
1945-55, a thesis on file at the American University, Washington, D.C.,
pp. 153-154.

North Korea received commitment for another round of aid from the East
European bloc during Kim Il-song's "friendship" visit throughout the countries
of Eastern Europe in 1956. The aid, to be used to finance imports from the bloc,
had reportedly been completed around 1959. This explains the relatively large

127

trade deficit that North Korea sustained from the bloc between 1956-59. It is reported that Poland's aid to North Korea, for instance, had amounted to a total of 364 million zlotys ($92 million) for the period 1954-59,[56] including the aid listed in table 35.

A few observations may be made on the post-Korean War trade statistics for 1953-69 between North Korea and the East European communist countries (table 36). First, although East Germany began trading with North Korea as early as 1953, it was not until 1956 that most countries of the bloc followed Germany's lead. Second, the volume of trade does not indicate any definite time pattern but rather irregular fluctuations until 1968. Since that time, the total value has made a definite upward jump. Third, North Korea had been consistently accumulating trade deficits except for the four years between 1963-66 and for 1969. The magnitude of trade deficits was largest during the 1950s, reaching a peak in 1959. This is no doubt accounted for by the bloc's economic aid, which continued until around 1960, thus pointing to a positive correlation between the size of the trade deficits and that of economic aid. As a specific example, North Korea's trade deficits with East Germany during 1953-55, which amounted to $26.3 million, is approximately equal to the 100-million-ruble ($25 million) economic aid provided by the latter for the same period. Fourth, the total trade value with the bloc has remained relatively small: in 1960-69 it averaged $47.4 million a year although there was an upward leap in 1968 and 1969. Since reaching a peak in 1959 (18.4 percent) the relative share of North Korean trade with the group to the total North Korean trade has been gradually declining (11.3 percent in 1969). Fifth, North Korean trade with both Bulgaria and Albania (not presented in the table) is probably very small.[57]

North Korean imports from East European communist countries are primarily capital goods such as machinery and equipment (table 37). According to fragmentary data (applying only to a limited number of countries and years) North Korean imports of machinery and transport equipment (engineering products) from Poland amounted to an annual average of $2.6 million between 1963-67, constituting 48.9 percent of the total North Korean imports from Poland for these five years. North Korean imports of engineering products from Czechoslovakia ran an annual average of $3.4 million, making up an overwhelming proportion, 82 percent, of the North Korean imports from Czechoslovakia for 1963-67. The corresponding figures for imports of the same products from East Germany for 1964-67 were $1.5 million and 42.3 percent, respectively.[58] During 1966 and 1967 North Korea

128

imported from Poland 25,000 and 48,000 tons of coke, respectively, in addition
to $2.8 and $3.0 million worth of machinery and transport equipment.[59]

North Korean exports[60] of such commodities as steel, machinery, tools,
semifinished products such as ferrous and nonferrous metals, chemical products,
and the like are significant indication of the degree of her industrialization,
although quantitative data are required for a more meaningful analysis.

Examination of imports suggests the probable North Korean requirements (de-
ficiencies)—precision instruments, special machines and tools, bearings, tires,
diesel engines and generators, synthetic rubber, wire rope, cable wire, coke,
and installation of steel pipe, power, and film plants. Relative importance of
each product in the composition of total trade must be known for a more definite
conclusion.

In at least one known instance, a reversal in the direction of technical
assistance has taken place: under the North Korea-Albania scientific and technical cooperation program North Korea sent her experts in rice cultivation to
Albania in March 1962.[61]

Trade with the Noncommunist World (NCW)

An integral part of the North Korean export drive has been to establish
trade contacts with the noncommunist world. Of all the NCW countries, North
Korea is especially desirous of maintaining close economic relations with Japan,
Hong Kong, and nations of Western Europe in order to obtain some of the industrial commodities essential to her economic development as well as a market for
her products. Since 1959, a year after all-out measures for export expansion
were taken, North Korea's trade with the NCW as a group has shown faster growth
than that with the communist countries as a whole. As a result the relative
share of North Korean trade with the NCW in her total trade has increased sharply
to constitute slightly more than one-fourth (from a mere 2.4 percent in 1959 to
27.3 percent in 1969). In absolute amounts, however, the total value of trade
with the entire NCW is still modest ($190.2 million in 1969).

Since 1961 Japan has been North Korea's largest trade partner among the
countries of the NCW. In the 1960s North Korea-Japan trade alone accounted for
an average of 53.3 percent (1961-67) of the total North Korean trade with the
group, although a slightly declining tendency was observed in 1969 (table 38).
The declining Japanese share in total NCW-North Korea trade in 1969 was due to a
faster growth in North Korea's trade with Western Europe, which significantly

TABLE 36

NORTH KOREAN TRADE WITH EASTERN EUROPEAN COMMUNIST BLOC, 1953-1969
(Million U.S. Dollars)[a]

North Korea's Exports to and Imports from	1953	1954	1955	1956	1957	1958	1959
I. Countries:							
1. Albania							
Exports							
Imports							
Total value							
2. Czechoslovakia							
Exports			0.0	0.8	1.1	1.5	6.1
Imports			4.7	12.5	16.9	11.8	23.8
Total value			(4.7)	(13.3)	(18.0)	(13.3)	(29.9)
3. East Germany							
Exports	0.0*	0.0*	0.1	1.7	2.5	2.9	5.2
Imports	7.1	11.7	7.6	8.3	6.8	5.5	8.4
Total value	(7.1)	(11.7)	(7.7)	(10.0)	(9.3)	(8.4)	(13.6)
4. Hungary							
Exports				0.2	1.0	0.2	0.6
Imports				3.9	2.9	4.3	4.5
Total value				(4.1)	(3.9)	(4.5)	(5.1)
5. Poland							
Exports				1.1	2.7	0.8	2.5
Imports				13.1	1.4	1.8	6.5
Total value				(14.2)	(4.1)	(2.6)	(9.0)
6. Rumania							
Exports						0.4	1.1
Imports						3.2	5.4
Total value						(3.6)	(6.5)
II. Group total:**							
Exports	0.0*	0.0*	0.1	3.8	7.3	5.8	15.5
Imports	7.1	11.7	7.6	37.8	28.0	26.6	48.6
Total value	(7.1)	(11.7)	(7.7)	(41.6)	(35.3)	(32.4)	(64.1)
Trade balance	-7.1	-11.7	-7.5	-34.0	-20.7	-20.8	-33.1

[a]Official rates of exchange used in dollar conversion.

*Less than $50,000.

**Group total for 1965-69 does not include Albania whose trade figures since 1965 have not been forthcoming.

Source: U.N., Yearbook of International Trade Statistics, various issues.

1960	1961	1962	1963	1964	1965	1966	1967	1968	1969
	0.3	0.3	0.7	0.6					
	0.2	0.2	0.5	1.3					
	(0.5)	(0.5)	(1.2)	(1.9)					
3.6	5.0	6.3	5.4	7.4	7.2	10.1	6.7	7.6	9.4
11.7	6.4	5.8	3.1	4.3	6.0	3.8	3.3	3.8	2.5
(15.3)	(11.4)	(12.1)	(8.5)	(11.7)	(13.2)	(13.9)	(10.0)	(11.4)	(11.9)
4.6	3.3	4.2	2.8	2.1	3.3	3.1	4.7	5.5	12.8
4.7	4.1	5.1	3.6	2.6	4.5	3.8	7.3	8.7	9.5
(9.3)	(7.4)	(9.3)	(6.4)	(4.7)	(7.8)	(6.9)	(12.0)	(14.2)	(22.3)
3.3	0.8	1.8	1.6	1.9	3.4	3.1	1.7	2.2	3.1
4.6	4.3	3.2	2.7	1.8	1.6	0.8	1.4	2.6	2.9
(7.9)	(5.1)	(5.0)	(4.3)	(3.7)	(5.0)	(3.9)	(3.1)	(4.8)	(6.0)
1.9	2.9	4.0	3.9	3.8	6.2	6.4	2.5	9.4	8.3
1.4	1.4	3.3	4.4	4.1	4.8	5.8	7.1	11.8	12.4
(3.3)	(4.3)	(7.3)	(8.3)	(7.9)	(11.0)	(12.2)	(9.6)	(21.2)	(20.7)
3.0	2.8	1.7	6.1	5.5	3.5	3.1	5.1	6.3	6.1
5.3	0.9	3.0	4.5	5.5	5.1	3.5	5.1	7.4	12.0
(8.3)	(3.7)	(4.7)	(10.6)	(11.0)	(8.6)	(6.6)	(10.2)	(13.7)	(18.1)
16.4	15.1	18.3	20.5	21.3	23.6	25.8	20.7	31.0	39.7
27.7	17.3	20.6	18.8	19.6	22.0	17.7	24.2	34.3	39.3
(44.1)	(32.4)	(38.9)	(39.3)	(40.9)	(45.6)	(43.5)	(44.9)	(65.3)	(79.0)
-11.3	-2.2	-2.3	1.7	1.7	1.6	8.1	-3.5	-3.3	0.4

TABLE 37

NORTH KOREA—EASTERN EUROPE: PRINCIPAL COMMODITIES TRADE

Country (1)	North Korean Exports to (2)	North Korean Imports from (3)	Basic Years of Information (4)	Date of First Trade Agreement (5)
Albania	High-speed steel, machine & spare parts, tools, rolled ferrous metal products, cement, copper wire, lorries, bite cap, vinyl chloride products	Copper, chrome ores, pitch, tobacco, fur	1962-65	April 14 1959
Czecho-slovakia	Machines, tools, instruments, high-speed steel, pig iron, magnesia clinker, magnesia bricks, electrolytic lead and zinc, leaf tobacco, canned fish, chemicals, cigarettes	Installations for power plants & film factories, diesel engines, diesel generators, mineral processing and power transforming machines, machine tools, automobile parts, gauges, bearings, tires, wire rope, cable wire, dyestuff, & other chemicals	1962-67	December 21 1954
East Germany	Rolled steel, magnesia clinker, graphite, electrolytic zinc & lead, ferrous metals, chemical & processed food products, leaf tobacco, silk fabrics, fruits	Textile equipment, industrial sewing machines, internal combustion engines, mining & power transforming machinery, telecommunication apparatus, farm & other chemicals, synthetic rubber, diesel generators, optical meters & other machine accessories, photographic materials	1963-67	February 26 1956
Hungary	Structural steel, machine tools, magnesia clinker, carbide, ferrous & non-ferrous metals, insulators, cement, fertilizers, marine products, fabrics, chemicals, hops	Accessories for ships and automobiles, electrical gauges & condensers, aluminum products, wire rope, filament, measuring instruments, vacuum tubes, communication facilities, medical supplies	1960-66	March 7 1956

132

TABLE 37, continued

(1)	(2)	(3)	(4)	(5)
Poland	Machines, magnesia clinker, tools, fluorite, talc power, nonferrous metals, structural steel, textiles, leaf tobacco	Mining & construction machines, food processing & electric power machinery, measuring instruments, outer rings of locomotive wheels, ship engines, axles, tires, synthetic rubber, chemicals, coke	1962-67	December 16 1955
Rumania	Rolled & special steel, silicon & pig iron, tool caps, magnesia clinker, nonmetal minerals, leaf tobacco, textiles, canned fish	Machines, installation & blueprints for a steel pipe factory, spare parts for tractors, aluminum wire, ball bearings, tires, pitch, coke, & other chemicals	1963-65	November 13 1956
Bulgaria	Magnesia clinker, nonferrous metals, silk fabrics, cement, plate glass, canned fish, high-speed wire, graphite, light industrial products	Cable & electric wire, rubber procuts, machines, chemicals, medical & pharmaceutical products	*	March 23 1956

*Not specified in the source; probably around 1960.

Sources: For Bulgaria, Yu Wan-sik, op. cit., p. 144.

For the rest, Korea News, various issues; Foreign Trade, various issues; FBIS, Pyŏngyang Radio Broadcast, April 26, 1962 and December 22 and 23, 1963; Yu Wan-sik, op. cit., pp. 143-144; Lee Joong-Koon, op. cit., pp. 22-24.

TABLE 38

NORTH KOREA'S TRADE WITH THE NONCOMMUNIST WORLD, 1954-1969
(In 1,000 U.S. Dollars)

North Korea's Exports to, and Imports from	1954	1955	1956	1957	1958
I. Japan:					
1. Exports	76	0	0.2	n.a.	0.9
(1) as percent of total exports to the noncommunist world (NCW)	(100.0)	(0.0)	(0.6)	–	(4.5)
2. Imports	0[a]	0	n.a.	n.a.	0.1
(2) as percent of total imports from the Free World	(0.0)	(0.0)	(–)	(–)	(0.2)
3. Total value	76	0	–	–	1
(3) as percent of total value of trade with the NCW	(100.0)	(0.0)	(–)	(–)	(1.2)
4. Trade balance	76	0	–	–	0.8
II. Hong Kong:					
1. Exports	0	0	0	0	5
(1) as percent of total exports to the NCW	(0.0)	(0.0)	(0.0)	(0.0)	(25.0)
2. Imports	0	0	0	5	7
(2) as percent of total imports from the NCW	(0.0)	(0.0)	(0.0)	(1.8)	(10.8)
3. Total value	0	0	0	5	12
(3) as percent of total value of trade with the NCW	(0.0)	(0.0)	(0.0)	(1.6)	(14.1)
4. Trade balance	0	0	0	-5	-2
III. The Noncommunist World:					
1. Exports	76	2	31	41	20
2. Imports	0[a]	6	27	278	65
3. Total value	76	8	58	319	85
4. Trade balance	-76	-4	4	-237	-45

[a]Negligible.

Sources: Ministry of Finance (Japan), Nihon gaikoku boeki nenkan (Annual Return of the Foreign Trade of Japan), Tokyo: Ministry of Finance, various issues; Nitcho boekino tebiki, p. 510; One Korea Yearbook, 1967-68, p. 426; U.N., Yearbook of International Trade Statistics, various issues; Ch'a Byŏn-kŏn, op. cit., p. 24.

1959	1960	1961	1962	1963	1964	1965	1966	1967	1968	1969
16	8	3,976	4,553	9,430	20,231	14,723	22,692	29,606	34,032	32,186
(0.4)	(0.1)	(53.9)	(66.6)	(78.0)	(86.6)	(65.0)	(67.2)	(75.2)	(-)	(36.9)
192	1,138	4,938	4,781	5,347	11,284	16,505	5,014	6,370	20,748	24,159
(4.2)	(18.6)	(33.2)	(73.2)	(38.7)	(51.8)	(45.0)	(15.9)	(21.9)	(41.1)	(23.5)
208	1,146	8,914	9,334	14,777	31,515	31,228	27,706	35,976	54,780	56,345
(2.5)	(9.7)	(41.8)	(69.8)	(57.0)	(69.9)	(52.6)	(42.4)	(52.5)	(-)	(29.6)
-176	-1,130	-962	-228	4,083	8,947	-1,782	17,678	23,236	13,284	8,027
537	2.797	1,838	719	749	1,708	1,782	4,239	2,587	4,373	3,300
(14.4)	(48.9)	(28.9)	(10.5)	(6.2)	(7.3)	(7.9)	(12.5)	(6.6)	(-)	(3.8)
199	723	529	348	82	453	205	397	324	457	422
(4.3)	(11.8)	(3.6)	(5.3)	(0.6)	(2.1)	(0.6)	(1.3)	(1.1)	(0.9)	(0.4)
736	3,520	2,367	1,067	831	2,161	1,987	4,636	2,911	4,830	3,722
(8.8)	(29.7)	(11.1)	(8.0)	(3.2)	(4.8)	(3.3)	(7.1)	(4.2)	(-)	(2.0)
338	2,074	1,309	371	667	1,255	1,577	3,842	2,263	3,916	2,878
3,732	5,721	6,426	6,840	12,090	23,352	22,666	33,768	39,367	n.a.	87,230
4,605	6,127	14,877	6,535	13,822	21,766	36,684	31,579	29,134	50,526	102,950
8,337	11,848	21,303	13,375	25,912	45,118	59,250	65,347	68,501	n.a.	190,180
-873	-406	-8,451	305	-1,732	-1,586	-14,018	2,189	10,233	n.a.	-15,720

raised the share of the NCW as a group in total North Korean trade. North
Korea's dependence on Japan is greater in her (North Korean) exports than in her
imports, with the implication that country origins of North Korean imports are
far more widely dispersed than countries to which her exports are destined.
Hong Kong is North Korea's second largest trade partner in noncommunist Asia,
although a poor second to Japan.

Trade balances with the NCW have been consistently unfavorable. In both 1965
and 1969, when the largest deficits ($14.0 million and $15.7 million, respectively) were incurred, they were due to an excess of North Korean imports from
the countries of Western Europe. The year 1966 marked the beginning of a sudden
and marked improvement in North Korea's trade balances with Japan which continued
through 1969. In her trade with Hong Kong, North Korea was a net exporter during
every year of the period 1959-69 with an upward trend for the trade surplus in
the latter part of the 1960s.

The small volume of trade carried on before the Korean War with the noncommunist world, especially of imports, virtually ceased to exist during and immediately after the war owing to the enforcement of embargos on North Korea by the
United States and its allies. This is evident in Japan-North Korea trade between
1949-52, as shown below. It is also presumed that there was no trade between the
two countries in 1953.

Japan-North Korea Trade, 1949-1952
(In 1,000 U.S. dollars)

	1949	1950	1951	1952
North Korean exports	195	209	10	0
North Korean imports	102	0	0	0
Total trade value	297	209	10	0
Trade balance	93	209	10	0

Source: Ministry of Finance (Japan), op. cit., 1949-1952.

Examination of the principal commodities that North Korea has been trading
with the noncommunist world since 1954 through 1968 based on the trade returns
of the partner countries (table 39) shows that on the export side the relative
importance of crude mineral products has been on the wane, although the absolute
amount exported has actually been rising. Since about 1960 exports of pig iron
became the largest single export item. Increased pig iron exports may be another
indication of the extent of the recovery and development in heavy industry, especially the metal processing industry. Zinc and its semifinished products have

been major export items throughout the period. Silk, corn, fish, and fish preparations have become steady export products.

On the import side, wheat and wheat flour have predominated since around 1960. For example, between 1965-68 imports of wheat and wheat flour were running an annual average of $10.1 million constituting 27.4 percent of the total imports from the noncommunist world. It is known that North Korea imported from Australia 45,000 tons of grains (most probably wheat, judging from the country of origin) in 1961; 75,000 tons of wheat through Japan (amounting to $4,991,700) in 1963; $6.5, $2.8, and $5.8 million of wheat and wheat flour, respectively, in 1965, 1966, and 1967.[62] Other sources include Greece ($5.5 million worth of unmilled wheat in 1966) and France ($3.5 million, $3.8 million, and $7.1 million worth of wheat and wheat flour, respectively, during 1965-67).[63] Sugar has been another food item imported consistently and at a substantial level. Nonfood commodities consist mainly of industrial equipment, parts, ferroalloys, iron and steel structural parts and other related items, indicating to some extent various deficiencies and requirements of North Korean industry.

An evaluation of the commodity composition of Japan-North Korea trade[64] based on data presented in table 40 and other available data[65] indicates the following: First of all, Japanese exports to North Korea (made up principally of machinery and semifinished products) are far more diversified than are North Korean exports to Japan (made up primarily of metals and metallic ores). This is what would be generally expected in the trade between highly industrially developed countries and less developed partners. Second, North Korean exports are predominantly made up of two categories—crude inedible materials and manufactured-goods-by-materials. They constituted 88.6 percent of total exports on the average during 1963-69. The second category is mainly made up of semifinished products such as steel products (mostly pig iron) and nonferrous metals (chiefly silver, lead, and zinc ingots) while the first is made up primarily of metallic ores (chiefly iron ores followed by zinc concentrates). The food and live animal category (mainly fish and fish preparations and corn) makes a poor third (7.3 percent). Other items of export to Japan include magnesia clinker, phosphorous, fluorspar, steatite, anthracite coal, graphite, and silk. Third, on the North Korean import side, three categories predominate: manufactured-goods-by-materials (38.7 percent), chiefly various manmade yarn, fishing nets, cord, paper and paper products, and steel products; machinery and transport equipment (30.0 percent), including various widely diversified electrical and nonelectric machinery and

TABLE 39

PRINCIPAL* COMMODITIES TRADED WITH THE FREE WORLD, 1954-1968
(1,000 U.S. DOLLARS)

Year	Imports		Exports	
1954	Total	Not specified	Total	76
			Crude minerals	75
1955	Total	6	Total	2
	Wood & other animal products	6	Unspecified merchandise	2
1956	Total	27	Total	31
	Unspecified merchandise	25	Unspecified ore & metal scrap	27
1957	Total	278	Total	41
	Dyeing and tanning extracts and materials	150	Unspecified crude materials	24
	Nitrogeneous fertilizers	56	Cotton yarn, fabrics and manufactures	14
1958	Total	65	Total	20
	Unspecified mining, construction, and industrial machinery	45	Animal and vegetable oils and fats	4
	Unspecified yarn fabrics and manufactures	6		
1959	Total	4,605	Total	3,732
	Sugar and sugar preparations	740	Rice and rice flour	1,294
	Ferroalloys	533	Nitrogeneous fertilizer	1,091
	Rubber tires and tubes	419	Pig and sponge iron	352
	Ball, needle & rolled bearings	402	Crude fertilizers and minerals except fuel	280
	Jute yarn, fabrics & manufactures	385	Corn	5
	Unspecified manufacture of metals	266		
	Cotton	264		
	Insulated cables and wire for electricity	258		
	Iron & steel structural parts & related manufactures	250		
1960	Total	6,127	Total	5,721
	Wheat and wheat flour	3,032	Pig iron	1,144
	Ball, needle & rolled bearings	707	Unspecified crude fertilizers & minerals	1,086
	Ferroalloys	481	Lead & semimanufactures	742
	Iron & steel structural parts, wire cables, netting & related manufactures	310	Rice	632
			Zinc & semimanufactures	563
			Unspecified oil seeds, oil nuts, and oil kernels	391
			Fish & fish preparations	341
1961	Total	14,877	Total	6,426
	Wheat & wheat preparations	8,174	Pig iron	1,060
	Unspecified electric machinery	1,123	Fish & fish preparations	603
			Zinc & semimanufactures	509
			Silk	488
			Unspecified ores & concentrates of non-ferrous metals	467

Year	Imports		Exports	
1962	Total	6,535	Total	6,840
	Wheat flour	452	Fish & fish preparations	408
	Waste materials from textile		Corn	712
	fibers	430	Silk	345
	Textile yarn fabrics	460	Nitrogen fertilizers	737
	Pig iron and ferroalloys	536	Pig iron	947
	Iron & steel tubes, pipes		Zinc & semimanufactures	357
	and fittings	1,287		
	Iron & steel structural parts,			
	wire cables, etc.	361		
1963	Total	13,822	Total	12,090
	Wheat	5,237	Fish & fish preparations	647
	Ferroalloys	1,527	Corn	2,021
	Iron and steel bars	787	Pig iron	4,058
			Zinc & semimanufactures	1,354
1964	Total	21,766	Total	23,352
	Sugar	3,000	Corn	1,384
	Ships and boats	4,207	Silk	1,216
	Manmade fibers	2,793	Iron ore and concentrates	3,546
	Ferroalloys	1,188	Pig iron	7,189
	Iron & steel tubes and pipes	1,484	Zinc & semimanufactures	3,966
1965	Total	36,684	Total	22,666
	Wheat and wheat flour	7,143	Fish & fish preparations	1,251
	Sugar flour	2,800	Silk	1,490
	Pumps, centrifuges, & filtering		Iron ore & concentrates	4,222
	machinery	4,631	Pig iron	4,478
	Ferroalloys	3,535	Zinc & semimanufactures	5,217
	Iron & steel bars, rods, etc.	2,444		
1966	Total	31,579	Total	33,768
	Wheat	9,340	Fish & fish preparations	1,703
	Wheat flour	3,787	Silk	1,875
	Sugar	2,600	Iron ore & concentrates	4,709
	Phosphatic fertilizers	2,311	Pig iron	6,763
	Trucks	2,693	Zinc & semimanufactures	4,051
1967	Total	29,134	Total	39,367
	Wheat	5,788	Iron ore & concentrates	5,582
	Wheat flour	7,111	Pig iron	10,137
			Iron and steel ingots	3,461
			Zinc & semimanufactures	4,879
1968	Total	50,526	Total	Not available
	Wheat	7,410		
	Sugar	5,500		
	Crude rubber, except synthetic	2,553		
	Machine tools	7,699		

*Principal commodities are defined for the purpose of this table as those which constitute more than five percent of the total each year.

Source: Based on the data on file at the U.S. Department of Commerce.

139

TABLE 40

JAPAN-NORTH KOREA TRADE: COMMODITY COMPOSITION, 1963-1969
(In 1,000 U.S. Dollars)

Description	North Korean Exports (1963-69)			North Korean Imports (1963-69)		
	Total	Annual Average	%	Total	Annual Average	%
0. Food and live animals	11,864	1,695	(7.3)	345	49	(0.4)
1. Beverages and tobacco	158	23	(0.1)	3	–	(–)
2. Crude materials, inedibles	63,493	9,070	(39.0)	3,074	439	(3.4)
3. Mineral fuels	5,593	799	(3.4)	354	51	(0.4)
4. Animal and vegetable oils & fats	23	3	(–	1,576	225	(1.8)
5. Chemicals	604	86	(0.4)	16,349	2,336	(18.3)
6. Manufactured-goods-by-materials	80,808	11,544	(49.6)	34,566	4,938	(38.7)
7. Machinery & transport equipment	74	11	(–)	26,820	3,831	(30.0)
8. Manufactured goods, miscell.	259	37	(0.2)	4,486	641	(5.0)
9. Other and unspecified	24	3	(–)	1,807	258	(2.0)

Sources: Nitcho boekino tebiki, pp. 511-540; Lee Joong-Koon, op. cit., pp. 35-37.

equipment; and a wide assortment of chemicals (18.3 percent). It is clear that Japan is not used as a source for food as far as North Korea is concerned. Some of the principal items of imports from Japan are steel pipe, wire rope, ferro-nickel, automobile tires and tubes, electric power condensers, agricultural chem-icals, ferroalloys, plasticizer, coconut oil, and fish hooks.

According to available data on the commodity breakdown of trade between Hong Kong and North Korea during 1956-61,[66] North Korean exports are mainly fish and fish preparations, crude fertilizers, zinc ores, pig and sponge iron, and crude minerals. Silk, fruits, and vegetables are items of some importance. The commodity composition of imports from Hong Kong fluctuates widely from year to year so that each year only one or two items completely dominate the trade. It may be speculated that the North Korean authorities use Hong Kong as the source for procuring whatever materials are currently in short supply in order to adjust possible unplanned short-run bottlenecks and unforeseen shortages. In 1959 imports of rubber accounted for 26.6 percent of the total imports from Hong Kong whereas metal manufactures amounted to 14.8 percent. In 1960 ball and roller bearings totaled 97.8 percent of imports. In 1961 nearly half (46.7 percent) of the total imports from Hong Kong was unwrought aluminum. Practically all (99.7 percent in 1959) of Hong Kong's exports to North Korea are reexports, a typical phenomenon with Hong Kong's exports.

North Korea at present maintains trade relations with an increasing number of noncommunist countries including Burma, the United Arab Republic, Yemen, India, Indonesia, Great Britain, West Germany, Italy, Switzerland, Lebanon, Guinea, Ceylon, Austria, Australia, Mexico, United Kingdom, Iceland, and others in addition to Japan and Hong Kong. The value of trade for most of these countries is very small. A perusal of the commodities traded points to the following observations. First, from developed nations like Japan and Western Europe, North Korea principally imports capital goods such as machinery and plants in exchange for industrial raw and semifinished materials (metals and metallic ores) and some agricultural products. A study[67] on North Korea's trade with Europe as a whole (excluding Eastern European communist countries) during 1965-68 shows that the commodity composition of her trade with Europe follows generally the same pattern as that of her trade with Japan, with one significant exception. North Korean exports to Europe have shown an extreme concentration in semifinished materials (accounting for about 90 percent of her exports on the average during 1965-68), crude materials (metallic ores) running a poor second (8 percent on the average of the total exports). As with North Korea-Japan trade, machinery and transport equipment have made up a substantial portion (32.0 percent) of North Korean imports from Europe. Unlike trade with Japan, imports of semifinished products ran a poor second to machinery. Second, North Korea exports industrial products to and imports raw materials and food grains from the underdeveloped countries of Asia and Africa. Third, judging from the fact that import items from these underdeveloped countries frequently include low-priority consumption goods, it appears that North Korean imports are used as means to achieve political diplomatic goals and possibly to enhance future export potential.[68]

Summary and Conclusion

Data presented in this chapter prima facie support other evidence indicating that North Korea has made substantial progress in import substitution and industrialization since the conclusion of the Korean War. The data are based on ever increasing absolute amounts of export of the products of industry, especially heavy industry, and the change in the commodity composition of foreign trade. North Korea was transformed from a raw-materials-exporting-and-capital-importing nation to a semifinished-products-exporting-and-capital-and-semifinished-products-importing nation. Import substitution seems to have occurred up to now mainly in

141

semifinished manufactured goods industries producing various metals and metal products. Her economy still depends heavily on importation of machinery and equipment including complete plants (constituting more than 20 percent of the total North Korean imports during 1959-68). Procurement of capital goods for development was made possible partly by North Korea's imports and, more importantly, by foreign aid and long-term credit from communist nations, chiefly the U.S.S.R. and Communist China. The amount of external aid and loans provided to North Korea which were estimated to be approximately $1.37 billion during 1949-62 ($557 million or 40.7 percent from the U.S.S.R., $517 million or 37.7 percent from Communist China, and the remainder, $296 million or 21.6 percent, from other communist countries)[69] have since dwindled, coinciding with the Soviet suspension of development aid during 1962-64 when the Soviet-North Korean relationship was at its lowest ebb. The Soviet development loans have since been resumed but at a greatly diminished amount. It is presumed that at this time North Korea receives a negligible amount of grant-type aid and a small amount, if any, of development loans from the communist countries taken as a whole.[70] Declining foreign aid was one of the factors responsible for the slow-down in the 1960s.

North Korea's trade is still predominantly with communist countries—with the Soviet Union and Communist China the two largest single partners. Since the 1960s her trade with the noncommunist world has been gradually increasing, Japan preempting this group. Trade balance has been unfavorable for North Korea throughout the period indicating that her imports have been financed by foreign aid and long-term credits, especially up to the early 1960s. The situation has somewhat improved in recent years. The sizable and consistent trade surplus that North Korea has been accumulating with Japan (and to a lesser extent with Hong Kong) is a notable exception. There have been some speculations[71] as to the factors contributing to the export surplus with Japan. First, the Japanese government still bans the issuing of entry visas to North Koreans, including trade personnel. Second, there is also in effect the Japanese government ban on the use of the delayed payment arrangement with North Korea. Third, the Japanese government still gives deference, though nominal, to the CoCom embargo. Fourth, Japanese demand for North Korean iron ore has increased rapidly. It is expected that as these trade barriers are removed the total volume of North Korea-Japan trade will grow faster, especially the latter's exports to the former, and as a result, the North Korean trade surplus will diminish.

North Korea has been a net importer of cereals in spite of the regime's claim that she is self-sufficient in food.[72] The fact that North Korea exports rice occasionally in the face of her imports of substantial amounts of other cereals seems to indicate that North Korea is sacrificing rice (traditionally its most favored grain) for wheat and forcing a change in the diet pattern of the populace. This is no doubt motivated by the gain in exchange arising from the fact that the price ratio of rice to wheat in international exchange is much greater than the ratio of nutritional value per unit of rice to wheat. In other words, by giving up overpriced rice (in terms of nutritional value) for wheat, more nutrition is made available after the exchange.[73]

How does rapid expansion in foreign trade jibe with North Korean adoption of a policy of establishing an independent and self-sufficient economy?[74] A plausible answer seems to be that North Korean leadership makes the distinction between how the policy is translated into domestic economic policy and external economic relations. Specifically, North Korea seems to show flexibility on the issue of the ways in which the doctrine of economic self-sufficiency and independence (self-reliance) is related to the external economic policy, while maintaining a more or less rigid position of the autarky for domestic policy, probably motivated by political reasons. Whenever expanded external economic contacts are deemed necessary for procuring required resources for general developmental need and to overcome economic crisis, North Korea shows no hesitation in pursuing its economic interests. Whereas for domestic consumption an economic policy based on the concept of the prima y of politics is more or less dogmatically followed, in external matters North Korea appears to put economics first whenever its interests are served without endangering the political integrity of the regime.[75] To be sure, political motives are present in her vigorous attempts to establish contacts with noncommunist countries including the "non-aligned" nations of Asia, Latin America, and Africa by means of diplomatic relations, trade, cultural exchange, technical cooperation, and every other conceivable means. The long-run political objectives of pushing trade with the noncommunist world seem to be to break through the political isolation and near embargo imposed on North Korea by the United States and its allies during and after the Korean War. Particularly, the North Korean regime appears desirous of winning the sympathy of these countries toward her side as against her southern counterpart. The ever increasing frequency with which North Korea has been sending trade missions—cultural or otherwise—to these countries in recent years may be the expression and confirmation of these objectives.

CHAPTER 5

An Overall Evaluation of
the North Korean Economy

Overall Growth and Change

Conclusions about the tempo and nature of economic development in North Korea, based on agriculture, industry, and foreign trade, are reinforced by overall indicators of growth and change. The overall indicators examined in this section are the magnitude and composition of national income, ownership pattern of national output, and occupational and geographical distribution of the population. They also add further dimensions to the nature of transformation in the North Korean economy.

National income, according to the Marxian practice which North Korean compilers of national-income statistics follow, includes the value of income generated only in the production of material goods and "productive services," but excludes services not directly related to production and distribution. For this reason nearly all personal and government services such as passenger transportation, private use of communications, public administration, internal security, public health, private housing, and the like are not included in national income.[1] Specifically, national income (kukmin sodŭk) in North Korea corresponds to Net National Product rather than to either gross national product or national income at factor cost: capital consumption allowance is subtracted but the turnover tax (sales tax) is included in the price.[2] Since nonmaterial production is excluded, it should be more correctly called Net Material Product. Like the Soviet Union, North Korea publishes indices on the total and composition of "gross social product" (sahoe ch'ong saengsan aek). Not much is known regarding its exact definition in North Korea. If the Russian practice is any indication, as it presumably is, this concept "represents the sum of the gross output of all the sectors, doublecounting and all. It is not to be confused with the national income. The purpose of such a total as this may appear far from obvious,..."[3]

Like other communist countries, North Korea has so far not made public a national income series in absolute money equivalents. However, the unprecedented disclosure of per capita income for 1966 in absolute value (and indirectly for 1962) made estimation of the won value of North Korean national income possible. This revelation came in the form of Kim Il-song's speech[4] in 1968 when he quoted North Korea's per capita national income in 1966 as 500 won, 1.2 times that of 1962. Estimation of the won value of national income series is derived by linking the disclosed information with available published indices of national income and published and projected population figures (see "Notes to Table 41," p. 148).

The national income of North Korea has increased considerably since 1946. In 1967 it was nearly 12.5 times that of 1946 and 8.6 times that of 1953 (table 41), registering an annual growth rate of 12.7 percent and 16.6 percent, respectively, during 1947-67 and 1954-67. Since the population has not increased substantially owing to war losses and the outflow of refugees to South Korea, the growth rate in per capita national income is equally impressive, amounting to 11.0 and 13.1 percent, respectively, for the two periods—1947-67 and 1954-67.

Since entering the 1960s, coinciding with the Seven Year Plan, the pace of overall economic progress as measured by national income began to drop sharply. Average annual rate of growth in national income declined to 8.9 percent during 1961-67, from 26.0 and 21.0 percent during the Three Year Plan (1954-56) and the Five Year Plan (1957-60), respectively. Relative slowdown (as indicated by the index of slowdown) in national income was not as pronounced as that in industrial output but worse than that in agricultural output.[5] The fact that no mention was made of the status of national income (as well as agricultural output) for 1970 in Kim Il-song's speech to the Fifth Congress suggests that the Seven Year Plan target of raising national income to 2.7 times the 1960 level by 1970 (originally by 1967) was not fulfilled.

In absolute amounts per capita income of North Korea rose from a mere 59 won in 1956 to 524 won in 1967. Using the conversion rate of 2.4 won per dollar used in foreign trade until toward the end of 1967, the dollar value of North Korea's per capita income amounted to $190, $202, $208, and $218, respectively, for 1964, 1965, 1966, and 1967 while (total) national income for those same years amounted to $2.3 billion, $2.5 billion, $2.6 billion, and $2.8 billion. Since the official exchange rate for international trade is hardly a meaningful measure of converting national income accounts of communist countries into Western currencies, exchange rates based on the concept of purchasing power parity is often used for

145

TABLE 41

OVERALL INDICATORS OF GROWTH AND STRUCTURAL CHANGE, 1946-1970

	1946	1949	1953
A. National Income:*			
1. National income (index)	100%	209	145
a. (In million 1966 won)[a]	546	1145	790
b. (In million 1966 won)[b]	(555)	(1160)	(807)
2. Per capita national income (index)	100%	201	158
a. (In 1966 won)[a]	59	119	93
b. (In 1966 won)[b]	(60)	(121)	(95)
3. Origin of national income by sectors (% composition)			
a. Industry	16.8	32.8	27.5
b. Agriculture	63.5	44.4	48.7
c. Capital construction[c]	–	4.4	9.4
4. Gross Industrial Product (GIP) as % of the combined total of GIP and Gross Agricultural Product	28%	47	42
5. Composition of national income according to ownership			
a. National income (NI) from socialized sectors	(14.8%)	(44.5%)	(45.6%)
(1) NI from state enterprises	14.6	40.3	39.4
(2) NI from cooperatives	0.2	4.2	6.2
b. NI from private enterprise	(85.2)	(55.5)	(54.4)
(1) NI from "transactions in small commodities"	64.2	46.6	51.2
(2) NI from "capitalist type of production"	21.0	8.9	3.2
B. Population:			
6. Total population (1,000)[d]	9257	9622	8491
a. Relative growth	100%	104	92
7. Occupational distribution of population (%)			
a. Laborers	12.5	19.0	21.2
b. Office workers	6.2	7.0	8.5
c. Agricultural cooperative members	–	–	–
d. Private farmers	74.1	69.3	66.4
e. Handicraftsmen, cooperatized	–	0.3	0.5
f. Private handicraftsmen	1.5	0.8	0.6
g. Private enterprisers	0.2	0.1	0.1
h. Merchants	3.3	1.7	1.2
i. Others	2.2	1.8	1.5
8. Distribution of population between urban & rural areas(%)[k]			
a. Urban areas			17.7
b. Rural areas			82.3

[a]Based on published per capita income of 500 won for 1966 as announced by Kim Il-song. [b]Based on per capita income of 510 won for 1966 in CCY, 1966-67, p. 227, which conflicts with Kim Il-song's announcement; see footnote "a" & first paragraph of "Notes" (p. 148). [c]Includes those investments in fixed assets which are considered "productive" according to the Marxian practice; for this reason, investments in fixed assets in education, culture, scientific research, public health, residential housing, & public administration are excluded, being classi-

1956	1960	1961	1962	1963	1964	1965	1966	1967	1970
319	683	810	869	928	1000[h]	1093	1160	1243	n.a.
1741	3722	4439	4713	5067	5461	5961	6320	6787	
(1778)	(3776)	(4517)	(4826)	(5148)	(5557)	(6059)	(6446)	(6890)	
316	584	681[f]	712[f]	742	775	822[f]	847	888	
186	345	402[f]	417[f]	438	457	485[f]	500	524	
(190)	(350)	(409)[f]	(427)[f]	(445)	(465)	(493)[f]	(510)	(532)	
34.0	53.4								
	(57.1)[e]			(60.6)[e]		(64.2)[e]			
31.4	27.0								
	(23.6)[e]			(21.5)[e]		(18.3)[e]			
6.7	5.3								
	(8.7)[e]			(9.2)[e]					
60	71	69	74	74	75	78			(74)[i]
(85.8%)	(100.0%)			(100.0%)					
50.3	65.0								
	(69.1)[e]			(74.0)[e]					
35.5	35.0								
	(30.9)[e]			(26.0)[e]					
(14.2)	(-)			(-)					
11.5	-								
	(-)			(-)					
2.7	-								
	(-)			(-)					
9359	10789	11043[g]	11302[g]	11568	11950	12290[g]	12640	12952[g]	13936[j]
101	117	119	122	125	129	133	137	140	151
27.3	38.3			40.1					
13.6	13.7			15.1					
40.0	44.4			42.8					
16.6	-			-					
1.1	3.3			1.9					
0.3	-			-					
-	-			-					
0.6	-			-					
0.5	0.3			-					
29.0	40.6			44.5		47.5			
71.0	59.4			55.4		52.5			

fied as noncapital construction. [d]Population as of end of year except the following: 1956, 1964 (Sept. 1); 1965 (Oct. 1); 1963 (Oct. 31); 1953, 1959 (Dec. 1).
[e]As of "gross social product"; see last paragraph of "Notes." [f]Estimate based on
interpolated population figures; see footnote "g". [g]Based on interpolation assum-
ing constant rate of growth. [h]Based on round numbers. [i]For 1969. [j]Derived from
announced total and per capita output figures for selected industrial products
for 1970. [k]Includes dependents.

Notes to Table 41

Kim Il-song's disclosure of per capita income for 1966 as 500 won was contradicted by other official sources (see, for example, CCY, 1966-67, p. 227, which cited it as 510 won). For this reason table 41 contains two series of estimates of the absolute value of national income based on both these figures. It is probable that Kim's figure may simply represent the result of rounding off, which would account for the difference.

The won value of total national income for 1962 and 1966 was derived by multiplying the announced per capita income by the population for each year. National income for other years was constructed by linking the 1966 value with the official indices of national income. Per capita income for other years was then derived by dividing the estimated total national income by the population for each year. To the extent that the population figures used are of different dates (although the majority are end-of-the-year figures) and some population figures are interpolations, the derived per capita income figures are subject to a margin of error and should be treated as such.

National income indices are supposedly based on constant prices and as a result the influence of price changes should be absent. However, there are tendencies inherent in index number construction which tend to inflate the real growth (see appendix B).

Since indices are often given only in round numbers (such as the information that national income in 1964 was 10 times that in 1946), the last one or two digits of estimated won value of national income, both total and per capita, may not be significant.

Since 1960 North Korea has for some reason stopped publishing the breakdown of national income according to origins (such as industry, agriculture) while continuing to publish the breakdown for gross social product. There are discrepancies between national income and the gross social product due to different degrees of grossness (or doublecounting) in each sector of the economy as well as in the total national product. This explains why the share of industry (whose degree of grossness is relatively larger than agriculture and other sectors) is higher for gross industrial product (57.1% in 1960) than for national income (53.4% in 1960). In spite of this any change in the relative share of sectors to the gross social product should reflect the direction in the shares of national income components, if not in the magnitudes. See, for estimates of won value of the gross social product, Pong S. Lee, "An Estimate of North Korea's National Income," Asian Survey, June 1972, pp. 522-523.

Sources for Table 41

1.—JPRS, Economic Report on North Korea, No. 79, p. 17; Korea News, No. 3, 1964, p. 4; No. 2, 1965, p. 14. 2, 3, 4, 5.—JPRS, ERNK, No. 108, pp. 8-9; according to CCY, 1958, p. 178, the figures for 1956 are 33.6, 32.6, and 5.8 percent, respectively, for industry, agriculture, and capital construction; figures for other years are consistent; see, for other years, CCY, 1958, p. 178; Hebanghu uri nara ŭi..., p. 252; and Chŏng, T'ae-sik, op. cit., p. 25; Statistical Summary of DPRK, 1946-63, pp. 8-9; Nodong sinmun, September 8, 1968, pp. 3-4. 6, 7, 8.—JPRS, The 1961 N. Korean Yearbook, pp. 470-471; see also ERNK, No. 79, p. 14; for other years, see CCY, 1958, p. 175; Cho Chae-son, op. cit., p. 120; Statistical Summary of DPRK, 1946-63, pp. 6-7; Area Handbook for North Korea, pp. 64-65; Pukhan yoram, 1968, p. 191; Nodong sinmun, November 3, 1970; Toitsu chosen nenkan (One Korea Yearbook), Tokyo: Toitsu Chosen Sinbunsha, 1964, p. 475.

such conversion. According to one Western estimate, the purchasing power parity exchange rate was approximately 1.66 won per dollar around 1965.[6] Using this rate, North Korea's per capita income for the same four years runs to $273, $292, $301, and $316, respectively, ranking her favorably among the world's developing economies. The dollar value of (total) national income converted at the purchasing power parity rate amounted to $3.3 billion, $3.6 billion, $3.8 billion, and $4.1 billion, respectively, for those four years. However, great care must be taken in comparing these income accounts with those of the noncommunist economies because of discrepancies arising from methodological differences in national income computation and definitions as well as the problem of conversion into a common currency.

There has occurred a striking and telling change in the composition of national income indicating the transformation of North Korea from a primarily agricultural to industrial economy (table 41). The relative position (contribution) of industry in the generation of national income has been increasing rapidly at the expense of agriculture. If the trend continues the share of industry and agriculture to national income would amount roughly to 60 and 20 percent by 1970, the remaining 20 percent coming from other sectors. The role of industry and agriculture reversed itself after 1946 (when the relative share of industry and agriculture was respectively 16.8 and 63.5 percent). The same trend is indicated also by the increasing share of industrial output in the combined total of gross industrial and agricultural product (table 41).

According to the breakdown of national income into types of ownership of enterprises, the socialization of North Korea has been completed in all sectors of the economy. Private ownership in all types of productive organizations had totally disappeared by 1958, with the exception of peasant garden plots. The major shift away from private ownership had not taken hold until after the Korean War. In 1953 national income still originated roughly equally from socialized and private sectors, although an overwhelming portion of private enterprise was made up of "small-scale establishments" (94.1 percent of national income from the private sector).

The transformation in the structure of the economy and of the ownership pattern is of course reflected in the occupational distribution of the North Korean population. Individual farmers who once made up more than 70 percent of the total labor force have entirely disappeared along with private handicraftsmen, entrepreneurs, and merchants, to be replaced by members of collectives, industrial

149

workers, and others. Another indicator of change is the shift in the population between urban and rural areas. Although prewar data are not available, there has been a drastic migration of population from rural areas to urban centers since 1953 when 82.3 percent of the total population of North Korea still lived in a rural setting. In 1965 the percentage was reduced to 52.5. Although no definition of urban and rural areas is given in the source, increasing urbanization is consistent with progress in North Korea's industrialization process. With the same trend continuing, the North Korean population would be divided roughly equally between the two areas by 1970. The percentage of rural population should approximately correspond to that of farm workers (both at collectives and state farms) in the labor force.

Per capita income by itself provides no direct measure of how well off the North Korean populace is economically, as it conceals the distribution of income and the portions of national output expended in capital formation and defense. Not atypically for a communist country, an average North Korean, though his lot has improved substantially, has not benefited fully from economic development. Priority development in heavy industry at the expense of the consumer and agricultural sector is one explanation. A high rate of defense spending is another. While sacrificing today's consumption for greater consumption tomorrow (North Korean strategy of high-level capital formation) does make long-run economic sense, resources allocated to national defense bring no such beneficial effects.

North Korea openly admits the relative backwardness of the consumer goods industry in terms of the variety—quality as well as quantity—of its products. As recently as November 1970, Kim Il, the First Vice-Premier, deplored in his reports to the Fifth Congress of the Workers' Party that:

> ...in our country, compared to the development of heavy industry, light industry has lagged far behind and the quality of its consumer goods is relatively behind their quantity. Daily necessities and processed foods lack both the variety and quantity of production.[7]

Under the circumstances it is not surprising that improvement of product quality constitutes a major Six Year Plan goal.

The policy of priority development of industry not only created an imbalance between industry and agriculture in terms of productive performance but it also was partially responsible for the industry-agriculture income difference as reflected by the proportions (Engel coefficients) of expenditures made by the farm and industrial workers for food (table 42). Changes in the Engel coefficients over the years suggest improvements in the standard of living of both the farm

and industrial workers despite the continuing gap. Income difference also is
quite pronounced even within agriculture between the collective farms and the
workers of the state farms which are organized and operated along the lines of
industrial enterprises. A report published in 1963 revealed that the average
daily share per member of the collective farm was 18 percent short of the comparable wage of the state farm workers.[8]

TABLE 42

ENGEL COEFFICIENT FOR FARM AND INDUSTRIAL-OFFICE WORKERS
(PERCENT), 1957-1963

	1957	1959	1960	1961	1962	1963
Farmers	77.2	66.4	64.8	57.9	58.9	
Industrial-office workers	58.7		47.3			45.5

Sources: Kim Song-jin, op. cit., p. 393; Statistical Summary of DPRK,
1946-64, p. 12.

All in all the study shows that North Korea has made a giant stride since
1945 in her drive toward industrialization and economic viability. Although recently her pace of growth has slowed, resulting in a readjustment of her economic plans, from all indications the dislocations of the early 1960s have long
been contained and her progress continues. While it would be difficult to dup-
licate the phenomenal growth during the Three Year Plan and Five Year Plan, the
prospect for fulfilling the less ambitious Six Year Plan seems favorable.

Calling the North Korean feat a miracle[9] perhaps overstates the case but
nevertheless dramatizes her achievements as evidenced by various indicators:
rapid growth and the absolute level (total and per capita) of national income
and of strategic industrial products (per capita output of 1,184 kilowatt hours
of electricity, 1,975 kilograms of coal, and 158 kilograms of steel in 1970); a
long-term change in the composition of national income in favor of industry;
change in the structure within the industrial sector in favor of heavy industry,
especially the machinery sector; change in the commodity composition of foreign
trade and evidence of significant import substitution as well as impressive
growth in exports; shifts in the occupational distribution of population in favor
of secondary industry at the expense of the primary; increasing urbanization of
population; and so on. Although lagging far behind industry and ridden with
seemingly insurmountable obstacles, growth in agriculture has not been unimpres-
sive. However, self-sufficiency in food has not yet been achieved; North Korea

is a substantial net importer of food. External aid from communist nations has played a vital role in her reconstruction and development. By and large, the official description of herself as having reached the stage of an "industrial" economy having graduated (through the "industrial-agricultural" stage) from the initial one of "agricultural-industrial" appears to be fairly correct. With nearly half of the population still deriving its livelihood from agriculture, however, the North Korean economy has a long way to go before it transforms itself into a truly industrial state.

North Korea as an Economic System

Slowdown in overall and industrial growth in the Soviet Union and Eastern European communist countries (except Albania) toward the end of the 1950s and beginning of the 1960s started a chain of drastic institutional reforms which resulted in significant liberalization and decentralization in central planning. These reforms, aimed primarily at avoiding the declining efficiency of a central command-type economic system, have as their basic thrust a shift of emphasis from administrative and bureaucratic control to economic and pecuniary incentives into the day-to-day decision making of individual productive units, thus introducing elements of liberalization in central planning and decentralization in control. It is the purpose of this section to appraise the nature and extent of reforms in North Korea's economic system which she patterned after the Soviet Union since the inception of the regime, particularly in the wake of North Korea's greatly reduced pace of economic growth since the 1960s and in the face of reform movements in the communist economies of Eastern Europe and the Soviet Union.

Examination of materials presented in previous chapters and elsewhere lead to the following summary concerning the change in nature of North Korea's economic system.[10]

(1) There has neither been any open discussion nor any allusion to the subject of reforming the economic system and introducing some measures of decentralization in the central planning.

(2) North Korea, as in the case of its counterparts in Eastern Europe, has not deviated from the basic tenets of state and collective ownership of productive resources and the commitment to the socialistic system and the monopoly of political power by the Communist Party and its regime.

152

(3) While there has been no evidence of any general, coordinated and consistent economy-wide liberalization movement, there have occurred scattered
cases of reforms, some of which coincide with those of Eastern Europe and her
own economic slowdown.

In agriculture these were: reorganizations in MTS in 1960 and 1966 which
provided added incentives to tractor operators by paying them according to their
productive contribution to the collective farms to which they were assigned
rather than through the fixed-fee system; the work-team bonus system introduced
after 1960 and, further, the subwork-team contract system which began in 1965 in
order to infuse built-in incentives and some decentralized decision-making on
the operations of the collective farms; lowering and eventually abolishing the
all-important agricultural tax-in-kind by the end of 1966; raising the prices of
selected farm products while lowering those of farm inputs such as agricultural
implements and machinery, accompanied by measures taken by the state to undertake
rural capital and housing construction projects which had hitherto been the main
responsibility of the collective farms themselves.

In industry reforms include some decentralization of industrial management
by means of emphasizing the role of local industry after 1958 through increased
county- and municipal-level control of local industrial enterprises as compared
to central and provincial control; replacement of the system of budget allocation
by an independent economic accounting system in the management of state enterprises; introduction in the mid-1960s of an intraenterprise incentive system
called the internal accounting system among various units of industrial
enterprises.

In other sectors of the economy, renovations took various forms. The first
concerns the peasant markets where surplus farm products—mostly nongrain products such as eggs, vegetables, milk, fish, poultry, rabbits, beef, mutton, seasonings, and the like—are sold at free market prices through the interaction of
demand and supply. Although peasant markets handle only an insignificant share
of the total retail trade in the distribution of consumer goods (0.6 percent in
1963), next to state-operated and cooperative stores (80.2 and 19.2 percent, respectively, in 1963), the goods offered in these markets are often of better
quality than those sold at state or cooperative stores. Although North Korea is
doctrinally opposed to the peasant markets, which are considered remnants of
capitalism,[11] these markets gained considerable headway by 1964. In that year
government officials were urged to take an active interest in these markets,

153

generally encouraging their smooth operation. According to a 1965 report there were more than 400 large and small peasant markets in existence, an average of about two per county.[12] These markets are used as a stop-gap device to provide consumers with much-needed relief in daily necessities which are in short supply. Lessening of blackmarket activities is also another reason for the tolerance.[13] Material incentives are also provided through price reduction in consumer goods as well as through wage increases. For example, a marked reduction in the prices of foodstuffs was reported in 1969, while the wages of workers, technicians, and office workers were raised by an average rate of 31.5 percent as of September 1, 1970, with higher rates applied to lower-wage earners.[14]

(4) There have been, on the other hand, countermovements offsetting any trend toward decentralization and liberalization. First of all, contrary to movements toward decollectivization in some East European countries, the scale of collective farm operation in North Korea has continued on an upward trend beginning with completion of collectivization in 1958 and amalgamation of all the collectives within each Ri into one single farm in the same year. A number of large-scale state general farms—countywide state agroindustry complexes—began to emerge in 1959. The creation of the Kun Agricultural Management Committee formed in 1961 brought local farm decision-making under the tighter control and closer supervision of the central government and made the Kun supersede the Ri as the lowest farm decision unit on all important agricultural problems.[15]

Introduction and continued emphasis on the Taean industrial management system is a clear example of North Korea's renewed and intensified reliance on political, ideological, and generally nonmaterial systems of motivating the workers and managers. The Taean system in industry is duplicated in every aspect of the economy where reliance on political indoctrination, mass mobilization,[16] and exhortations have been intensified. Such nonpecuniary incentive systems as the Chŏllima movement, Chŏngsan-ri spirit, and such mass production campaigns as "Pyŏngyang speed," "Kangsŏn speed," "Carrying-one-more-load movement," "Run-while-carrying-loads-on-head-and-back," "Watching-the-early-star movement," and "Let's-fulfill-the-plan-as-a-present-for-Marshall-Kim-Il-song's-birthday," as well as translating national economic goals into so many "heights to scale" permeate every aspect of the life of the North Korean.

The most significant and revealing testimony to trends in North Korea's economic system comes from the decision of her leadership to further tighten and strengthen central planning through what the regime calls the "unified planning system" and the "detailed planning system" introduced, in the words of Kim Il-song, "to further tighten the democratic centralist discipline in overall economic management and to develop our economy in a more planned and balanced way."[17] Under "unified planning," introduced as a policy in February 1962,[18] regional planning commissions were created in March 1964 for the first time in cities, counties, and provinces under the direct control of the State Planning Commission (SPC) in the capital city of Pyŏngyang, while at the same time SPC branches were also established at each enterprise. Further, planning departments and offices in all sectors of the economy, including those of ministries and other central governmental agencies, were placed under the jurisdiction of the SPC as well as under the organs to which they belonged insofar as planning work was concerned.[19] Regional planning commissions were not established to decentralize the planning process; on the contrary, they were created to centralize the process further and to eliminate planning and actions influenced by local and bureaucratic interests.[20] Thus the "unified planning" system was initiated to coordinate and execute economic planning from the center down to regions, localities, and individual enterprises with a more direct, unified, and centralized control, and place it under the closer supervision of the central government and its planning agency. Introduced subsequently and in conjunction with "unified planning," "detailed planning" purports

> ...to closely link general economic development with the management activities of every factory and enterprise and to elaborate plans to suit the actual conditions in all branches of the national economy, localities and enterprises, so that all indices can mesh with one another squarely down to details.[21]

All in all, at a time when central planning is being significantly altered and the market mechanism is being increasingly enlisted, at least at the micro-level in the Soviet Union and Eastern Europe, there is no evidence in North Korea of a general and consistent economy-wide trend toward reforms aimed at decentralizing the central planning. Also, there has been no change in the existing pattern of state and collective ownership and control of productive enterprises. Except for minor and scattered cases of innovations which tend to be stop-gap devices, the North Korean system has not diverged fundamentally from the Stalinistic command system which characterized the pre-Liberman Soviet model.

The reasons for the behavior of the North Korean leadership running counter to the pattern of high correlation between the incidence of economic slowdowns and the timing of the reforms in Eastern Europe and the Soviet Union[22] appear

partly economic and partly noneconomic. Students of comparative economic systems conjecture a positive correlation, other things being equal, between the
stage of economic development and the vigor of instituted reforms as observed
among the countries of Eastern Europe and the Soviet Union.[23] In this sense the
lack of reforms in North Korea may simply be attributable to her still relatively
early stage of development. More importantly and credibly, political considerations must have figured large in North Korea's response to liberalization movements in the communist economies of Europe and to her own economic slowdown. An
economy-wide liberalization would be

> ...neither consistent with the existing ideological, political, and power
> structure, nor be compatible with the personality cult of the present ruler.
> Any regime which possesses the degree of doctrinal rigidity that North Korea
> manifests would fear that any such relaxation could open a Pandora's box and
> cause loss of control. The North Korean leaders may have decided that con-
> tinuation of centralized economic decision-making is a sure avenue to cen-
> tralized political control (for military, ideological and cultural reasons)
> and, perhaps, the only road for the perpetuation of the regime.[24]

The North Korean Model of Economic Development

Finally, in the way of concluding this study, the following model is advanced to describe the essentials of North Korean economic development based on
the materials presented in the study and their evaluation.

(1) The North Korean leadership is committed to economic development via
rapid industrialization. North Korea's achievements in industrialization in the
post-Korean War era has been ultimately a function both of a high rate of investment (20.2 and 16.0 percent, respectively, for 1956 and 1960 and an average of
17.6 percent during 1961-67 as a share of national income)[25] and of the expanding
urban labor force. To channel a large share of current output into investment,
consumption has been depressed at a tolerable minimum. Peasants and the agricultural sector have shared the brunt of the burden of development through forced
savings, especially up to the middle of the 1960s.

(2) The North Korean development model is characterized by a large defense
burden, particularly since 1967. Since the sudden leap in defense expenditures,
its share in national income jumped to an average of 20.0 percent (between
1967-70) from an average of 3.1 percent (during 1956-66) while its share in the
national budget increased to an average of 31.2 percent (1967-70) from a 4.3 percent average (1956-66). Such a high rate of defense spending cannot but depress

consumption further or constrain the rate of investment. After a continued high
rate of defense spending in 1971 (31.1 percent), however, planned military spending in 1972 shows a marked decline (17.0 percent)[26] although it is still substantially higher than that during 1956-66. A chain of dramatic turns in international events occurred in recent years which are expected to reduce tension surrounding Korea and may, as a result, lead to further reduction of North Korea's
military spending. These events include the opening of a dialogue between the
United States and Communist China on one hand and improvement in the United
States-U.S.S.R. relationship on the other, as demonstrated by President Nixon's
visit to China and the Soviet Union in 1972. As dramatic was the direct contact
and dialogue between North Korea and South Korea initiated in 1971 which culmin-
ated in a joint communique of July 4, 1972, between the two governments in which
both sides agreed to take positive measures to reduce tension and military threat
and pursue a policy of unification through peaceful means. A successful consequence of the North-South détente must surely reduce military expenditures further in favor of investment in the nondefense sector and in consumption, with
favorable impacts on economic growth and the standard of living of the average
North Korean.

(3) North Korea's industrialization, made possible by infusing a large quantity of labor force and capital into industry, has been accompanied by a rapid
and fundamental change in the composition of national output and the labor force.
Nowhere is the structural change more crystallized than in the machine-building
industry (and to a lesser extent in the industrial raw-materials industry) which
grew from a minor sector to become a significant industry, regarded by the planners as the "kingpin" and a symbol of North Korea's success in industrialization
and modernity. A declining share of agriculture in national output and in the
labor force, increasing urbanization of population, an expanding share of the
products of heavy industry in the composition of exports, agriculture-industry
income gap, and so on are all corollaries of the structural change in the makeup
of national output in favor of industry, particularly heavy industry.

(4) North Korea remains one of communism's most centralized, socialized,
and planned economies. Her dogmatic adherence to the Stalinistic development
model will continue as long as the present regime is in power. Readiness to institute reforms and liberalize economic decision-making does not appear to be
North Korea's response to calls for accelerated growth or to slowdowns. While
stop-gap renovations may be resorted to and tolerated, the precedence of politics

and ideology and, most important, the perpetuation of the regime will continue to be prime considerations.

(5) Mass movements, exhortations, political campaigns, "socialistic competition," and the like have been widely and consistently relied upon as substitutes for pecuniary incentives. Intensity of these movements and campaigns tends to reach a peak during the last phase of each economic plan as evidenced by the heightened activities during 1959-60 and 1970 or whenever "the going gets rough." As occurred around 1959-60 and thereafter, these movements tend to create sectoral imbalances, secondary disruptions, overambitious targets, and planning errors. Defaulting of product quality is another consequence. Moreover, mobilization of the general populace, even if successful, would have economic limitations. Except in the areas of such highly labor-intensive projects as food processing, irrigation facilities, and construction of unpaved roads, continued substitution of labor for capital will produce, after a point, very small or near zero marginal output. Eventually, expansion in labor must be accompanied by an increased supply of capital or other inputs.

(6) North Korea has enjoyed a continuity of political control and relative political stability, one of the preconditions of economic growth. To be sure, purges and lack of basic liberties have characterized North Korean life, and Kim Il-song has been an absolute dictator since the beginning of the regime with the monolithic Communist Party under his tight rein. But North Korea has been generally free from the kind of factionalism, frequent revolutions, corruption, ineptitude, inflation, unemployment, and so on that demoralized and undermined many an emerging economy. Such stability has probably exerted some favorable influence on the economy. On the other side of the ledger, political stability achieved under such conditions also works to dampen the private incentives of the populace.

(7) A rapid expansion in investment in human capital, especially in technical education, has been high in the North Korean priority in order to channel it toward growth-supporting activities. Improvement in human capital, a necessary ingredient of growth, must have substantially contributed toward productivity gains. North Korea was reportedly successful in eradicating illiteracy within a few years after the division of Korea. Apart from the vigorous adult education campaigns and an early institution of compulsory and free education on the grade school level, the successful early abolition of Chinese characters and compulsory use of Korean phonetics must have greatly facilitated North Korea's campaign against illiteracy. Since 1967 North Korea went even further by adopting a free

158

nine-year compulsory system of education with greater emphasis on technical education, the first such program in the Far East. (Both China and Japan have six-year compulsory systems with tuition partially free.) Beyond the level of primary education, North Korea has exerted all-out efforts to increase the supply of technical-scientific personnel by expanding the enrollment at and resources of technological colleges, vocational schools, and "factory colleges," and by sending selected groups of students abroad (primarily to the Soviet Union) for scientific and technical education. The whole educational system seems to be geared to the goals of industrialization as the school system

> ...incorporates a theory-practice concept of education in which the theories of the classroom are translated into active participation in government-directed labour units designed to consolidate the student's learning and also to assist the government in its effort to industrialize the country...[27]

As a result of the aggressive technical and scientific educational program there has been an impressive growth in the number of engineers, technicians, and other specialists available (table 43).

TABLE 43

NUMBER OF ENGINEERS, TECHNICIANS, AND SPECIALISTS
1953, 1960, 1963, AND 1964

Type of Specialist	1953[a]	1960[b]	1963[a]	1964[a]
Engineers	1,837	11,991	32,955	43,544
Assistant engineers	6,763	57,978	95,150	136,250
Specialists and technicians	13,272	63,497	95,549	113,712
Of which: college graduates	(n.a.)	(26,005)	(52,589)	(66,347)
Total	21,872	133,466	223,654	293,506

[a]As of October 10; [b]as of November 15.

Source: CCY, 1965, p. 482.

(8) Economic application of North Korea's policy of independence and self-reliance (Chuch'e) within the communist bloc nations appears to be two-pronged. Domestically, it has been translated into more or less rigid measures and exhortations for motivating the masses to be nationalistic and proud of the economy they are constructing by their own hands without external help.[28] Externally, however, this policy has been much more flexible. A policy of self-reliance works as an effective countermeasure to dwindling foreign aid. While refusing formally to join the communist bloc network of specialization and trade, the

value of North Korea's trade has been increasing at a rapid rate. As evidenced by her willingness to incur large amounts of trade deficits with the U.S.S.R. in the latter part of the 1960s, North Korea will continue, as she has in the past, to use foreign trade as means to acquire requisite capital and other resources for development. Pragmatism and economic rationality seem to be guiding principles of the policy as it relates to foreign economic relations. This seems to be especially true of her trade relations with the advanced countries of the West, including Japan.

(9) North Korea suffered a sizable loss in population from the war dead and from the outflow of refugees before and during the Korean War. Since both these categories comprise largely males of productive ages, this drain on the labor force, coupled with the initial (relatively) lower population density has made North Korea a labor-scarce country, a rarity among overpopulated Asian economies. For example, the total North Korean population, in a slightly larger land area, is far less than half that of South Korea. Although the long-run effects of the population loss are uncertain as yet, one probable impact which seems to be shaping up in North Korea is that the population drain has laid conditions favorable for introducing mechanization in industry, agriculture, and other sectors of the economy. The relative scarcity of labor would make the mechanization and automation economically feasible and desirable without putting too much pressure on employment. On the other hand, it would make the social (or alternative) cost of maintaining a large army relatively higher and produce short-run bottlenecks in the form of labor shortages of one kind or another. The problem of labor shortage is of such magnitude as to make rationalization of the labor administration through improved allocation and regulation (of labor) a major goal of the Six Year Plan.

(10) From all accounts and judging from the rapid reconstruction and development during the Three Year Plan and Five Year Plan periods, North Korea seems to have effectively utilized foreign aid in its program for industrialization.[29] This makes North Korea's model unique among the world's many aid-receiving aspirants of development. Perhaps, centrally planned, coordinated use of foreign aid integrated into the total national plan and the small size of the economy may explain this in part. Corruption and mismanagement universally associated with foreign aid among the majority of aid recipients probably have been absent.

As North Korea embarks upon the task of successfully fulfilling the current Six Year Plan, the leadership would like to see the quality of life of the masses rise faster than it has and the gap between various sectors narrowed. However, the basic tenets of the plan fail to reveal any fundamental shift in the long-run North Korean economic strategy. In this sense the model presented above may not only be used for extracting possible lessons for development but also for purposes of prediction as well.

Appendix A: Economic Plans

North Korea, since 1947, has instituted six distinct economic plans, each of which expresses the broad and specific economic goals to be achieved during the plan period. Following is a brief summary of the broad aims of these plans.

One Year Plans of 1947 and 1948 ("Peaceful Construction" Period)

1. Strengthen economic ties with the U.S.S.R. and other socialist nations based on international specialization with the bloc.

2. Develop both heavy industry, particularly the machine-building sector, and light industry to correct the colonial nature of the industrial structure left behind by the Japanese.

3. Consolidate and raise the leading role of state-controlled enterprises.

4. Continue to reconstruct Japanese-destroyed and -neglected enterprises and resume operation of idle plants.

5. Establish the independent accounting system for various enterprises.

6. Increase the role of state and cooperative commercial networks.

7. Reform and improve the railroad transportation system.

8. Solve the food problem as the basic task of agriculture. Encourage industrial crops to provide raw materials to light industry.

For specifics, see:

For 1947, Chosŏn chungang yŏngam (CCY) (Korean Central Yearbook), Pyŏngyang: Korean Central News Agency, 1949, pp. 80-81; Institute for Economic and Legal Research, Academy of Science, Haebanghu uri naraŭi inmin kyŏngje palchŏn (Development of People's Economy in Our Country Since Liberation), Pyŏngyang: Academy of Science Publishing House, 1960, pp. 45-48; Korean Affairs Institute, Chosen no keizai (Economy of Korea), Tokyo: Oriental Economist Press, 1956, pp. 62-67.

For 1948, CCY, 1950, pp. 273-274; Haebanghu uri naraŭi inmin kyŏngje palchŏn, p. 50; Chosen no keizai, pp. 67-70.

Two Year Plan: 1949-50 ("Peaceful Construction" Period, continued)

1. Complete restoration of destroyed and idle plants and concentrate on constructing new industrial plants and facilities and enlarging those in existence.

2. Emphasize development of metallurgical, steel, machinery, parts, ship-building, chemical, railroad and automobile transportation industries, and mining.

3. Consolidate results of the land reform, enlarge sown and cultivated areas, and increase output, especially of rice and industrial crops.

4. Strengthen further the role of state and cooperative commercial networks to facilitate the commodity circulation between urban and rural centers.

5. Develop textile, artificial fiber, rubber, shoe, and glass industries.

For specifics, see:

CCY, 1950, pp. 56-66; Chosen no keizai, pp. 70-72.

Three Year Plan: 1951-53

Planned (through a cabinet decision of June 20, 1950) but not carried out due to the outbreak of the Korean War. Completion of rehabilitation (to the Japanese level) and "enforcement" of industrialization were to be the main objectives.

For specifics, see:

Haebanghu uri naraŭi inmin kyŏngje palchŏn, p. 53.

Three Year Plan: 1954-56 (Postwar Reconstruction Period)

1. Reconstruct the war-torn economy on the basis of the principle of "priority development of heavy industry with simultaneous development in agriculture and industry."

2. Raise industrial output of 1956 to 2.6 times that of 1953 and 1.5 times that of 1949.

3. Raise output of principal grains in 1956 to 119 percent of that in 1949. Recover and reconstruct idle land while maintaining higher utilization of land in general. Expand irrigation. Develop industrial crops, seri-culture, livestock, and fruits. Increase the number of agricultural machinery and tractors. Strengthen state farms.

4. Expand freight and passenger transportation facilities as well as the number of trucks and marine transporters.

For specifics, see:

Haebanghu uri naraŭi inmin kyŏngje palchŏn, pp. 112-113; CCY, 1954-55, pp. 50-60; Ch'ae Hŭi-jŏng, "Economic Policy of the Korean Labor Party for the Construction of Socialism in the Northern Parts of the Republic," Kyŏngje kŏnsŏl (Economic Construction), November 1956, pp. 2-21.

Five Year Plan: 1957-60(61)

Actually, the Five Year Plan lasted only four years, to 1960, as its targets were claimed to have been fulfilled within two and a half years after its insti-tution in 1957. The remaining period through 1960 was designated as a "transition" or "buffer" period to prepare for the following economic plan. This is why the Seven Year Plan dates from 1961 instead of 1962.

1. Complete elimination of any remnants of the colonial industrial structure.

2. Establish a firm foundation for industrialization and basically solve problems of food, shelter, and clothing.

3. Continue the policy of priority development of heavy industry.

4. Provide material and technical conditions for future large-scale introduction of modern and mass production techniques and equipment.

5. Raise industrial output by 2.6 times.

6. Complete collectivization of farms as well as socialization of private merchants and entrepreneurs.

7. Assign priority on grain production while simultaneously developing industrial crops, livestock, sericulture, and fruits. Raise output per acre through increased use of fertilizers, expansion of irrigation, and introduction of advanced techniques of farming. Raise land utilization rate.

For specifics, see:

CCY, 1956, pp. 86-101; Pak Chu-ryŏng, Inminŭi pongni hyangsangŭl wihan uri nara kyŏngje chŏngch'aek (Economic Policy of Our Country to Raise the Welfare of the People), Pyŏngyang: State Publishing House, 1958, pp. 71-90.

Seven Year Plan: 1961-67 (Extended to 1970)

Slowdowns in growth rates and reverses in production compelled North Korea to extend the plan officially to three additional years to the end of 1970.

1. Continue the policy of priority development of heavy industry. Specifically, during the first three years, emphasis is to be on consolidating the foundation of heavy industry ("to put meat on the skeleton" of heavy industry developed so far) with a view toward assisting the development of agriculture and light industry. During the remaining four years, emphasis is to be placed on expanding heavy industry further with improved technology so as to strengthen decisively the material and technical basis for socialism.

2. Develop rapidly the machine-building industry, which is the fundamental task of heavy industry.

3. Facilitate rapid growth of the chemical industry as a principal supplier of fertilizers to agriculture and various raw materials to light industry.

4. Emphasize double cropping. Increase output of grains both for food and animal feed.

5. Pursue mechanization of agriculture, expansion of consumer goods, and improvement in their quality.

6. Raise the target-year level of national income, industrial output, and agricultural output, respectively, to 2.7 times, 3.2 times, and 2.4 times the 1960 level.

For specifics, see:

Documents of the Fourth Congress of the Workers' Party of Korea, Pyŏng-
yang: Foreign Language Publishing House, 1961, pp. 53-84; Terao Goro,
Chosen sono kita to minami (Korea: North and South), Tokyo: New Japan
Publishing House, 1963, pp. 118-124.

Six Year Plan: 1971-76

1. "Consolidate and carry forward the accomplishments of industrialization
   and advance technical revolution to new heights in order to cement further the material and technical foundations of socialism and free the
   working people from arduous labor in all fields of the national economy."

2. Emphasize in industry qualitative growth and sectoral balances and
   strengthen self-sufficiency in industrial raw materials. Priority is
   given to developing power and extractive industries and to raising the
   quality of industrial products in general.

3. Raise agricultural productivity through technical improvements and highly
   intensive methods of production.

4. Raise the final year national income and industrial output, respectively,
   to 1.8 times and 2.2 times (14 percent per annum) the 1970 level. Output
   of grains is to reach 7 to 7.5 million tons, including 3.5 million tons
   of rice per year, by 1976.

For specifics, see:

Kim Il-song, "Report on the Work of the Central Committee to the Fifth
Congress of the Workers' Party of Korea," Nodong sinmun, November 3,
1970; Kim Il, "Concerning the Six-Year Plan for the Development of
People's Economy," Nodong sinmun, November 10, 1971; Joseph S. Chung,
"The Six Year Plan (1971-76) of North Korea: Targets, Problems and Pros-
pects," Journal of Korean Affairs, July 1971, pp. 15-26.

During the so-called "peaceful construction" of the pre-Korean War period,
the basic target of North Korean planning was to exceed the output level and efficiency attained during the Japanese occupation, ending in August 1945. An all-
out effort at rehabilitation and reorganization was made necessary by deterioration of productive facilities during World War II, some willful destruction by
the outgoing Japanese, and the mass withdrawal of trained Japanese personnel at
all levels. This was the basic purpose to which the two successive One Year
Plans of 1947 and 1948 and the Two Year Plan of 1949-50 were geared. Subsequently, North Korea had to pass through another period of rehabilitation, this
time reconstructing an economy torn by the Korean War. The Three Year Plan of
1954-56 had as its main task the regaining of the pre-Korean War output level.
Although the Three Year Plan was officially designated the "Post-war Reconstruction Plan," actual reconstruction for the majority of industrial products was not
generally achieved until toward the end of the Five Year Plan.

Due to the earlier termination of the Five Year Plan, the Seven Year Plan*
was introduced in 1961, one year earlier than the original timetable. The Seven
Year Plan thus started was transformed into a de facto Ten Year Plan. In sharp
contrast to unparalleled and continuous high growth during the Three Year Plan
and Five Year Plan, the Seven Year Plan was beset by setbacks from its inception.
Reverses and slowdowns spread throughout the economy and forced the government
to readjust the plan and extend it three more years to the end of 1970.

---

*The Seven Year Plan was initially conceived as the second Five Year Plan,
judging from the fact that the Five Year Plan was often referred to as the First
Five Year Plan in various North Korean literature. For instance, as late as
October 1959 Kim Il, First Vice-premier, was referring to the Second Five Year
Plan as starting from 1961.

Appendix B: Organization, Availability and Reliability of North Korean Statistics

Since 1952 the collection, computation, tabulation, and reporting of statistical data have been centralized in the Central Statistical Bureau (CSB) of the State Planning Commission (chart 4). Its functions are specifically:

1. To collect, analyze, and submit to the government the statistical data necessary for national administration and economic control.

2. To conduct statistical investigations concerning the pursuance of economic planning and study the causes for plan failures.

3. To unify and standardize statistical computational system, reports, and forms.

4. To construct various "balances" of national economy for economic planning.

5. To publish final results of the national economic plans.

The subordinate departments of the CSB which specialize in certain sectors or aspects of the economy include such statistical divisions as Industrial, Agricultural, Capital Construction, Transportation, Cultural and Population, Labor and Economic Balances, and Finance. The Advisory Committee reviews statistical methodology and the Mechanical Computation Laboratory has the responsibility of mechanizing computation procedures. Local, regional, and provincial sections carry out statistical duties within the respective administrative districts under the supervision of the CSB.[1]

The thorniest problem faced by students of the North Korean economy concerns the availability and reliability of official economic statistics. To begin with, these data are extremely hard to come by due to the secretive nature of the North Korean regime. Further, even those few statistics that are made available are more often than not fragmentary, misleading, and discontinuous. Once the trickle of information has been made available, the lingering question is how reliable are the statistics published under the auspices of the Communist government of North Korea. In what follows, an attempt will be made to advance certain hypotheses and observations about this credibility issue.

CHART 4

NORTH KOREAN STATISTICAL AGENCIES: ORGANIZATIONAL CHART

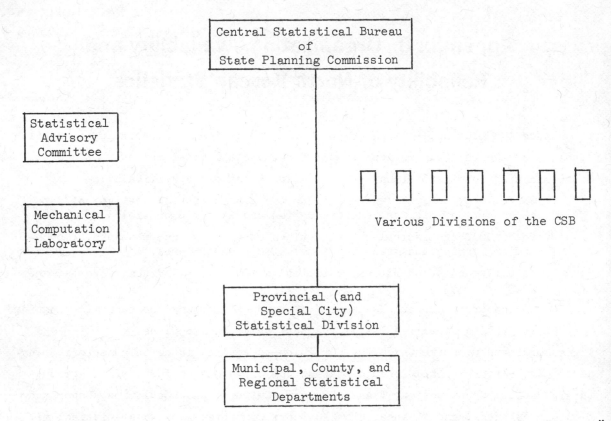

Source: "The System of Computation and Statistics of the People's Economy," in Kongŏp kiŏpso kyŏngje (Economics of Industrial Enterprises), Pyŏngyang: State Publishing House, 1957, Chapter II, pp. 54-85.

1. Suppression of selective data does not imply that North Korea is either miserly in the collection, compilation, and utilization of economic data or is less than concerned about their reliability. On the contrary, the operational needs of a planned economy such as North Korea probably require more data, greater in detail and extent of coverage, standardization, and accuracy than do market-oriented economies. Such slogans as "Strict Observation of Regulations on Computation and Statistics is the Necessary Condition for the Development of People's Economy" attest to this.[2] Soviet concern for reliability has been by now well documented.[3]

2. There may not be a necessary relationship between secrecy and fabrication. There seems to be no evidence to indicate that North Korea uses a double

bookkeeping system: those data selected for publication for external or domestic consumption do not differ from records circulated among the inner circles of the Central Statistical Bureau (CSB) of the State Planning Commission. The same conclusion tested for the U.S.S.R. by captured documents seems to apply generally to Communist China as well.[4] First of all, no such practice (double bookkeeping) has been uncovered. Second, at the level of the CSB there are no apparent motives to distort. It is the highest reporting agency. This must be contrasted with microlevel reporting wherein there are motives to "pad" the output claims on the part of the individual workers and managers of a plant and peasant workers on the state or collective farms. Fabrication at the highest level amounts to cheating oneself unless double sets of records are kept. If deliberately false reports exist, the CSB itself is a victim: published figures may correctly reflect data available at the Central Statistical Bureau, yet they could be wrong due to "padding" by the reporting agencies. Third, there is the requirement for greater accuracy for planning and coordination among different agencies, enterprises, and so on at all levels of the economy. Putting out false information regarding the economy will mislead the planning process and cause intersectoral imbalances and create general chaos.

3. Published data seem to be by and large internally consistent relative to certain obvious mathematical and technical relationships existing among different variables. Several consistency tests performed on industrial output data seem to bear out this point. To be sure, internal consistency is not the same as statistical accuracy.

4. Statistics in absolute or physical terms such as the output of major industrial and agricultural commodities and transportation data seem to be far more correct and reliable than those in index numbers.[5] There are, however, ambiguities because of vague or unexplained definitions and aggregation methods. For instance, it is not explained in many North Korean statistics what exactly constitutes such groupings as underwear, marine products, footwear, and so on. Also, such classifications as "large" or "small," "rich" or "poor" farmers, and the like are seldom accompanied by notes defining them. Another source of ambiguity is associated with output figures of products requiring more than two sets of units of measurement for precise reckoning. For example, output figures of such items as textiles state the length without exception but rarely mention the width of the article.

171

5. Greatest potential source for statistical inflation arises from the possibility of cheating and error at the microlevel reporting by individual enterprises and collective farms. Although such a tendency exists in all economies (motivated by tax evasion, industrial rivalry, and so on) there are factors in North Korea which make its reporting more susceptible for statistical tampering at the lower echelons of the North Korean reporting hierarchy. First, in the North Korean economy, economic performance and rewards of individual workers, peasants, and managers are fundamentally based on the fulfillment of planned quotas as reflected by the predominance of a piece-rate wage system and bonuses. In such a system there is a built-in tendency for the workers, enterprises, and lower administrative units to exaggerate the output figures.[6] Statistical "padding" also takes the form of fulfilling the quantitative quota at the expense of quality. The resulting abundance of shoddy goods has posed a major problem for industry and for consumers.[7] The problem of low product quality applies equally to heavy and light industry and covers a wide range of products such as tractors, coal, metal products, cement, fabrics, automobiles, shoes, and other daily necessities.[8] There are, on the other hand, some limits to this tendency: the close link between output and distribution has a constraining effect—that is, what is produced is expected to be delivered—and pilfering and other more or less illegal transactions and the like tend to be concealed. In addition, inflating output may not prove advantageous to the enterprise managers in the long run: exaggerated output figures may overrate the productive capacity of the plant and result in increased quotas in the ensuing years. North Korea's heavy reliance on nation- and economy-wide exhortations and mass movements compounds the problem of statistical "padding." One notices unusually large production claims made around 1958-59 in the wake of the introduction in 1958 of the Chŏllima Movement which was inspired by and patterned after the Chinese Great Leap Forward Movement. Studies based on input-output relationships point to substantial over-reporting in the official production figures for machinery and, to a lesser extent, for fuel and coal centered around 1958-59,[9] as well as for agricultural output between 1959-61.[10] Such a movement, by placing stress on "socialist competition" among the individual workers, work brigades, and plants for the "coveted" titles of Chŏllima "heroes," would result in exaggerated production claims and sectoral imbalances causing, in time, disruptions in input-output relationships. These movements through their secondary repercussions nearly turned the North Korean economy into chaos around 1959. This partly explains the designation of 1960 as a "buffer year," a year of readjustment.

6. North Korean index numbers are generally not accompanied by vital information such as that concerning the base year, price or quantity weights, treatment of new products, index formulas, definitions of terms and groupings, and sampling methods. This fact makes it very difficult to assess the extent and nature of potential statistical biases associated with particular index numbers of concern. Biases in index numbers arise from problems inherently connected with aggregations and are not confined to communist countries. North Korean index numbers, especially the growth indexes, like those of many other developing economies, probably contain an upward bias.[11] There are several likely reasons for this conjecture. First, chances are that new products are introduced, as they actually have been in substantial varieties and quantities in the past, at the initial high costs of pilot plants or experimental production. Since their relative price would generally fall with a subsequent increase in output, this practice would tend to give undue weight to new products. This is known as the "new product effect" and is related to the so-called Gerschenkron effect which, based on the Soviet experience, states that there is a negative correlation through time between relative outputs and relative prices. This has been so in the case of Communist China.[12] The new product effect would tend to increase progressively until such a time as the price weights for new products were adjusted. Second, an upward bias is likely to occur from growing commercialization and specialization of a developing economy like North Korea. Goods and services which were formerly either self-consumed or did not enter the exchange network would be excluded or inadequately imputed in aggregate indexes. As these goods and services become produced by enterprises with growing specialization and interdependence, they come to be included in the aggregates. To be sure, mistaking increasing interdependence for growth in total output with the resultant upward bias is common to all developing economies.

7. Extension of nationalization and collectivization have most probably contributed toward exaggerated growth by increasing statistical coverage and control of output. Since "socialization" (transformation of all productive units into state enterprises and producers' cooperatives in industry, and state farms and collective farms in agriculture) was accomplished in 1958, growth indexes and production figures for the years after 1958 probably contain a marked upward bias while the quality of statistical reporting might have improved somewhat. There is speculation that statistical inflation in agriculture since 1958 occurred owing principally to farm reorganization in the aftermath of collectivization

and the resultant change in the procedure of statistical reporting.[13] Since
nationalization of large industrial enterprises was already accomplished before
the Korean War, agricultural output figures have been affected more than those
of industrial output. The move toward collectivization was seriously made only
after the Korean War and accomplished quite abruptly.

8. Another source for upward bias attributable to technical factors is the
doublecounting problem common to all communist economies. It arises from the
communist practice of counting interenterprise production more than once in the
valuation of output. This adds to the usual problems involved in measuring output due to "grossness." It may be argued that insofar as the growth rates are
concerned the "gross" factor may not pose a serious problem as long as the same
practice is consistently used throughout the time period under study, the period
under concern is relatively short, or there has been no appreciable change in
the structure and organization of industry. Absorption and merger of small industrial plants into larger state plants tend to reduce the extent of doublecounting while addition of new plants, new processes, increased specialization
and decentralization tend to increase it. Both of these have taken place in
North Korea and it is difficult to determine which of these opposing forces has
been stronger. As would be expected, the degree of grossness is larger for gross
industrial output than for the gross agricultural output due to greater interdependence among industrial enterprises. This is reflected by the fact that the
share of industry in the combined value of gross industrial and agricultural output rose from 34 percent in 1956 to 74 percent in 1969 while the share of industry in national income originating from industry and agriculture increased from
25 to 65 percent during the same period.[14]

9. Insofar as the rates of growth are concerned the so-called "law of equal
cheating" may be applied with caution. Theoretically, to the extent that the
proportion of falsification, omission, grossness, errors, and the like remains
stable, rates of growth would not be affected. It is difficult, however, to
ascertain the extent of changes in these factors over the years. It will suffice
to add that growth rates over a short span of time would in general be more reliable in this connection than over the longer run.

10. Omission, rather than falsification, tends to be the communist means of
concealing any unfavorable development. This means that if, for example, output
of a certain series declines, the production figures for the series tend to be
omitted to conceal current failure and, instead, emphasis is placed on the data

of the series in which output has shown gains. The relative abundance of published economic data during the high growth period of the Five Year Plan and the recent conspicuous withdrawal of previously published statistical series tend to confirm the existence of a positive correlation between economic performance and the amount of official published data. Gradual withholding of output data coincided with the beginning of the Seven Year Plan when the number of reported production figures suddenly dwindled. A quick comparison of the statistical section of North Korean Central Yearbooks—say of 1965 with that, for example, of 1961—will bring home this point. Output figures on only a handful of products have been made public for 1964, 1965, and 1970 while there is a complete lack of information on physical data on production for the years between 1966-69. Complete blackout of statistical data started with 1966 in a year in which Gross Industrial Output actually declined (by 3 percent) for the first time since 1945. In addition to the paucity of data, the timing and circumstances surrounding the publication of data bear some interesting speculation. Up to 1964 the official announcements of national output data for a given year were made public by the Central Statistical Bureau predictably around the middle of the first month in the succeeding year. Not only was the date of public announcement of the 1964 figures postponed until toward the end of 1965 but they came in the form of a report by Kim Il at the Second Conference of the Workers' Party held in October 1966.[15] In addition, the 1965 figures were made public only in terms of percentage indexes over 1964 and, for the first time, were not accompanied by absolute physical production data for the major industrial and agricultural products. Moreover, every one of the products whose figures were made known for 1964 had shown production gains over the previous years, information on others being totally withheld. Also, after a complete blackout between 1966-69, what little information published for 1970 came in the form of Kim Il-song's report to the Fifth Congress of the Workers' Party in November 1970. Further, for the first time since North Korea introduced economic plans after 1947, North Korea withheld the planned Gross Agricultural Output for 1976, the target year for the Six Year Plan. As a matter of fact the last year for which the agricultural output figure (in index) was made public is 1963. Agriculture continues to be the weakest link in the North Korean economy. This pattern of behavior on the part of the North Korean authorities seems to confirm the contention that North Korean statistics on production in physical quantities are relatively more reliable and that the ambiguous percentage figures, omission, and delay, rather than deliberate falsification, appear to be the regime's means of concealing unfavorable developments.

11. Aside from common errors associated with insufficient training of statistical personnel, clerical oversights, observation and measurement errors, and the like, deliberate falsification of economic data poses problems. To be sure, manipulation of one kind or another probably is resorted to by all countries for military, political, and economic reasons. The fact that all statistical data are controlled by the monolithic CSB and that all the regulations and controls are designed to promote the interest of the communist regime and the party suggests that a totalitarian nation like North Korea would be tempted to manipulate data to its advantage. In this connection, some observers suspect the probability that the achievements of the Three Year Plan and Five Year Plan were overstated by the regime in order to vindicate the position of the party leadership after purging those who opposed and criticized the priorities and strategies as outlined in the economic plans.[16] By and large, however, North Korea appears to resort to either omitting or to publishing data which are "literally correct but functionally and operationally meaningless or false" simply to conceal the facts.[17] In the long run there is a limit to fabrication unless backed by actual performance as exemplified by Communist China's retracting of production claims in the wake of the Great Leap Forward and North Korea's open admission of retrenchment during the Seven Year Plan.

12. Due to the paucity of published compendia of statistics, searching for statistics and "reading between the lines" in leaders' speeches is an unavoidable but all-important source for information. This is a familiar occupational hazard for students of North Korea. Also, official statistics may be supplemented and checked by travelogues although great care must be taken to discern the ideological bias of the travelers. Fortunately, official foreign trade statistics can be checked by trade returns of partner countries or, as actually happens, these can be substituted for the scarce North Korean official data on foreign trade.

In summary, North Korean economic data must be scrutinized carefully for their reliability. Although they seem more or less internally consistent, North Korea presents them in an ambiguous manner or withholds them in times of poor economic performance. Physical data tend to be more reliable than those made available only in index numbers. Although North Korean authorities may actually resort to outright falsification if it serves political expediency, they themselves are concerned about the reliability of data submitted by lower echelons. Omission appears to be their chief means for concealing or downplaying poor performance. While there are technical factors inherent in the nature of statistical methodology that tend to distort statistics, these are not confined to North Korea or communist countries alone. By and large, North Korean data are usable if handled with extreme care and investigated critically.

Notes

2: The Agricultural Sector

1. See, for the breakdown of major food crops produced in North Korea and South Korea in 1944, Chosŏn kyŏngje yŏnpo, 1948 (Annual Economic Review of Korea, 1948) (Seoul: Bank of Korea, 1948), I, pp. 43-51.

2. Chosŏn kyŏngje yŏnpo, 1948, I, p. 28.

3. Ibid., I, p. 375; Chosŏn chungang yŏngam, 1949 (CCY) (Korean Central Yearbook) (Pyŏngyang: Korean Central News Agency, 1949), p. 71.

4. For the complete text of the "Law Concerning Land Reform in North Korea," see CCY, 1949, pp. 70-71.

5. Namboku chosenno genjo (Current Situation of South and North Korea) (Tokyo: Research Department of Asahi Daily, 1962), Vol. 2, p. 114.

6. United Nations, Report of the U.N. Commission for the Unification and Rehabilitation of Korea (UNCURK), General Assembly, Official Records: 6th Session, Supplement No. 12 (A/1881), p. 28.

7. CCY, 1949, p. 72.

8. Korean Affairs Institute, Chosen no keizai (The Economy of Korea) (Tokyo: Oriental Economist Press, 1956), p. 60.

9. Yi Chong-p'al, Nongŏp hyŏptong johapŭi chŏngch'i kyŏngjejŏk kongkohwarŭl wihan myŏtkaji munje (Several Problems Concerning the Political and Economic Consolidation of Agricultural Cooperatives) (Pyŏngyang: Korean Labor Party Publishing House, 1960).

10. U.S. Department of State, North Korea: A Case Study in the Technique of Takeover, Department of State Publication 7118 (Washington: U.S. Government Printing Office, 1961), p. 59; Report of the UNCURK, loc. cit.

11. Parts of this and the following sections on collective and state farms are based on expanding, revising, and updating "A Pattern of Agricultural Development: Size, Organization and Work Incentives of the North Korean Collective and State Farms," in Joseph S. Chung [ed.], Patterns of Economic Development: Korea (Kalamazoo, Michigan: Korea Research and Publications, Inc., in cooperation with the Graduate School of Western Michigan University, 1966), pp. 55-79.

12. This paragraph is based on Kajimura Hideki, "A Note on the Collectivization Movement (1953-58) in North Korea," Chosen gakuho (Journal of Korean Studies) (Tokyo: April, 1966), pp. 279-321; Namboku chosenno genjo (Current Conditions of South and North Korea), Vol. 2 (Tokyo: Asahi Newspaper Research Department, 1962), pp. 128-133; Agricultural Cooperativization in DPRK (Pyŏngyang: Foreign Languages Publishing House, 1958), pp. 8-9.

13. Hong Tal-sŏn, "Socialistic Transformation of Agriculture in Our Country," Academy of Science, Institute of Economic and Legal Research, 8.15 haebang 15 junyŏn kinyŏm kyŏngje ronmunjip (Economic Essays Commemorating the 15th Anniversary of 8.15 Liberation) (Pyŏngyang: Academy of Science Publishing House, 1960), pp. 61-65.

14. Ibid., p. 71. No definition of "rich farmers" is given in the source.

15. Agricultural Cooperativization in DPRK, p. 81.

16. O Hyŏn-sang, Kyŏngje chisik (Economic Knowledge) (Pyŏngyang: State Publishing House, 1957), pp. 178-80; Democratic People's Republic of Korea (Pyŏngyang: Foreign Languages Publishing ouse, 1958), p. 224; Philip Rudolph, North Korea's Political and Economic Structure (New York: Institute of Pacific Relations, 1959), p. 52.

17. DPRK, p. 224. The concept of workday points will be treated later.

18. For the complete text of the Standard Rules Concerning Agricultural Cooperatives, see Saikinno chosenno kyodo nojo (Recent Cooperative Farms in Korea) (Tokyo: Nihon chosen kenkyusho, 1967), pp. 97-106.

19. Joan Robinson, "Korean Miracle," Monthly Review, January 1965, p. 546.

20. Kyŏngje kŏnsŏl (Economic Construction), Pyŏngyang, May 1956, p. 137; Institute for Economic and Legal Research, Academy of Science, Haebanghu uri nara ŭi inmin kyŏngje palchŏn (Development of People's Economy in Our Country Since Liberation) (Pyŏngyang: Academy of Science Printing Office, 1960), pp. 45-48.

21. For the complete text of the Cabinet Decision No. 125 "Concerning the Amalgamation and Expansion in the Scale of Operation of Agricultural Cooperatives," see CCY, 1959, pp. 126-127.

22. Hong Tal-sŏn, op. cit., p. 73.

23. Joint Publications Research Service (JPRS), Economic Report on North Korea (ERNK), No. 79, Washington, D.C.: JPRS, 1963, p. 32.

24. CCY, 1961, p. 181.

25. JPRS, ERNK, No. 79, p. 32.

26. Agricultural Cooperativization in DPRK, p. 73.

27. Ro Hang-mok, "Several Problems Concerning the Labor Formation in the Agricultural Cooperatives," Kyŏngje kŏnsŏl, April 1958, p. 22.

28. Saikinno chosenno kyodo nojo, p. 15.

29. Complete text of the law consisting of 11 articles appears in CCY, 1950, p. 40.

30. O Hyŏn-sang, op. cit., p. 171.

31. Fire farming consists in growing crops by planting them on the virgin soil after a piece of forest land is burned off. The ash deposits from the burnt vegetation improve the soil fertility to a limited extent. When the field ceases to yield well, it is abandoned. In Korea the fire field ordinarily is used two or more years before moving on to a new field but the abandoned plot is commonly exploited again in ten or twenty years. Thus the fire field which is seldom very fertile may pass into a permanently cultivated land. Fire farming is open to the criticism that it often causes erosion and laterization. The product of the laterization process is laterite, an infertile

soil composed of various mixtures of iron hydroxides, aluminum, and perhaps quartz. Another objection is that although ashes may fertilize the soil somewhat, the fire destroys most of the humus, thereby reducing the fertility. In the words of one expert, "because of the vegetable matter that fire devours, the impoverishment of the soil due to the disappearance of the forest, and the erosion that occurs on soils deprived of plant cover, fire farming consumes far more wealth than it produces." See Shannon McCune, _Korea's Heritage_ (Rutland, Vermont: Charles E. Tuttle Company, 1956), pp. 86-89, and V. D. Wickizer and M. K. Bennett, _The Rice Economy of Monsoon Asia_ (Stanford, California: Stanford University, Food Research Institute, 1941), pp. 12-13. The quote is from the latter source, p. 13.

32. Kim Chang-sun, _Pukhan siponyŏn sa_ (The Fifteen-Year History of North Korea) (Seoul: Chimungak, 1961), p. 200.

33. U.S. Department of State, _North Korea: A Case Study..._, p. 57.

34. _Chosen minshushugi jinmin kyowakokuni okeru kanryoshugito bunpashugini taisuru toso_ (The Struggle Against Bureaucratism and Factionalism in the People's Democratic Republic of Korea) (Tokyo: Tokyo kensetsu tsushin sha, 1953), p. 20.

35. U.S. Department of State, _Land Reform in North Korea_, DRF-Information Paper No. 419, May 11, 1951, p. 2.

36. U.S. Department of State, _North Korea: A Case Study..._, p. 59; _Report of the UNCURK_, loc. cit.; U.S. Department of State, _Land Reform in North Korea_, loc. cit.

37. Kim Chang-sun, op. cit., pp. 200-201.

38. O Hyŏn-sang, op. cit., pp. 172-173.

39. Kim Chang-sun, op. cit., p. 201.

40. Kim Il-song, "Uri nara sahoejuŭi nongch'on munjee kwanhan t'eje" (Thesis Concerning the Socialist Agrarian Question in Our Country), _CCY_, 1965, pp. 5-22.

41. _CCY_, 1965, pp. 150-151.

42. JPRS, _1962 North Korean Yearbook_, p. 214.

43. "Inspiration by the Great Programme for Socialist Rural Construction," _Korea News_, Pyŏngyang, No. 8, 1964, p. 1; _CCY_, 1965, p. 151; _Pukhan ch'onggam, 1945-68_ (General Survey of North Korea) (Seoul: Institute of Communist Bloc Affairs, 1968), p. 346.

44. For a complete text of the decree, see _Chosen shiryo_ (Source Materials on Korea), Tokyo: June 1966, pp. 2-3.

45. Academy of Science, Institute of Economic and Legal Research (Pyŏngyang), _Chosenni okeru shakai shugino kiso kensetsu_ (Construction of the Foundation of Socialism in Korea), translated into Japanese by Kim Kwang-ji and Ko (Tokyo: New Japan Publishing House, 1962), p. 131.

46. Kim Il-song, "Uri nara sahoejuŭi nongch'on munjee kwanhan t'eje," p. 20.

47. Kim Wŏn-sam, "A Balanced Improvement in the Lives of Workers, Office Workers and Farmers," _Kyŏngje Yŏn'gu_ (Economic Study), Pyŏngyang, No. 3, 1965, pp. 15-22.

48. _Pukhan ch'onggam, 1945-68_, pp. 246-247.

49. Information in this and following paragraphs on the Kun farm management committee is based on: "Concerning the Organization of Kun Agricultural Co-operative Management Committee in North Korea," Chosen kenkyu geppo (Monthly Report on Korean Studies), Tokyo, December 1962, pp. 67-70; Kim Taek-hyŏn, "The Creation of the Kun Co-operative Farm Management Committee and Further Development of the Alliance of Workers and Peasants," Kŭlloja, No. 7, 1963, pp. 24-30; Chŏn Yong-sik, "Party's Agricultural Policy," Nodong sinmun (Worker's Newspaper), Pyŏngyang, March 13, 1964, pp. 2-4. The last two articles also appear, respectively, in ERNK, No. 88 & No. 121.

50. Kim Song-jin, Uri nara esso ui nongch'on munje haegyŏl ŭi yŏksajŏk kyŏnghŏm (Historical Experience in the Solution of Agricultural Problems in Our Country) (Pyŏngyang: Korean Labor Party Press, 1965), p. 341.

51. Quoted in Hong Tal-sŏn "The Superiority of the Kun Cooperative Farm Management Committee," Nodong sinmun, December 25, 1962.

52. See, in this connection, "Strengthening Enterprise-type Guidance Over Cooperative Farm Management," Nodong sinmun, June 9, 1965.

53. Korea News, April 20, 1962, p. 12.

54. Yu Kwan-chil, "Several Problems in the Guidance of the Agricultural Cooperative Management Committee by the Kun Party Committees," Kŭlloja, January 3, 1963, pp. 27-31. See also Kyŏngje chisik (Economic Knowledge) (Pyŏngyang: Korean Labor Party Publishing House, 1963), p. 288.

55. CCY, 1965, p. 151.

56. Kŭlloja (Workers), Pyŏngyang, December 20, 1963, pp. 26-32.

57. See Kim Il-song, "Summary Report of the Work of the Central Committee to the Fifth Congress of the Workers' Party of Korea," Nodong sinmun, November 3, 1970.

58. Kyŏngje chisik, pp. 498-501; Pukhan yoram, p. 114; Pukhan ch'onggam, 1945-68, pp. 345-347.

59. O. Hyŏn-sang, op. cit., p. 138.

60. Idem.

61. For the complete text of the law concerning the work standards passed in 1962, see Saikinno chosenno kyodonojo, pp. 107-128.

62. Kyŏngje chisik, pp. 370-371.

63. Kyŏngje kŏnsŏl, September 1954, p. 105.

64. Academy of Science, Uri nara inmin kyŏngje esŏ saengsanryŏk kwa saengsankwangye ŭi hosang chagyong (Inter-relationship Between Productivity and Relations of Production in the People's Economy of Our Country) (Pyŏngyang: Academy of Science Publishing House, 1960), p. 132.

65. Idem.

66. Ibid., p. 131; Kyŏngje chisik, p. 374.

67. Lee Il-yong, "A Few Problems Presented by the 1962 Annual Final Distribution Task in the Cooperative Farms," Minju chosŏn (Democratic Korea), November 17, 1962; Kyŏngje chisik, p. 374.

68. This paragraph is based on Yi Il-yong, op. cit.

69. "The Subteam Group Contract System on Cooperative Farms," Kŭlloja, No. 24 (Workers), December 20, 1965, pp. 2-10; CCY, 1966-67, p. 208.

70. Nodong sinmun, February 13, 1968.

71. Agricultural Commission of the DPRK, "Accurate Implementation of Work for Fiscal 1962 Settlement of Accounts and Distribution," Nongmin sinmun (Farmers' Newspaper), November 27, 1962, p. 4; Nodong sinmun, November 14, 1965, p. 2.

72. Hong Tal-sŏn, Urinara nongch'on bumunesŏ mulchiljŏk kwansim ŭi ch'angjojŏk jŏkyong (Creative Application of the Principles of Material Incentives in the Farm Management Sector of Our Country) (Pyŏngyang: Academy of Science Publishing House, 1963), p. 208.

73. JPRS, The 1961 North Korean Yearbook, p. 229.

74. Pukhan yoram, 1968, p. 120.

75. Academy of Science, Uri nara inmin kyŏngje esŏ saengsannyŏk kwa saengsan-kwangye ŭi hosang chagyong, pp. 111-113.

76. Kyŏngje chisik, p. 281.

77. As of January 1961, there were 3,872 villages and 170 counties. Kim Chang-sun, op. cit., pp. 248, 251.

78. Academy of Science, Uri nara inmin kyŏngje eso saengsannyok kwa saengsan-kwangye ŭi hosang chagyong, p. 112.

79. Hong Tal-sŏn, op. cit., p. 2.

80. Idem.

81. Yi Sok-nok, "The Superiority and Vitality of the New System of Guidance in Agriculture," Kŭlloja, December 1962, pp. 26-38.

82. O Hyŏn-sang, op. cit., p. 174.

83. CCY, 1961, pp. 182-183.

84. Academy of Science, Uri nara inmin kyŏngje esŏ saengsannyŏk kwa saengsan-kwangye ŭi hosang chagyong, p. 124.

85. JPRS, The 1961 North Korean Yearbook, p. 229.

86. See Pukhan yoram, 1968, pp. 117-118, for the organizational chart of the MTS.

87. CCY, 1961, p. 183.

88. Academy of Science, Uri nara inmin kyŏngje esŏ saengsannyok kwa saengsan-kwangye ŭi hosang chagyong, pp. 118-128.

89. Pukhan yoram, 1968, pp. 117-118.

90. "Drive for Farm Mechanization," Far Eastern Economic Review, Hong Kong, February 25, 1960, p. 403.

91. This and other examples in this paragraph regarding farm machinery and their operation were originally cited in Yi Sok-nok, op. cit., pp. 26-38; and Yi Yang-chon, "Mechanization of Farming is Central Task of Agricultural Management," Minju chosŏn, November 15, 1962, p. 2.

92. See, for example, JPRS, The 1961 North Korean Yearbook, p. 261.

93. See, in this connection, Joseph S. Chung, "The Six Year Plan (1971-76) of North Korea: Targets, Problems and Prospects," Journal of Korean Affairs, July 1971, pp. 17-18.

94. Andrew J. Grajdanzev, Modern Korea: Her Economic and Social Development under the Japanese (New York: Institute of Pacific Relations, 1944), p. 88.

95. Haebanghu uri nara ŭi inmin kyŏngje palchŏn, p. 98.

96. Yi Chong-p'al, op. cit., p. 115.

97. Robert A. Scalapino, "North Korea," a prepared statement before the Subcommittee on Asian and Pacific Affairs, House of Representatives Foreign Affairs Committee, June 10, 1971, reprinted in Journal of Korean Affairs, July 1971, p. 33. Prof. Scalapino does not cite the original source.

98. DPRK, p. 217.

99. Pyŏngyang Radio Broadcast, August 28, 1962.

100. Idem.

101. North Korea received shipments of various crop seeds along with breeding animals from Communist China in the past. In 1963, such shipments included "over 670 kinds of seed grains, more than 200 kinds of industrial crop seed, and over 200 kinds of vegetable seed, 15 kinds of breeding animals." Korea News, No. 1, 1964, p. 21.

102. Shin Nak-sam, "State Control Over Grain Processing," Sangŏp (Commerce), April 1963, pp. 9-11.

103. DPRK, p. 221.

104. Nodong sinmun, November 10, 1970.

105. Idem.

3: The Industrial Sector

1. Chosen no keizai, p. 58; Japanese destruction of Aoji Petroleum Plant in the face of the advancing Soviet Army was reported in a Japanese source, Mikio Yamana, Chosen sotokufu shuseino kiroku (Record of the Final Period of the Government-General of Korea) (Tokyo: Yuho kyokai, 1956), pp. 1-2.

2. For detailed information on the development of hydroelectric power and mineral resources in Korea, see Shannon McCune, Korea's Heritage, pp. 219-224.

3. Chosŏn kyŏngje yŏnbo, 1948, I, p. 102.

4. See, for the breakdown of industrial output in 1942 and mineral output in 1944, Chosŏn kyŏngje yŏnbo, 1948, I, p. 101; George M. McCune, Korea Today (Cambridge, Massachusetts: Harvard University Press, 1950), p. 58.

5. This section is a revised and updated version of the author's article, "The North Korean Industrial Enterprise: Control, Concentration and Managerial Functions," Robert K. Sakai [ed.], Studies on Asia, 1966 (Lincoln: University of Nebraska Press, 1966), pp. 165-185.

6. For the complete text of the decree, see CCY, 1949, p. 73.

7. Chosen no keizai, p. 61.

8. Idem. The source does not specifiy the precise meaning of the percentage figure.

9. For a summary of the entire decision, see George M. McCune, op. cit., pp. 186-187.

10. V. Gryaznov, Sotsialisticheskaya industrializatsiya v KNDR, 1945-1960gg (Socialist Industrialization in the KPDR, 1945-1960), Moscow: Izd. "Nauka," 1966, as reviewed by George Ginsburg in The Journal of Asian Studies, February 1972, pp. 425-427.

11. North Korea: A Case Study in the Technique of Takeover, pp. 78-79.

12. Ray Cromley, "North Korea Sovietized," The Wall Street Journal, May 5, 1947, p. 4.

13. North Korea: A Case Study in the Technique of Takeover, p. 79.

14. Ibid., p. 114.

15. Haebanghu uri nara ŭi inmin kyŏngje palchŏn, p. 179.

16. O Hyŏn-sang, Kyŏngje chisik (Economic Knowledge) (Pyŏngyang: State Publishing House, 1957), pp. 129-130, and Kyŏngje chisik: kongŏp, nongŏp, sangŏp (Economic Knowledge: Industry, Agriculture and Commerce) (Pyŏngyang: Korean Labor Party Publishing House, 1963), pp. 7-10.

17. Nodong sinmun, November 3, 1970.

18. Chŏng Tae-sik, Chŏngch'i kyŏngjehak tokbon (Primer on Political Economy), Vol. I (Pyŏngyang: Korean Labor Party Publishing House, 1960), p. 204.

19. Pak Sang-kun, "How to Provide Working Capital," Chaejŏng kŭmyung (Finance and Banking), No. 7, July 1964, p. 9; Yi Ki-hong, "What is the Independent Economic Accounting System?" Kyŏngje chisik, February 1960, pp. 36-39; and "What is the Independent Accounting System: Lecture on the Economy of the Republic," Minju ch'ŏngnyŏn (Democratic Youth), December 25, 1959, p. 3.

20. See Kim Tu-chil, "Qualitative and Quantitative Indices in Factory Operation," Kŭlloja (The Worker), July 1963, pp. 46-48; Cho Wong-hong, "What Significance Does the Quality Index Have in Enterprise Activities?" Kŭlloja, July 20, 1965, pp. 44-47; and Kongŏp kiŏpso kyŏngje, Chapter XV.

21. Kyŏngje chisik: kongŏp, nongŏp, sangŏp, p. 196.

22. Report Orally Submitted to the March 1954 Plenum of the Central Committee of the Workers' Party of Korea as quoted in Kongŏp kiŏpso kyŏngje, pp. 349-350.

23. The following is a list of selected large-sized firms around 1963:

Firms	Number of Workers
Pyŏngyang Cotton Textile	11,500
Kangsŏn Steel (Pyŏngyang)	11,000
Hŭngnam Fertilizer (Hamhŭng)	8,000
Yongsŏng Machinery (Hamhŭng)	6,500
The 2.8 Vinalon (Hamhŭng)	5,600
Pyŏngyang Silk Textile	5,500

Source: Hama Takeo, "North Korea's Industry and Agriculture," Dairiku mondai (Continental Affairs), May 1965, p. 55.

24. Kim Il, "Concerning Further Development of Local Industries," Chŏnguk chibang sanŏp mit sĕngsan hyŏpdong chohap yŏlsŏngja taewhae munhŏnjip (Documents for Nationwide Local Industries and Producers Cooperatives Enthusiasts Meeting) (Pyŏngyang: Korean Labor Party Publishing House, 1959), p. 28.

25. Pak Yun-kun, "Further Completion of the Form and Method of Industrial Management in Our Country," 8.15 haebang 15 chunyŏn kinyŏm kyŏngje ronmumjip, pp. 128-129.

26. Kim Il, Chŏnguk chibang sanŏp mit sĕngsan hyŏpdong chohap yŏlsŏngja taewhae munhŏnjip, p. 6.

27. Pak Yong-song, "Formation of a Firm Foundation of Local Industry and Its New State of Development," Kŭlloja, September 20, 1962, pp. 16-23, and JPRS, 1963 North Korean Central Yearbook, p. 153.

28. Chu Chang-yon, "Significance of Establishing a Local Industrial Base in Building Socialism in Our Country," Nodong sinmun, June 7, 1963, p. 3.

29. Pak Yun-kun, op. cit., pp. 140-142.

30. Based on a table in Kyŏngje chisik, October 1962, p. 25.

31. This paragraph is based on a lecture on economic geography offered by the Pyŏngyang Teachers College as it appeared in Kyŏngje chisik, May 1963, pp. 37-40.

32. Pak Yong-song, loc. cit.

33. Nodong sinmun, February 25, 1970.

34. "Our Country's Cooperative Management," Kyŏngje kŏnsŏl, February 1958, p. 65.

35. Academy of Science, Institute of Economic and Legal Research, Chosenni okeru shakai shugi no kiso kensetsu (Construction of the Foundation of Socialism in Korea) (Tokyo: New Japan Publishing House, 1962), p. 69.

36. Nam Chun-wha, "Socialistic Transformation of Private Commerce and Industry," Academy of Science, Institute of Economic and Legal Research, 8.15 haebang 15 chunyŏn kinyŏm kyŏngje nonmunjip (Economic Essays Commemorating the 15th Anniversary of the 8.15 Liberation) (Pyŏngyang: Academy of Science Publishing House, 1960), pp. 114-117; CCY, 1961, p. 175.

37. O Hyŏn-sang, op. cit., pp. 129-130.

38. CCY, 1961, p. 175.

39. JPRS, 1963 North Korean Central Yearbook, p. 152.

40. Nodong sinmun, November 10, 1970.

41. See, for the classification of industries in North Korea, "Classification of Industries and the Place of the Extracting Industry," Kyŏngje chisik, December 1962, pp. 38-39. Classification of industry into producer goods and consumer goods corresponds to the usual Marxian practice of distinguishing between the industrial sectors; that is, Department I (means of production) and Department II (consumer products). They are also referred to as Group A and Group B industries, respectively.

42. Kim Il, "Concerning Current Tasks for the Socialist Economic Construction," Nodong sinmun, October 11, 1966, pp. 2-5.

43. It is drawn in part from the author's article, "North Korea's Seven Year Plan (1961-70): Economic Performance and Reforms," Asian Survey (Berkeley: University of California), pp. 527-545.

44. See, for discussion on the Eastern European countries and the U.S.S.R., Harry G. Shaffer, "Economic Reforms in the Soviet Union and East Europe: A Comparative Study," _Proceedings of the Association for Comparative Ecomics_ (De Kalb: Northern Illinois University, 1970), pp. 1-35; Alexander Erlich, "Economic Reforms in Communist Countries," _Dissent_, May-June 1967, pp. 311-319.

45. Shaffer, "Economic Reforms in the Soviet Union and East Europe: A Comparative Study," p. 3.

46. _Nodong sinmun_, November 3, 1970.

47. _Idem_.

48. Kim Il, "On the Six Year Plan (1971-1976) for Development of the National Economy of the DPRK," _Nodong sinmun_, November 10, 1971.

49. _Ibid_.

50. See, in this connection, B. C. Koh, "North Korea and Its Quest for Autonomy," _Pacific Affairs_, Fall-Winter, 1965-66, pp. 294-306.

51. See, for instance, Ilpyong J. Kim, "The Chinese Communist Relations with North Korea," _The Journal of Asiatic Studies_, Seoul, December 1970, pp. 60-67.

52. Pak Tong-un, "Communist China's Impact on North Korea," _The Journal of Asiatic Studies_, Seoul, September 1966, pp. 48-49.

53. _Pukhan ch'onggam_, _1945-68_, p. 323.

54. _Nodong sinmun_, November 3, 1970.

55. Kim Il, "Concerning Current Tasks for the Socialist Economic Construction," _Nodong sinmun_, October 11, 1966.

56. See _Yŏnku nonjip_ (Collection of Treatises), Seoul, May 1971, pp. 53-58.

57. Chung Kiwon, "The North Korean People's Army and the Party," _The China Quarterly_, April-June 1963, pp. 118-119.

58. Hama Takeo, _op. cit._, pp. 50-57.

59. Joungwon Alexander Kim, "The 'Peak of Socialism' in North Korea: The Five and Seven Year Plans," Jan S. Prybyla, _Comparative Economic Systems_ (New York: Appleton-Century-Crofts, 1969), pp. 412-427. The quotation is from p. 415.

60. Kim Il, "On Six Year (1971-1976) Plan for Development of the National Economy of DPRK," _Nodong sinmun_, November 10, 1971.

61. _CCY_, 1968, p. 154; Baik Bong, _Kim Il-song_, _Biography_, Vol. III, pp. 35-38.

62. See, for an instructive survey of Chinese influence on North Korea, Ilpyong J. Kim, _loc. cit._

63. See, in this connection, Joseph S. Chung, "A Model of the Post-Reconstruction Stagnation: North Korea's Seven Year Plan," _Asian Forum_, October 1969, pp. 30-36.

64. P. H. M. Jones, "Poor Results in Pyŏngyang," _Far Eastern Economic Review_, March 26, 1964, p. 669.

4: Foreign Trade

1. *Chosen no keizai*, p. 125.

2. For a list of trading firms, their lines, and officials as existed around 1965-66, see Yu Wan-sik, "An Analysis of Foreign Trade of North Korea," *The Journal of Asiatic Studies*, September 1967, Seoul, Korea, pp. 104-114; *CCY*, 1965, p. 499.

3. *The 1961 North Korean Yearbook*, p. 285.

4. "Newly Established Material Incentive Measures to Increase the Production of Export Goods," *Chaejŏng kŭmyung* (Finance and Banking), February 1961, pp. 37-39.

5. The Council for Economic and Industry Research, Inc., *Foreign Assistance Activities of the Communist Bloc and their Implications for the United States* (Washington: U.S. Government Printing Office, 1957), p. 60.

6. *The 1961 North Korean Yearbook*, p. 286.

7. O Hyŏn-sang, *op. cit.*, pp. 254-258; Yu Wan-sik, *op. cit.*, pp. 124-132.

8. O Hyŏn-sang, *op. cit.*, p. 334; *Foreign Trade*, No. 2, 1967, Pyŏngyang, pp. 3-5.

9. *Nitcho boekino tebiki* (Handbook of Japan-North Korea Trade) (Tokyo: Japan-North Korea Trade Association, 1970), p. 438; *Nitcho boeki* (Japan-North Korea Trade), Tokyo, January 1968 (No. 18), p. 29.

10. The following is the list of exchange rates applied with other currencies around 1970:

    1 ruble = 6.17 won
    1 yuan = 1.05 won
    1 Hong Kong dollar = 0.44 won
    1 Swiss franc = 0.61 won

    Source: *Nitcho boekino tebiki*, p. 438.

11. Estimate by Lee Joong-Koon. See his article, "Foreign Trade of North Korea, 1955-68," a paper delivered at the International Conference on the Problems of Korean Unification in Seoul, Korea, August 24-29.

12. This paragraph is based on Chong-Sik Lee, "Notes on North Korean Import and Export of Cereals," *Journal of Korean Affairs*, January 1972, pp. 54-56.

13. Mah Feng-hwa, "Foreign Trade," Alexander Eckstein, Galenson & Liu [ed.], *Economic Trends in Communist China* (Chicago: Aldine Publishing Co., 1968), pp. 684-686; *Ajia keizai junpo*, end of the month issue, January 1963, p. 3.

14. *Quarterly Economic Review: China, Hong Kong, North Korea*, December 1963, p. 13.

15. U.S. Department of State, *North Korea: A Case Study...*, p. 108.

16. *Ibid.*, p. 108.

17. See Lee Joong-Koon, *op. cit.*, pp. 11-21, for detailed data and analysis. The author borrowed heavily from Prof. Lee's article on this topic.

18. See, for example, the 1966 trade agreement in *The People's Korea*, April 13, 1966.

19. Lee Joong-Koon, *op. cit.*, pp. 15-16.

20. Shinn Rinn-sup et al., _Area Handbook for North Korea_, p. 370.

21. Professor David Felix comments, relative to Franklyn D. Holzman's article on Soviet Bloc terms of trade, that the accepted evidence is that the nominal prices of Soviet exports to the satellites, when the official ruble-dollar exchange rate is used for comparison, have been generally well above dollar prices of Soviet exports to nonbloc countries. But the same conversion shows that satellite export prices to the Soviet Union were also higher than their export prices to nonbloc countries. It is not at all clear, therefore, that one does not largely cancel out the other. See, in this connection, Chapter IX (Settling the Terms of Trade) of P. J. D. Wiles' _Communist International Economics_ (New York: Frederick A. Praeger, 1969).

22. U.S. Department of State, _North Korea: A Case Study..._, p. 109.

23. _Northern Korea_, 'Independent Satellite', p. 9.

24. "Why Try to Smear Achievements of Pyongyang Economic Seminar?" _Nodong sinmun_, September 7, 1964.

25. Subsequently, in 1953, interest charge was lowered to 1 percent. Repayment was also postponed so that the loan which was cut by half was to be repaid in ten years starting in 1957.

26. This paragraph is based on a speech by Kim Il-song titled "Progress Report on the Visit to the Soviet Union of the DPRK Government Delegation," which appears in _Kim Il-song sŏnjip_, Vol. 2, pp. 354-377.

27. For details of the agreement, see _Kim Il-song sŏnjip_, Vol. 4, pp. 61-65, and "Soviet-Korean Negotiations in Moscow, September 11-19, 1953," supplement to the _New Times_, No. 39, September 26, 1953.

28. U.S. Department of State, _The Sino-Soviet Economic Offensive in the Less Developed Countries_ (Washington, D.C.: U.S. Government Printing Office, 1958), p. 16.

29. _The 1961 North Korean Yearbook_, p. 97.

30. _Ibid._, p. 96.

31. See, for example, _Nodong sinmun_, October 28, 1963 (Editorial section).

32. _Far Eastern Economic Review_, April 9, 1964, pp. 79-80; September 17, 1964, p. 504.

33. _Area Handbook for North Korea_, p. 370.

34. _Ibid._, p. 80.

35. _Far Eastern Economic Review_, April 9, 1964, p. 80, based on _Pravda_, March 16, 1964; _The People's Korea_, January 15, 1964, p. 4.

36. The 2.8 Vinalon Factory is the pride of the North Korean chemical industry. It is located in the industrial city of Hamhŭng and is a complex composed of approximately 50 large and small buildings with floor space of 130,000 square meters. It is claimed to have been built in one year by North Korean scientists and technicians. Over 3,000 miles of large and small pipes, over 200,000 meters of electric wires and cables, over 15,000 sets of modern machinery and other equipment were said to have been supplied by 300 factories for the construction of this factory. It began to produce and supply

its products in August 1961. In 1963 the annual rate of vinalon production was about 10,000 tons and it is boasted that in several years it will rise to 20,000-30,000 tons a year. By comparison, the world production of vinalon in 1958 was 12,000 tons. It is also claimed that 20,000 tons of vinalon, which makes superior cloth, is the equivalent in cotton of 200,000 chongbo of land and 600,000 man-days of labor. The People's Korea, March 6 and March 13, 1964.

37. Kim Sam-gyu, Konnichi no chosen (Korea Today) (Tokyo: Kawade Shobo, 1956), pp. 34-35.

38. Ajia Seikei Gakkai, Chugoku seiji keizai soran (Survey of China's Politics and Economy) (Tokyo: Tokyo Daily Labor Press, 1954), p. 214.

39. Ajia Seikei Gakkai, Chuka jinmin kyowakoku gaiko shiryo soran (Survey of the Diplomatic Data of the People's Republic of China) (Tokyo: Hitotsubashi Shoten, 1960), pp. 472-475.

40. Union Research Institute, Communist China 1949-59, Vol. II (Hong Kong: Union Research Institute, 1961), pp. 80-81.

41. It was reported that the Chinese vessel "Peace No. 60" anchored on June 15, 1964, at the Nampo port for the first time under the treaty and that this marked the opening of a regular service line between Nampo and Shanghai. Korea News, No. 18, 1964, p. 25.

42. Area Handbook for North Korea, pp. 373-374.

43. Samsonov, op. cit., pp. 7-10; Ch'a Byŏn-lon, "North Korea's Trade and Its Characteristics," Kukje munje (Journal of International Studies), Seoul, October 1972, p. 24.

44. Ibid., p. 10.

45. Yuan-dollar rate of 2.462 effective during 1953-54 was used, based on Shanghai telegraphic transfer rates compiled from newspaper daily quotations by Wu Yuan-li in his An Economic Survey of Communist China (New York: Bookman Associates, 1956), p. 489.

46. Information on the treaty is based on Kim Il-song sŏnjip, Vol. 4, pp. 65-68; Chugoku seiji keizai soran, 1962, p. 738. See Jen-min jih-pao (People's Daily), Peking, November 21 and 24, 1954, for reports of grant.

47. Han Kyung, "Chinese People's Economic and Technical Assistance in the Reconstruction and Development of Post-War People's Economy," Kyŏngje kŏnsŏl (Economic Construction), October 1954, pp. 11-23.

48. CCY, 1961, pp. 136-137; Chugoku seiji keizai soran, 1964, p. 683.

49. Yoon T. Kuark, "North Korea's Industrial Development During the Post-War Period," The China Quarterly, April-June 1963, p. 61.

50. Based on various issues of Korea News; Foreign Trade, No. 2, 1966, p. 3; The People's Korea, January 15, 1969, p. 3 (for the 1969 agreement); Yu Wan-sik, op. cit., p. 143.

51. FEER (Far Eastern Economic Review) 1965 Yearbook, p. 233; Korea News, February 10, 1962, p. 13.

52. Trade returns of Cuba on file at the U.S. Department of Commerce.

53. Korea News, No. 34, 1963, pp. 11-12.

54. _Korea News_, various issues.

55. _Foreign Trade_, No. 1, 1967, p. 4.

56. _The 1961 North Korean Yearbook_, p. 114.

57. This is surmised from the fact that such information is excluded in the U.N. trade yearbook. It includes the trade volume with principal partners only.

58. United Nations, Economic Commission for Europe, _Bulletin of Statistics on World Trade in Engineering Products_, various issues.

59. R. A. Pense, "The Mineral Industry of North Korea," a preprint of the U.S. Department of the Interior, _Minerals Yearbook_, 1968, as quoted in Lee Joong-Koon, _op. cit._, p. 22.

60. According to a source, North Korean exports to Poland during 1966 and 1967 included 87,000 and 24,000 tons, respectively, of magnesite; 10,621 and 7,009 tons of talc; 1,390 and 5,540 tons of fluorspar; and 207 and 927 tons of lead metal. See _Idem_.

61. Foreign Broadcast Information Service (FBIS), _Pyŏngyang Radio Broadcast_, March 10, 1962.

62. Lee Joong-Koon, _op. cit._, p. 42.

63. _Idem_.

64. For details concerning history and politics of economic relations between North Korea and Japan, see Kiwon Chung, "Japanese-North Korean Relations Today," _Asian Survey_, April 1964, pp. 788-803; Yu Wan-sik, _op. cit._, pp. 150-153; and _Nitcho boekino tebiki_, pp. 17-73.

65. Miyahara Masahiro, "Japan-North Korea Trade, Past and Present," _Chosen kenkyu_ (Korean Studies), August 1964, Tokyo, pp. 5-13; _Nitcho boekino tebiki_, pp. 511-540.

66. For 1956-57, see _FEER_, September 4, 1958, p. 320. Data for 1958 are missing. For 1959, see _FEER_, March 20, 1960, p. 668. Information for 1960-61 is based on data on file at the U.S. Department of Commerce.

67. Lee Joong-Koon, _op. cit._, pp. 40-42.

68. See, in this connection, Kim yu-gap, "A Study of the Foreign Policy of North Korea Toward Southeast Asia," _The Journal of Asiatic Studies_, September 1967, pp. 55-84.

69. _Area Handbook for North Korea_, p. 369.

70. Janos Horvath, "Grant Elements in Intra-Bloc Aid Programs," _The ASTE_ (Association for the Study of Soviet-Type Economies) _Bulletin_, Fall 1971, pp. 11-15.

71. Lee Joong-Koon, _op. cit._, pp. 43-47.

72. Clearly, Mrs. Joan Robinson was either not aware or overly enthusiastic when she wrote after her short visit to North Korea in October 1964 that:
    > Cut off from its rice bowl in the South, the North has built up its agriculture by irrigation and improved farming methods. It now produces 5 million tons of grain (58 percent rice) which feeds the population of 12 million comfortably and permits a small export of surplus.
    See J. Robinson, _op. cit._, p. 542.

73. See, for interesting discussion of this subject, Lee Chong-Sik, "Notes on North Korean Import and Export of Cereals," Journal of Korean Affairs, January 1972, pp. 54-56.

74. As an expression of this policy, North Korea has refused to join the communist bloc-wide network of specialization and trade within the framework of CMEA (Council for Mutual Economic Assistance) which she has been attending as an observer since 1957.

75. Kim Tae-su, "North Korea's Line of Self-Reliance Viewed from the Point of Her External Policy," Kukje munje (Journal of International Studies), Seoul, May 1971, pp. 29-30.

5: An Overall Evaluation
of the North Korean Economy

1. For an account of the Soviet methodology involved in national income computation, see M. C. Kaser, "Estimating the Soviet National Income," Economic Journal, March 1957, pp. 83-101.

2. O Hyŏn-sang, op. cit., p. 289; Chŏng Tae-sik, op. cit., p. 287.

3. Alec Nove, op. cit., p. 274.

4. Speech made at the twentieth anniversary meeting of the founding of the DPRK on September 7, 1968, Nodong sinmun, September 8, 1968, pp. 2-5.

5. See Joseph S. Chung, "North Korea's Seven Year Plan (1961-70): Economic Performance and Reforms," Asian Survey, June 1972, pp. 528-529.

6. See, for a pioneering and innovative work, Pong S. Lee, "An Estimate of North Korea's National Income," Asian Survey, June 1972, pp. 518-526.

7. Nodong sinmun, November 10, 1970.

8. Saikinno chosenno kyodo nojo, p. 10.

9. Joan Robinson, op. cit., p. 541.

10. Parts of this section are drawn from Joseph S. Chung, "North Korea's Seven Year Plan: Economic Performance and Reforms," pp. 539-545.

11. For North Korea's official attitude toward the peasant markets, see Kim Il-song, "On Some Theoretical Problems of Socialistic Economy," The People's Korea, March 26, 1969; Kŭlloja, No. 7, 1969, pp. 44-50.

12. Area Handbook for North Korea, pp. 361-363.

13. The People's Korea, April 29, 1970.

14. Nodong sinmun, September 1, 1970.

15. See, for political implications of the Kun's role, The Journal of Asian Studies, February 1970.

16. See, for an illuminating article on this subject, Kim Il-Pyong, "The Mobilization System in North Korean Politics," Journal of Korean Affairs, April 1972, pp. 3-15.

17. Nodong sinmun, November 3, 1970.

18. Ryu Hun, _Study of North Korea_ (Seoul: Research Institute of Internal and External Affairs, 1968), p. 236.

19. _Ibid._, pp. 236-237; _Pukhan ch'onggam_, 1945-68, p. 315; _Nodong sinmun_, November 3, 1970.

20. _Nodong sinmun_, November 3, 1970.

21. _Idem._

22. See, for example, Harry G. Shaffer, "Economic Reforms in the Soviet Union and East Europe: A Comparative Study," pp. 18-23.

23. See, for example, "Those Economic Reforms Behind the Iron Curtain: An Interview with Professors Abram Bergson, John Montiac, and Arthur Smithies," _Challenge_, May-June 1967, pp. 18-23.

24. Quotation from Joseph S. Chung, "North Korea's Seven Year Plan...," p. 545.

25. Ratios of state investment to national income in each period. For the period 1961-67, the investment figure used is the average annual amount for 1961-69 since such a figure is lacking for 1961-67. Because of an upward trend in state investment over time, the rate of investment for 1961-67 based on this figure should show some inflation.

26. _Nodong sinmun_, April 30, 1972.

27. This paragraph including the quotation is based on Yang Key P. and Chee Chang-Boh, "North Korean Educational System: 1945 to Present," _North Korea Today_, ed. Robert A. Scalapino (New York: Frederick A. Praeger, 1963), pp. 125-140.

28. Joan Robinson, _op. cit._, p. 547.

29. Yoon T. Kuark, "North Korea's Industrial Development During the Post-War Period," _The China Quarterly_, April-June 1963, pp. 62-63.

Appendix B

1. Based on "The System of Computation and Statistics of the People's Economy," _Kongŏp kiŏpso kyŏngje_ (Economics of Industrial Enterprises) (Pyŏngyang: State Publishing House, 1957), pp. 54-85.

2. Taken from the title of an article by Hwang, Do-yun, _Kyŏngje kŏnsŏl_ (Economic Construction), Pyŏngyang, June 1955, pp. 13-23.

3. See, in this connection, Gregory Grossman, "Soviet Concern with Reliability," _The Soviet Economy_, ed. Harry G. Shaffer (New York: Appleton-Century-Crofts, 1963), pp. 10-15.

4. See Lynn Turgeon, _The Contrasting Economies_ (Boston: Allyn and Bacon, Inc., 1963), pp. 27-28; also Turgeon's article "On the Reliability of Soviet Statistics," _The Review of Economics and Statistics_, February 1952, pp. 75-76; Alexander Eckstein, "Economics and the Study of Mainland China's Development," _The American Economist_, V, November 1961, p. 2; and Li, Choh-ming, _Economic Development of Communist China_ (Berkeley and Los Angeles: University of California Press, 1959), p. 3.

5. Most Soviet experts believe this to be the case for Russian figures. See, for example, Naum Jasny, _Essays on the Soviet Economy_ (New York: Frederick A. Praeger, 1962), p. 17; Alec Nove, _The Soviet Economy_ (New York: Frederick A. Praeger, 1965), pp. 323-330; Edward Ames, _Soviet Economic Processes_ (Homewood, Illinois: Richard Irwin, Inc., 1965), pp. 10-12.

6. It was reported, for instance, that in 1954 a certain marine processing enterprise under the supervision of the Ministry of Marine Affairs included in its output figure twice the value of the semifinished products amounting to 55 million won (old currency). Also, the Komusan Cement Factory falsified its report on output in 1954 by 4,000 tons. Hwang, Do-yun, _op. cit._, pp. 13-23.

7. Kim Il, "Concerning the Six Year Plan (1971-76) for the Development of the People's Economy of the DPRK," _Nodong sinmun_, November 10, 1970.

8. _Ibid._

9. See chapter 3 of this book.

10. See chapter 2 of this book.

11. See, for an analysis of upward bias in North Korea's industrial output, Pong S. Lee, "Overstatement of North Korean Industrial Growth, 1946-63," _Journal of Korean Affairs_, Silver Springs, Maryland, July 1971, pp. 3-14.

12. Ta-chung Liu and Yeh, _The Economy of the Chinese Mainland_ (Princeton, New Jersey: Princeton University Press, 1965), p. 58. Professor Yuan-li Wu also confirms this fact.

13. U.S. Department of State, Bureau of Intelligence and Research, _The Role of Agriculture in North Korea's Development_, Washington, D.C.: Research Memorandum RSB-105, June 21, 1962, pp. 9-11.

14. See Kim Il-song, "Summary Report of the Work of the Central Committee to the Fifth Congress of the Workers' Party of Korea," _Nodong sinmun_, November 3, 1970.

15. Kim Il, "Concerning Current Tasks for the Socialist Economic Construction," _Nodong sinmun_, October 11, 1966.

16. Pong S. Lee, _op. cit._; Glenn D. Paige and Dong Jun Lee, "The Post-War Politics of Communist Korea," in Robert A. Scalapino [ed.], _North Korea Today_ (New York: Frederick A. Praeger, 1963), pp. 20-23; _Pukhan ch'onggam, 1945-68_ (General Survey of North Korea) (Seoul: Research Institute of Communist Bloc, 1968), pp. 319-321.

17. Yoon T. Kuark, "Economic Development Contrast Between South and North Korea," in Joseph S. Chung, _Patterns of Economic Development: Korea_, p. 194.

Bibliography

Korean-language Sources

Books, Monographs, and Yearbooks

Bank of Korea. Chosŏn kyŏngje yŏnbo, 1948 (Annual Economic Review of Korea, 1948). Seoul: Bank of Korea, 1948.

_____. Kyŏngje yŏnggam, 1949 (Economic Yearbook, 1949). Seoul: Bank of Korea, 1949.

Charyŏk kaengsaeng kwa charipchŏk minjok kyŏngje ŭi kŏnsŏl ŭn uri hyŏngmyŏng sŭngni ŭi tambo (Self-revival and the Construction of the Self-supporting Economy Are the Security for the Victory of Our Revolution). Pyŏngyang: Korean Workers' Party Publishing House, 1963.

Cho, Chae-sŏn. Chosŏn minjujuŭi inmin konghwaguk sahoe kyŏngje chedo (Social and Economic System of the People's Republic of Korea). Pyŏngyang: Korean Workers' Party Publishing House, 1958.

_____. Kwadogi ŭi issŏsŏ ŭi chosŏn nodongdang ŭi kyŏngje chŏngchaek (Economic Policy of the Korean Workers' Party in the Period of Transition). Pyŏngyang: Korean Workers' Party Publishing House, 1958.

Ch'ŏllima chagŏppan undong (Ch'ŏllima Work-team Movement). Pyŏngyang: Trade Union Publishing House, 1960.

Chŏn, Yong-sik. Chŏnhu uri dang kyŏngje kŏnsŏl ŭi kibon nosŏn (Our Party's Basic Lines of Economic Construction in the Post-war Period). Pyŏngyang: Korean Workers' Party Publishing House, 1961.

Chŏng, Rae-hwang. Nongŏp hyŏptong chohap esŏ sahoejuŭi wŏnch'ik ŭn ŏtŏkye silhyŏn toenŭnka (How Can Collective Farms Perform Effectively Under the Socialistic System?). Pyŏngyang: Korean Workers' Party Publishing House, 1959.

Chŏng, T'ai-sik. Chŏngch'i kyŏngjehak dokbon: Sahoejuŭi pyŏn (Primer on Political Economy: Socialism). Pyŏngyang: Korean Workers' Party Publishing House, 1960.

Chŏnguk chibang sanŏp mit saengsan hyŏptong chohap yŏlsŏngja taehoe munhŏnjip (Documents of the Nationwide Local Industries and Producers Cooperatives Enthusiasts' Meeting). Pyŏngyang: Korean Workers' Party Publishing House, 1959.

Chosŏn chungang yŏngam [CCY] (Korean Central Yearbook). Various annual issues. Pyŏngyang: Korean Central News Agency.

Chu, Ch'ang-nyŏng. Sahoejuŭi ha esŏ kyehoekchŏk palchŏn pŏpch'ik (Principles of Planned Development of People's Economy Under the Socialistic System). Pyŏngyang: Korean Workers' Party Publishing House, 1960.

DPRK, Academy of Science, Institute of Economic and Legal Research. Chibang sanŏp palchŏn esŏ hoekkijŏk chŏnbyŏn ŭl iruk'in chosŏn nodongdang chungang wiwŏnhoe 6-wŏl chŏnwŏn hoeŭi nonmunjip (Collection of Theses from the June Plenary Conference of the Central Committee of the Korean Workers' Party Which Made an Epoch-making Turning Point for the Development of Our Local Industry). Pyŏngyang: Academy of Science Printing Office, 1959.

_____. Haebanghu uri nara ŭi inmin kyŏngje palchŏn (Development of the People's Economy Since the Liberation). Pyŏngyang: Academy of Science Printing Office, 1960.

_____. 8.15 haebang 15 chunyŏn kinyŏm kyŏngje nonmunjip (Economic Essays Commemorating the 15th Anniversary of the 8.15 Liberation). Pyŏngyang: Academy of Science Printing Office, 1960.

_____. Sahoejuŭi kŏnsŏl esŏ kodeahan chŏnjin ŭl iruk'in chosŏn nodongdang chungang wiwŏnhoe 9-wŏl chŏnwŏn hoeŭi nonmunjip (Collection of Theses from the September Plenary Meeting of the Central Committee of the Korean Workers' Party Which Had Brought Spectacular Development for the Construction of Socialism). Pyŏngyang: Academy of Science Printing Office, 1958.

_____. Uri nara esŏ ŭi sahoejuŭi kŏnsŏl ŭi taegojo (The Climax of Socialist Construction in Our Country). Pyŏngyang: Academy of Science Printing Office, 1959.

_____. Uri nara inmin kyŏngje esŏ saengsannyŏk kwa saengsan kwangye ŭi hosang chagyong (Inter-relationship Between the Productivity and the Relations of Production in the People's Economy of Our Country). Pyŏngyang: Academy of Science Printing Office, 1960.

DPRK, State Planning Commission, Central Statistical Bureau. Chosŏn minjujuŭi inmin konghwaguk inmin kyŏngje palchŏn t'onggyejip, 1946-60 (Statistical Returns of the Development of the People's Economy of the Democratic People's Republic of Korea, 1946-60). Pyŏngyang: State Publishing House, 1961.

Hong, Tal-sŏn. Uri nara nongch'on kyŏngni pumun esŏ mulchilchŏk kansim ŭi wŏnch'ik ŭi ch'angjojŏk chagyong (Creative Application of the Principle of Material Incentives in the Field of Agricultural Economy in Our Country). Pyŏngyang: Academy of Science Printing Office, 1963.

Kibon kŏnsŏl saŏp balchŏnŭl wihan uri dang ŭi chŏngchaek (Our Party's Policy for the Development of the Basic Construction Work). Pyŏngyang: Korean Workers' Party Publishing House, 1961.

Kim, Ch'ang-man. Kisul injae yangsŏng saŏp ŭl kaesŏn kanghwahal te taehayŏ (On the Question of Improving and Strengthening the Technical Training Programs). Pyŏngyang: Korean Workers' Party Publishing House, 1960.

Kim, Ch'ang-sun. Pukhan siponyŏn sa (The Fifteen-year History of North Korea). Seoul: Chimungak, 1961.

Kim, Chun-jŏm. Inmin ŭi mulchil munhwa saenghwal hyangsang ŭl wihan uri dang ŭi chŏngchaek—8.15 haebang 15 chunyŏn kinyŏm (Our Party's Policy for the Development of People's Material Life: the 15th Anniversary of National Independence Day). Pyŏngyang: Korean Workers' Party Publishing House, 1960.

Kim, Ha-myŏng. Chosŏn kyŏngje chiri: sang (Economic Geography of Korea: Vol. 1).
Pyŏngyang: State Publishing House, 1958.

Kim, Han-ju. Chosŏn minjujuŭi inmin konghwaguk esŏ ŭi nongŏp hyŏptong hwa undong
ŭi sŭngni (Victory of the Agricultural Cooperatization Movement in the Democratic People's Republic of Korea). Pyŏngyang: Korean Workers' Party Publishing House, 1959.

Kim, Hyo-sun. Inmin chŏngkwŏn kanghwa wa inmin kyŏngje puhŭng palchŏn ŭl wihan
chosŏn inmin ŭi t'ujaeng (1945-48) (Struggle of the Korean People for the
Strengthening of the People's Political Power and the Reconstruction of
People's Economy). Pyŏngyang: Korean Workers' Party Publishing House, 1957.

Kim, Il. Inmin kyŏngje modŭn pumun esŏ kisul hyŏksin undong ŭl chŏnmyŏnjŏk ŭro
chŏn'gae halte taehayŏ (On the All-out Development for Technical Renovation
in All Aspects of the People's Economy). Pyŏngyang: Korean Workers' Party
Publishing House, 1960.

_____. Kongŏp saengsanp'um ŭi chil ŭl chego halte taehayŏ (On the Question of
Improving the Quality of Industrial Products). Pyŏngyang: Korean Workers'
Party Publishing House, 1959.

_____. Nongch'on kyŏngni wa kŭpsokhan pokku palchŏn ŭl wihan nodongdang ŭi
kŭmhu t'ujaeng taech'aek e kwan hayŏ (On the Future Struggling Measures of
the Korean Workers' Party for Rapid Reconstruction and Development in Rural
Management). Pyŏngyang: Korean Workers' Party Publishing House, 1954.

Kim, Il-song. Chosŏn inmin ŭi minchokchŏk myŏngjŭl 8.15 hebang 15 junyŏn
kyŏngchuk taehoeessŏ han boko (Report at the Celebration Meeting of the Fifteenth Anniversary of the August Fifteenth Liberation, Korean People's
National Holiday). Pyŏngyang: Korean Workers' Party Publishing House, 1960.

_____. Kim Il-song sŏnjip (Selected Works of Kim Il-song). Vol. 4. Pyŏng-
yang: Korean Workers' Party Publishing House, 1960.

_____. Kisul hyŏngmyŏng ui sŏngkwajŏk suhaeng ŭl wihayŏ (For Successful
Achievement of the Technical Revolution). Pyŏngyang: Korean Workers' Party
Publishing House, 1961.

_____. Sahoejuŭijŏk nongch'on kyŏngni ŭi chŏnghwakhan unyong ŭl wihayŏ (For
the Accurate Operation of Socialistic Agricultural Management). Pyŏngyang:
Korean Workers' Party Publishing House, 1960.

_____. Uri nara sahoejuŭi nongch'on munje e kwanhan t'eje (Theses on the
Socialistic Agricultural Problems in Our Country). Pyŏngyang: Korean Workers' Party Publishing House, 1964.

Kim, Myŏng-san. Chŏngch'i kyŏngjehak kaeyo (The Outline of Political Economy).
Pyŏngyang: State Publishing House, 1963.

Kim, Sang-hak. Uri nara kongŏp palchŏn esŏ ŭi saengsannyŏk paech'i e taehayŏ
(Concerning the Allocation of the Productivity in the Development of Our
Country's Industry). Pyŏngyang: Academy of Science Printing Office, 1956.

Kim, Se-hwal. Uri nara hwahak kongŏp ŭi palchŏn chŏnmang (Outlook for the Development of the Chemical Industry in Our Country). Pyŏngyang: Korean Workers'
Party Publishing House, 1959.

Kim, Song-jin. Uri nara esŏ ŭi nongch'on munje haegyŏl ŭi yŏksajŏk kyŏnghŏm
(Historical Experience in the Solution of Agricultural Problems in Our Country). Pyŏngyang: Korean Workers' Party Publishing House, 1965.

Konghwaguk ch'anggŏn 10-chunyŏn ŭl majihanŭn nongch'on kyŏngni (Agricultural Management on the Occasion of the Tenth Anniversary of the Founding of the Republic). Pyŏngyang: National Agricultural Publishing House, 1958.

Kyŏngje sangsik: kongŏp, nongŏp, sangŏp (Commonsense of Economics: Industry,
Agriculture and Commerce). Pyŏngyang: Korean Workers' Party Publishing
House, 1960.

O, Hyŏn-sang. Kyŏngje chisik (Economic Knowledge). Pyŏngyang: State Publishing
House, 1957.

Pak, Chu-ryŏng. Inminŭi pongni hyangsangŭl wihan uri nara kyŏngje chŏngch'aek
(Economic Policy of our Country to Raise the Welfare of the People). Pyŏngyang: State Publishing House, 1958.

Pukhan ch'onggam, 1945-68 (General Survey of North Korea, 1945-68). Seoul: Institute for Communist Bloc Affairs, 1968.

Republic of Korea, Ministry of Information. Pukhan yoram, 1968 (Handbook of North
Korea, 1968). Seoul: Ministry of Information, 1968.

Sahoejuŭi ha esŏ ŭi inmin kyŏngje ŭi kyehoekchŏk kyunhyŏngjŏk palchŏn pŏpch'ik
(Principle of Planned and Balanced Development of the People's Economy Under
Socialism). Pyŏngyang: Korean Workers' Party Publishing House, 1960.

Sahoejuŭi nongch'on kyŏngni esŏ kiŏpchŏk pangbŏb ŭi ch'angjojŏk chagyong (Creative
Application of Industrial Methods in the Socialistic Agricultural Management).
Pyŏngyang: Academy of Social Science Printing Office, 1964.

Sŏ, Chang-hun. Konghwaguk inmin kyŏngje palchŏn kyehoek kwa inmin saenghwal
hyangsangŭi kwanghwalhan chŏnmang (Broad Prospects for the Development Plans
of the People's Economy and the Improvement of the People's Livelihood in Our
Republic). Pyŏngyang: State Publishing House, 1954.

Sŏ, Kŭm-ja. Charyŏk kaengsaeng kwa charipchŏk minjok kyŏngje (Self-reliance and
Independent National Economy). Pyŏngyang: Korean Workers' Party Publishing
House, 1963.

Sŏ, Nam-wŏn. Pukhan ui kyŏngje chŏngchaek kwa sengsan kwanri (North Korea's Economic Policy and Production Control). Seoul: Asiatic Research Institute,
Korea University, 1966.

Sŭngnihan taean ŭi kyŏnghom (The Successful Experiences of the Taean Method).
Pyŏngyang: Korean Workers' Party Publishing House, 1963.

Tongnip ch'aesanje wa suiksŏng wŏnka wa kagyŏk (Independent Accounting System,
Profits, Costs and Prices). Pyŏngyang: Korean Workers' Party Publishing
House, 1960.

Yi, Chong-pal. Nongŏp hyŏndong chohap ŭi chŏngch'i kyŏngjechŏk kongkohwarŭl wihan
myŏtkachi munje (Several Problems Concerning the Political and Economic Consolidation of Agricultural Cooperatives). Pyŏngyang: Korean Workers' Party
Publishing House, 1960.

Yi, Myŏng-sŏ., Chi, Ŭn-sŏp., and Kim, Hyŏk-chin. Uri nara esŏ ŭi sahoejuŭi kŏnsŏl
ŭi tae kojo (Greater Progress in the Socialist Construction of Our Country).
Pyŏngyang: Academy of Science Printing Office, 1959.

Articles from Periodicals

"Analysis of Growth of Industrial Production." Kyŏngje chisik (Economic Knowl-
    edge) (Pyŏngyang), February 1963, 39-40.

Ch'ae, Hŭi-jŏng. "Economic Policy of the Korean Labor Party for the Construc-
    tion of Socialism in the Northern Part of the Republic." Kyŏngje kŏnsŏl
    (Economic Construction) (Pyŏngyang), November 1956, 2-21.

Cho, Wong-hong. "What Significance Does the Quality Index Have in Enterprise
    Activities?" Kŭlloja (Workers) (Pyŏngyang), July 20, 1965, 44-47.

Chŏng, Byŏng-sik. "The Growth of National Income and the Improvement of Living
    Conditions in North Korea." Kyŏngje yŏnku (Economic Research) (Pyŏngyang),
    September 1963, 16-27.

"Classification of Industries and the Place of the Extracting Industry." Kyŏngje
    chisik, December 1962, 38-39.

"Concerning the First Five-Year Plan (1957-1961) for the Development of People's
    Economy in the Democratic People's Republic of Korea." Kyŏngje kŏnsŏl,
    March 1958, 2-11.

"Data on Economic Development in 1962." Kyŏngje chisik, February 1963, 44-48.

"Development of People's Economy of Our Country in 1961." Kyŏngje chisik,
    February 1962, 41-42.

DPRK, State Planning Commission, Central Statistical Bureau. "Report Concerning
    the Summary Performance in the Reconstruction and Development of the
    People's Economy of the DPRK During the Three-year Period of 1954-56."
    Kyŏngje kŏnsŏl, March 1957, 81-90.

_____. "Report of the Central Statistical Bureau of the State Planning Com-
    mission Concerning the Development of People's Economy and Culture in the
    DPRK During 1949-1955." Kyŏngje kŏnsŏl, May 1956, 132-145.

_____. "Report of the Central Statistical Bureau of the State Planning Com-
    mission Concerning the Fulfillment of the 1958 Development Plans in the
    People's Economy of the DPRK." Kyŏngje kŏnsŏl, February 1959, 65-71.

Han, Kyŏng. "Chinese People's Economic and Technical Assistance in the Recon-
    struction and Development of the Post-war People's Economy." Kyŏngje kŏnsŏl,
    October 1954, 11-23.

Han, Ung-chon. "People's Economy in Our Country on the Road to Development."
    Kyŏngje kŏnsŏl, November 1957, 19-30.

Hwang, Do-yun. "Strict Observance of Regulations on Computation and Statistics
    Is the Necessary Condition for the Development of People's Economy."
    Kyŏngje kŏnsŏl, June 1955, 13-23.

Kim, Chong-ŭi. "Correct Evaluation and Computation of Work-days in Agricultural
    Cooperatives." Kyŏngje kŏnsŏl, June 1956, 44-55.

Kim, T'aek-hyŏn. "The Creation of the Kun Cooperative Farm Management Committee
    and Further Development of the Alliance of Workers and Peasants." Kŭlloja,
    July 1963, 24-30.

Kim, Tu-chil. "Qualitative and Quantitative Indices in Factory Operation."
    Kŭlloja, July 1963, 46-48.

Kim, Wŏn-sam. "A Balanced Improvement in the Lives of Workers, Office Workers and Farmers." Kyŏngje yŏnku, March 1965, 15-22.

"Law Concerning the First Five-Year Plan (1957-1961) for the Development of People's Economy in the DPRK." Kyŏngje kŏnsŏl, July 1958, 11-33.

"Newly Established Material Incentive Measures to Increase the Production of Export Goods." Chaejŏng kŭmyung (Finance and Banking) (Pyŏngyang), February 1961, 37-39.

O, Paek-ryong. "Industrial Development of Our Country During 1948-1958." Kyŏngje kŏnsŏl, September 1958, 24-29.

"Our Country's Cooperative Management." Kyŏngje kŏnsŏl, February 1958, 65.

Pak, Yong-sŏng. "Formation of a Firm Foundation of Local Industry and Its New Stage of Development." Kŭlloja, September 1962, 16-23.

Ro, Hang-mok. "Several Problems Concerning the Labor Formation in Agricultural Cooperatives." Kyŏngje kŏnsŏl, April 1958, 21-26.

Shin, Nak-sam. "State Control over Grain Processing." Sangŏp (Commerce) (Pyŏngyang), April 1963, 9-11.

"Ten-Year Industrial Development in Our Country." Kyŏngje kŏnsŏl, August 1955, 32-52.

Yi, Chu-yŏn. "Improvement in People's Material and Cultural Life in the Northern Section During the Ten Years." Kyŏngje kŏnsŏl, August 1955, 74-90.

Yi, Ki-hong. "What Is the Independent Economic Accounting System?" Kyŏngje kŏnsŏl, February 1960, 36-39.

Yi, Sŏk-nok. "The Superiority and Vitality of the New System of Guidance in Agriculture." Kŭlloja, December 1962, 26-38.

Yu, Kwan-chil. "Several Problems in the Guidance of the Agricultural Cooperative Management Committee by the Kun Party Committees." Kŭlloja, January 3, 1963, 27-31.

Articles and Special Reports from Newspapers

Ahn, Yong-man. "The Independent Accounting System." Nodong sinmun (Workers' Daily) (Pyŏngyang), July 9, 1966.

Chŏn, Yong-sik. "Party's Agricultural Policy." Nodong sinmun, March 13, 1964.

Chu, Chang-yong. "Significance of Establishing a Local Industrial Base in Building Socialism in Our Country." Nodong sinmun, June 7, 1963.

DPRK, Agricultural Commission. "Accurate Implementation of Work for the Fiscal 1962 Settlement of Accounts and Distribution." Nongmin sinmun (Farmers' Newspaper) (Pyŏngyang), November 27, 1962.

Hong, Tal-sŏn. "The Superiority of the Kun Cooperative Farm Management Committee." Nodong sinmun, December 25, 1962.

Kim, Ha-kwang and Hong, Su-il. "Enormous Superiority of Integrated National Planning System." Minju chosŏn (Democratic Korea) (Pyŏngyang), March 18, 1965.

Kim, Il. "Concerning Current Tasks for the Socialist Economic Construction." _Nodong sinmun_, October 11, 1966.

_____. "On the Six Year Plan (1971-1976) for Development of the National Economy of the DPRK." _Nodong sinmun_, November 10, 1971.

Kim, Il-song. "Summary Report of the Work of the Central Committee to the Fifth Congress of the Workers' Party of Korea." _Nodong sinmun_, November 3, 1971.

"Strengthening Enterprise-type Guidance Over Cooperative Farm Management." _Nodong sinmun_, June 9, 1965.

"Why Try to Smear Achievements of Pyongyang Economic Seminar?" _Nodong sinmun_, September 7, 1964.

Yi, Il-yong. "A Few Problems Presented by the 1962 Annual Final Distribution Task in the Cooperative Farms." _Minju chosŏn_, November 17, 1962.

Yi, Kun-hwan. "The Internal Accounting System Is an Important Form of Organizing and Mobilizing the Masses for the Control of Enterprises." _Nodong sinmun_, September 15, 1965.

Yi, Yang-chon. "Mechanization of Farming is Central Task of Agricultural Management." _Minju chosŏn_, November 15, 1962.

Japanese-language Sources

Chosen jinmin keizai keikaku ni tsuite (On Korean People's Economic Plan). Osaka: Zai nichi chosen shizen kagakusha kyokai, 1954.

Chosen minshushugi jinmin kyowakoku kokumin keizai hatten tokeishu, 1946-1963 (Statistical Summary of the Development of the People's Economy in the DPRK, 1946-63). Tokyo: Chosen kenkyusho, 1965.

Chosen minshushugi jinmin kyowakokuno suisangyo (Marine Industry of the DPRK). Tokyo: Nihon chosen kenkyusho, 1967.

"Concerning the Organization of the Kun Agricultural Cooperative Management Committee in North Korea." _Chosen kenkyu geppo_ (Monthly Review of Korean Studies) (Tokyo), December 1962, 67-70.

DPRK, Academy of Science, Institute of Economic and Legal Research. _Chosenni okeru shakaishugino kiso kensetsu_ (Construction of the Foundation of Socialism in Korea). Tokyo: New Japan Publishing House, 1962.

DPRK, State Planning Commission, Central Statistical Bureau. "Summary of the Plan Fulfillment of the People's Economy of the DPRK in the First Half of 1962." _Chosen shiryo_ (Data on Korea) (Tokyo), August 1962, 43-55.

Hama, Takeo. "North Korea's Industry and Agriculture." _Dairiku mondai_ (Continental Affairs) (Tokyo), May 1965, 55-56.

Hiroshi, Sakurai. "The Mechanization of North Korean Agriculture." _Ajia keizai_ (Asian Economy) (Tokyo), November 1965, 1-35, 64-75.

Hocho kishadan. _Kita chosenno kiroku_ (The Record of North Korea). Tokyo: Shindoku shosha, 1960.

Hwang, To-hyŏng. Sengo ni okeru waga kuni no keizai (Post-war Economy of Our Country). Pyŏngyang: Foreign Languages Publishing House, 1957.

Japan, Ministry of Foreign Affairs. Chosen benran (Handbook of Korea). Tokyo: Japan Institute of International Affairs, 1961.

"Japan-Korea Trade in the First Half of 1962." Nitcho boeki (Japan-Korea Trade) (Tokyo), September 1962, 11-19.

Kajimura, Hideki. "A Note on the Collectivization Movement (1953-58) in North Korea." Chosen gakuho (Journal of Korean Studies) (Tokyo), April 1966, 279-321.

Kankoku keizai gaikan (General Survey of the Korean Economy). Tokyo: Japan Ministry of Foreign Affairs, 1961.

Kim, Sam-gyu. Konnichi no chosen (Korea Today). Tokyo: Kawade shobo, 1956.

Kimura, Yasuji. Chosen nomin kaihoshi (History of the Liberation of Korean Peasants). Yokosuka, Japan: Cultural Korea Co., 1947.

Kita chosen ni okeru tochi kaikaku (Land Reform in North Korea). Tokyo: Chosen keizai kenkyusho, 1948.

Kita chosen no keizai 1949-50 nen no kensetsu jokyo (The State of Development of the North Korean Economy During 1949-50). Tokyo: Sekai keizai kenkyusho, 1950.

Korean Affairs Institute. Chosen no keizai (The Korean Economy). Tokyo: Oriental Economist Press, 1956.

Miya, Masahiro. "North and South Korean Economy Under Stress." Ekonomisuto (Economist) (Tokyo), February 13, 1968, 38-41.

Miyahara, Masahiro. "Japan-North Korea Trade, Past and Present." Chosen kenkyu (Korean Studies) (Tokyo), August 1964, 5-13.

Namboku bundan go no chosen keizai—Sono antei kozo kenkyu eno shoronteki kosatsu (The Korean Economy after the South-North Division: An Introductory Inquiry into the Study of Stability and Structure). Tokyo: Nihon keizai kenkyujo, 1951.

Namboku chosenno genjo (Current Conditions of South and North Korea), vol. 2. Tokyo: Asahi Newspaper Research Department, 1962.

Nitcho boekino tebiki (Handbook of Japan-North Korea Trade). Tokyo: Japan-North Korea Trade Association, 1970.

Saiko jinmin kaigi daiichiji kaigi gijiroku (Documents of the First Congress of the Supreme People's Assembly). Tokyo: Korean Affairs Institute, 1949(?).

Sobieto nempo, 1958 (Soviet Annual). Tokyo: Nikkan rodo tsushinsha, 1958. Contains information on Soviet-North Korean relations. Successor to Sobieto nenkan, 1954-55.

Terao, Goro. Chosen sono kita to minami (Korea: North and South). Tokyo: New Japan Publishing House, 1963.

_____. 38 dosen no kita (North of the 38th Parallel). Tokyo: New Japan Publishing House, 1963.

Toitsu chosen nenkan, 1964 (One Korea Yearbook, 1964). Tokyo: Toitsu chosen shimbunsha, 1964.

Toitsu chosen nenkan, 1967-68 (One Korea Yearbook, 1967-68). Tokyo: Toitsu chosen shimbunsha, 1967.

Yamana, Mikio. Chosen satokufu shuseino kiroku (Record of the Final Period of the Government-General of Korea). Tokyo: Yuho kyokai, 1956.

English-language Sources

Books, Monographs, and Yearbooks

Agricultural Cooperativization in D.P.R.K. Pyŏngyang: Foreign Languages Publishing House, 1958.

Chung, Joseph S. [ed.]. Patterns of Economic Development: Korea. Kalamazoo, Michigan: Western Michigan University and Korea Research and Publications, Inc., 1966.

Democratic People's Republic of Korea. Pyŏngyang: Foreign Languages Publishing House, 1958.

Documents and Materials of the Third Congress of the Workers' Party of Korea, April 23-29, 1956. Pyŏngyang: Foreign Languages Publishing House, 1956.

Documents of the Fourth Congress of the Workers' Party of Korea. Pyŏngyang: Foreign Languages Publishing House, 1961.

Documents of the National Congress of Agricultural Cooperatives. Pyŏngyang: Foreign Languages Publishing House, 1959.

DPRK, State Planning Commission, Central Statistical Bureau. Statistical Returns of National Economy of the DPRK (1946-1960). Pyŏngyang: Foreign Languages Publishing House, 1961.

Facts About Korea. Pyŏngyang: Foreign Languages Publishing House, 1961.

Grajdanev, Andrew J. Modern Korea. New York: Institute of Pacific Relations, 1944.

Joint Publications Research Service (JPRS). Compilation of Statistics on the Development of the People's Economy of the Korean Democratic People's Republic, 1946-1960. Washington, D.C.: Joint Publications Research Service, no. 18763, 1963.

_____. Development of the National Economy and Culture of the People's Democratic Republic of Korea (1946-59). (English translation of the Russian-language material of the same title). JPRS no. 4148, 1959.

_____. Economic and Statistical Information on North Korea. JPRS no. DC-901, 1959.

_____. Economic Progress and Development of Foreign Economic Relations of North Korea, by Nikolai Ivanovich Samsonov. JPRS no. 878-D, 1959.

_____. Economic Reports on North Korea (ERNK). Various issues.

_____. Information from the 1962 North Korean Yearbook. JPRS no. 21631, 1963.

_____. Information from the 1965 North Korean Yearbook. JPRS no. 35146, 1966.

_____. The 1961 North Korean Yearbook. JPRS no. 17890, 1963.

_____. North Korean Central Yearbook, 1964. JPRS no. 35218, 1966.

_____. North Korean Study on the Economy of Industrial Establishments. (English translation of the Korean-language material of the same title.) JPRS nos. 1537-N, 1550-N, 1585-N, 1598-N, 1620-N, 1959.

_____. Translations on North Korea. Various issues.

Kim, Il-song. All for the Post-war Rehabilitation and Development of the National Economy. Pyŏngyang: Department of Cultural Relations with Foreign Countries, DPRK Ministry of Culture and Propaganda, 1954.

_____. All for the Post-war Rehabilitation and Development of the National Economy: Report Delivered at the Sixth Plenum of the Central Committee of the Workers' Party of Korea on August 5, 1963. Pyŏngyang: Foreign Languages Publishing House, 1961.

_____. For Socialist Economic Construction in Our Country. Pyŏngyang: Foreign Languages Publishing House, 1958.

_____. Theses on the Socialist Agrarian Question in Our Country Adopted at the Eighth Plenary Meeting of the Fourth Central Committee of the Workers' Party of Korea on February 25, 1964. Pyŏngyang: Foreign Languages Publishing House, 1964.

Kim, Sang-hak. Development of Socialist Industry in the DPRK. Pyongyang: Foreign Languages Publishing House, 1958.

Korean Handbook. Pyongyang: Foreign Languages Publishing House, 1959.

McCune, George M. Korea Today. Cambridge, Massachusetts: Harvard University Press, 1950.

McCune, Shannon. Korea's Heritage. Rutland, Vermont: Charles E. Tuttle Co., 1959.

National Economic Development in the DPRK, 1945-1960. Pyongyang: Foreign Languages Publishing House, 1960.

Paige, Glenn D. The Korean People's Democratic Republic. Stanford: Stanford University Press, 1966.

Pauley Commission. Report on Japanese Assets in Soviet-occupied Korea to the President of the United States. Washington, D.C., 1946.

Rudolph, Philip. North Korea's Political and Economic Structure. New York: Institute of Pacific Relations, 1959.

Ryu, Hun. Study of North Korea. Seoul: Research Institute of Internal and External Affairs, 1968.

Scalapino, Robert A. (ed.). North Korea Today. New York: Frederick A. Praeger, 1963.

Shinn, Rinn-sup et al. Area Handbook for North Korea. Washington, D.C.: U.S. Government Printing Office, 1969. (DA Pam no. 550-81)

United Nations. Report of the United Nations Commission for the Unification and Rehabilitation of Korea. (General Assembly Official Records: Sixth Session) Supplement no. 12 (A/1881) New York, 1951.

_____. Yearbook of International Trade Statistics. New York, 1955-71.

United States, Department of State. Korea: 1945-1968. (Department of State Publication 3305.) Washington, D.C.: U.S. Government Printing Office, 1948.

_____. Land Reform in North Korea. (DRF-Information Paper no. 419.) Washington, D.C., May 11, 1951.

_____. North Korea: A Case Study in the Technique of Takeover. (Department of State Publication no. 7118.) Washington, D.C.: U.S. Government Printing Office, 1961.

_____. Bureau of Intelligence and Research. The Role of Agriculture in North Korea's Development. (Research Memorandum RSB-105.) Washington, D.C., June 21, 1962.

Yang, Key P. "The North Korean Regime: 1945-1955." An unpublished M.A. thesis on file at the American University, Washington, D.C., 1958.

Articles

Chung, Joseph S. "Economic Development of North Korea, 1945-70: A Survey," in Politics and Government of Korea. Washington, D.C.: Research Institute on Korean Affairs, 1972, 216-234.

_____. "A Model of Post-Reconstruction Stagnation: North Korea's Seven Year Plan." Asian Forum (Washington, D.C.), October 1969, 30-36.

_____. "The North Korean Industrial Enterprise: Size, Concentration and Managerial Functions," in Robert K. Sakai [ed.], Studies on Asia, 1966. Lincoln, Nebraska: The University of Nebraska Press, 1966, 165-185.

_____. "North Korea's Economic System and Development: Recent Trends and Their Implications on Unification." Journal of Asiatic Studies (Seoul), December 1970, 261-277. Also reprinted in The Proceedings of the International Conference on the Problems of Korean Unification. Seoul: Asiatic Research Center, Korea University, 1971.

_____. "North Korea's Seven Year Plan (1961-70): Economic Performance and Reforms." Asian Survey, June 1972, 528-545.

_____. "The Six Year Plan of North Korea, 1971-76: Targets, Problems and Prospects." Journal of Korean Affairs (Washington, D.C.), July 1971, 15-26.

Chung, Kiwon. "Japanese-North Korean Relations Today." Asian Survey, April 1964, 788-803.

Cromley, Ray. "North Korea Sovietized." The Wall Street Journal, May 5, 1947.

"Drive for Farm Mechanization." Far Eastern Economic Review (Hong Kong), February 25, 1960, 403.

Jones, P. H. M. "Korea Felix." Far Eastern Economic Review, July 5, 1962, 32-34.

Juhn, Daniel Sungil. "The North Korean Managerial System at the Factory Level." Journal of Korean Affairs, April 1972, 16-21.

Kim, Il-pyong. "The Mobilization System in North Korean Politics." Journal of Korean Affairs, April 1972, 3-15.

Kim, Il-song. "On Some Theoretical Problems of Socialistic Economy." The People's Korea (Tokyo), March 26, 1969.

Kim, Joungwon Alexander. "The 'Peak of Socialism' in North Korea: The Five and Seven Year Plans," in Jan S. Prybyla, Comparative Economic Systems. New York: Appleton-Century-Crofts, 1969, 412-427.

Koh, B. C. "North Korea and Its Quest for Autonomy." Pacific Affairs, Fall and Winter, 1965, 294-306.

Kuark, Yoon T. "North Korea's Agricultural Development During the Post-war Period." China Quarterly, April-June 1963, 82-93.

_____. "North Korea's Industrial Development During the Post-war Period. China Quarterly, April-June 1963, 51-64.

Lee, Chong-sik. "Land Reform, Collectivization and the Peasants in North Korea." China Quarterly, April-June 1963, 55-81.

_____. "Notes on North Korean Import and Export of Cereals." Journal of Korean Affairs, January 1972, 54-56.

Lee, J. K. and Donald Wellington. "North Korea's Trade with the West: 1956-68." Journal of Korean Affairs, April 1971, 25-33.

Lee, Pong S. "An Estimate of North Korea's National Income." Asian Survey, June 1972, 518-526.

_____. "Overstatement of North Korean Industrial Growth: 1946-1963." Journal of Korean Affairs, July 1971, 3-14.

Porter, C. and W. L. Holland. "North Korea's Economic Development." Far Eastern Survey, no. 24, November 1955, 171-173.

Robinson, Joan. "Korean Miracle." Monthly Review, January 1965, 545-548.

Scalapino, Robert A. "The Foreign Policy of North Korea." China Quarterly, April-June 1963, 30-50.

Shabad, Theodore. "North Korea's Postwar Recovery." Far Eastern Survey, 25, no. 6, June 1956, 81-91.

Yang, Key P. and Chee Chang-boh. "North Korean Educational System: 1945 to Present." China Quarterly, April-June 1963, 125-140.

Yu, Wan-sik. "An Analysis of Foreign Trade of North Korea." The Journal of Asiatic Studies, September 1967, 104-114.

Index

Cooperatives: agricultural, 10-17, 23-32, 55; industrial, 61-62, 71-72
Corn, 45, 47-53; export of, 137
Cotton, 47-51, 66; see also Textiles
Crops: production of, 44-46, 52; see also by name
Cuba: aid to, 126; trade with, 125-26
Czechoslovakia: aid from, 127; trade with, 128, 130-32

Decentralization, 152-56; agricultural, 153; industrial, 66-69, 153
Defense expenditures, 94, 156-57
Diesel fuels, 115-16; see also Fuels
Draft power, 39, 54

East Germany: aid from, 127; trade with, 128, 130-32
Eastern Europe, 152-56; aid from, 92, 126-27; trade with, 125, 126-29; see
    also by country
Economic plans: One Year Plan (1947), 1, 163, 166; One Year Plan (1948), 1,
    163, 166; Two Year Plan (1949-50), 1, 163-64; Three Year Plan (1954-56),
    1-2, 145, 164, 166; Five Year Plan (1957-61, 60), 1-2, 91, 104, 145,
    164-65; Seven Year Plan (1961-67, 70), 1-2, 29, 52, 85, 90-99, 104, 119,
    145, 165-67; Six Year Plan (1971-76), 1-2, 47, 52, 56, 91-92, 96, 150-51,
    166
Economic reforms, 152-56
Education, 158-59
Electricity: exports of, 121, 123; hydroelectric, 57, 119-20; production of,
    57, 78-79, 81, 86-87, 89; in rural areas, 48-49; state investment in,
    74-75
Energy sources: atomic power, 120; draft power, 39, 54; fuels, 78-79, 81,
    91-92, 106, 115-16, 117; electric power, 48-49, 57, 74-75, 78-79, 81,
    86-87, 89, 119-20, 121, 123; horsepower, 37-38; thermal power, 120
Engel coefficients, 150-51
Enterprise method, 22
Enterprises: private, 59-62, 71, 88, 102, 146-47, 149; state, 62-67, 88,
    146-47, 153
Equipment: import of, 103, 106-07, 115, 117, 128-29, 137, 140-42
Europe, see Eastern Europe; Western Europe
Exchange: foreign, 103; rates of, 104, 145-46, 188
Exports, 104-08; promotion of, 102, 103; see also Foreign trade and by product

Farms: collective, 10-17, 23-32, 55; income from, 17, 23-32; labor, 16-18,
    24-28; and laterization, 180-81; mechanization of, 36-41; private, 11,
    13, 55, 149; state, 11, 32-36
Fertilizers: export of, 113, 140; use of, 47-49, 51, 52, 55
Fire farming, 180-81
Fish: export of, 137, 140
Flying Horse movement, see Chŏllima movement
Food: export of, 58, 108, 115, 116, 137, 191; import of, 50-52, 56, 107, 116,
    137-40, 143, 151-52; shortage of, 2, 163; see also Crops
Foreign aid: from China, 92-93, 108, 121-24, 126, 142; decline in, 92-93,
    103, 142, 159; from Eastern Europe, 92, 126-27; and industrial growth,
    92-93, 97, 103, 160; for reconstruction, 84, 92; from U.S.S.R., 92, 93,
    118-20, 126, 142
Foreign exchange, 103; rates of, 104, 145-46, 188

Foreign trade: administration of, 101-04; with communist world, 102-03,
    108-29, 130-33, 142, 159-60; with noncommunist world, 104, 108, 109,
    111, 115, 129, 134-43; value and composition of, 104-08; see also by
    country
Forestation, 42, 43
France: trade with, 137
Fruit: export of, 108, 115, 140; production of, 43, 46, 53
Fuels: import of, 92, 106, 115-16, 117; and industrial growth, 78-79, 81-82,
    91

Gasoline, 115-16; see also Fuels
Germany, see East Germany; West Germany
Gold: export of, 113, 117
Grains: corn, 45, 47-53, 137; export of, 58, 108, 115, 116, 137; import of,
    50, 52, 107, 116, 137, 143; oats, 45; production of, 43-53; rice, 47-53,
    58, 108, 115, 116, 143, 191; wheat, 107, 116, 137, 143
Great Britain: trade with, 141
Greece: trade with, 137
Gross Agricultural Product, 44-46, 80, 146-47; see also Agriculture
Gross Industrial Product, 76, 78-82, 146-47; see also Industry
Gross National Product, see National income
Gross Social Product, 144, 146-47, 148
Guinea: trade with, 141

Hong Kong: trade with, 103, 129, 134-46, 140, 142
Horsepower, 37-40
Human capital, 158
Hungary: aid from, 127; trade with, 130-32
Hydroelectric power, 57, 119-20

Iceland: trade with, 141
Illiteracy, 158
Imports, 101, 104-07; see also Foreign trade and by product
Income: farm, 17, 23-32; national, 144-49, 157; per capita, 145-49; tax on, 17
Independent accounting system, 64-65
India: trade with, 141
Industrialization, 2, 76, 90-98, 151-52; and agriculture, 9-10, 20, 56, 156;
    as goal, 2, 73, 156; and trade, 141-42
Industry: growth of, 76, 78-81, 90-100; heavy, 2, 57-59, 73-74; and Japanese
    occupation, 1, 57-59, 163; light, 73-75; local, 66, 68-70; nationalization
    of, 59-72, 100, 173; private, 59-62; production, 78-82, 84-90, 96-97,
    146-47; state investment in, 72-75, 156; structural change in, 77-80,
    82-84, 98, 157; 2.8 Vinalon Factory, 120, 189-90
Investment, state: in agriculture, 41-43, 55; in industry, 72-75, 156
Iron ore, 58; export of, 122, 136, 140, 142
Irrigation, 42-43, 48-49, 51, 52, 55
Italy: trade with, 141

Japan, 100, 166; and agriculture, 4-5, 17, 44-45, 54; education in, 159; and
    industry, 1, 57-59, 99, 100, 163; trade with, 103, 104, 108-09, 129,
    134-37, 140-42, 160

Kangwŏn Province, 19
Kim Il, 85, 150, 175

Kim Il-song: and agriculture, 11, 16, 19-20, 22, 53, 175; and economy, 145,
    148, 158; and foreign trade, 127; and industry, 63, 66, 68, 85, 91, 93,
    97, 175; on per capita income, 145, 148
KimKwa-bong, 120
Korean War, effects of: on agriculture, 11, 12, 46, 54; on foreign trade,
    104, 136; on population, 160
Kun (county), 21-23; agricultural management committees of, 21-23, 35, 36, 154

Labor, 2; farm, 16-18, 24-28; shortage of, 92, 94, 160; urban, 156
Land: cultivable, 46-51; fragmentation of, 4-5, 7, 10; laterization of, 180-81;
    reform, 5-10; speculation, 9; tax, 17; tenure pattern, 4-5, 9, 12-13, 55;
    utilization of, 4, 47-49, 51, 55
Landlords, 5, 6-10, 12
Laterite, 180-81
Latin America: trade with, 141, 143
Lebanon: trade with, 141
Livestock, 42-54 passim

Machine-building industry, 2, 58-59, 73-82 passim, 157
Machinery: import of, 103, 106-07, 115, 117, 128-29, 137, 140-42
Machine-tractor stations (MTS), 36-41, 153
Mao Tse-tung, 120
Markets, peasant, 13, 153-54
Metallurgy industry, 74-75, 78-79, 81; see also by metal
Mexico: trade with, 141
Military aid, 121
Mining industry, 74-75, 91
Mongolia: trade with, 125
MTS, 36-41, 153

National income, 144-49, 157; per capita, 145-49
Nodong sinmun, 23
Noncommunist world: trade with, 104, 108, 109, 111, 115, 129, 134-43; see also
    by country
North Hamgyŏng Province, 19; state farm in, 34
North Hwanghae Province, 19
North Pyŏngan Province, 19
North Vietnam: trade with, 126; U.S. bombing of, 93

Oats, 45
Occupations, 4, 146-47, 149, 157, 159
Oil, 92, 106, 116, 117; see also Fuels
Owner-tenants, 4

Peasants: and land reform, 5-10; markets, 13, 153-54
People's Republic of China, see China, People's Republic of
Plans, see Economic plans
Poland: aid from, 127, 128; trade with, 126, 128-29, 130, 132, 191
Population, 15, 99, 146-48; distribution of, 146-47; loss from war, 160
Potatoes, 48-51, 53
Producer goods, 77-81
Profit: and state enterprises, 65-66
Provinces: and agricultural tax-in-kind, 19; state farms in, 34
Provisional People's Committee, 5, 59, 102
Pyŏngyang City, 69-70, 93, 119, 155

Railroads, 58, 123, 124, 163
Reconstruction (from Korean War), 1-2, 91, 95, 98, 164; aid for, 84, 92
Rice, 143; export of, 58, 108, 115, 116, 191; production, 47-53, 191
Rubber: import of, 140
Rumania: aid from, 127; trade with, 130, 132
Ryongyun County: state farm in, 34

Sericulture, see Silk
Silk: culture of, 43-44, 48-49, 51, 53, 54-55; export of, 108, 137, 140
Socialization, 61, 88, 100, 149, 174; see also Collectivization; Cooperatives
South Hamgyŏng Province, 19
South Hwanghae Province, 19; state farm in, 34
South Korea: and agriculture, 4-5; military in, 94; population in, 99, 160
South Pyŏngan Province, 19
Soviet Union, see U.S.S.R.
Stalinistic command economy, 90-92, 100, 157-58
State Planning Commission (SPC), 1, 85, 169-70
Statistics, economic, 52, 169-77; Central Statistical Bureau, 85, 169-71;
    doublecounting, 80; fabrication of, 170, 176, 194; "grossness," 80, 174;
    index numbers, 173; "law of equal cheating," 174; "new product" effect,
    80; omission of, 52, 85, 90, 145, 174-75; reliability of, 170-77; upward
    bias of, 50, 76, 82-83, 95-99, 148, 171-72
Steel: export of, 113, 114-15, 122, 125, 126, 137; production, 106
Sugar: import of, 126, 137
Switzerland: trade with, 141

Taean industrial management system, 63-64, 100, 154
Tariffs, 103
Taxes: agricultural, 9, 17-21, 24, 56; on imports, 103; income, 17; tax-in-
    kind, 9, 17, 19, 24, 56
Tenants, 4-10, 12
Textiles: Chinese aid for, 124; cotton, 47-51, 66; export of, 108, 137, 140;
    industrial output of, 78-79, 81; production of, 66, 69-70, 84, 86-87, 89;
    silk, 43-44, 48-49, 51, 53, 54-55, 108, 137, 140; Soviet aid for, 119;
    state investment in, 74-75; vinalon, 120, 189-90
Thermal power, 120
Tobacco: export of, 115
Trade, see Foreign trade

Unggi County: state farm in, 34
Union of Soviet Socialist Republics, see U.S.S.R.
United Arab Republic: trade with, 141
United Nations Forces, 121
United States of America: trade with, 109, 143; and Vietnam, 93, 94
U.S.S.R., 152, 155-56; aid from, 92-93, 118-20, 125, 142; aid to, 118, 120;
    and education, 159; and gross social product, 144; occupation by, 57, 59;
    and Stalinistic command economy, 90n, 100; state farm in, 32; trade with,
    50, 104, 108-20, 160, 189; and use of statistics, 171, 173

Vietnam: and U.S., 93, 94
Vinalon: production of, 120, 189-90

West Germany: trade with, 141
Western Europe: trade with, 108, 129, 141; see also by country